D1452652

Enlightened Despotism in Russia: The Reign of Elisabeth

American University Studies

Series IX

History

Vol. 14

PETER LANG

New York · Berne · Frankfurt am Main · Paris

James F. Brennan

ENLIGHTENED DESPOTISM IN RUSSIA

The Reign of Elisabeth, 1741–1762

PETER LANG

New York · Berne · Frankfurt am Main · Paris

Library of Congress Cataloging-in-Publication Data

Brennan, James F.
  Enlightened Despotism in Russia.

  (American University Studies. Series IX,
History; vol. 14)
    Bibliography: p.
    1. Soviet Union – History – Elizabeth,
1741 – 1762. 2. Elizabeth, Empress of Russia,
1709 – 1762. I. Title. II. Series.
DK161.B74   1987   947'.062   85-18081
ISBN 0-8204-0262-1
ISSN 0740-0462

CIP-Kurztitelaufnahme der Deutschen Bibliothek

Brennan, James F.:
Enlightened Despotism in Russia : The Reign of
Elisabeth, 1741 – 1762 / James F. Brennan. –
New York ; Berne ; Frankfurt am Main : Lang,
1987.
  (American University Studies : Ser. 9,
  History ; Vol. 14)
  ISBN 0-8204-0262-1

NE: American University Studies / 09

© Peter Lang Publishing, Inc., New York 1987

Printed by Weihert-Druck GmbH, Darmstadt (West Germany)

TO MY PARENTS

ACKNOWLEDGMENTS

For the purposes of researching this book several libraries were consulted. First, the Library of the university of Helsinki with its excellent collection and its extraordinarily helpful staff in particular Elisabet Tokoi. The Saltykov-Shchedrin Library in Leningrad provided me with the essential Sanktpeterburgskyia Vedomosti for most of the period covered. Much research was also undertaken in the Bibliothèque nationale where in addition to several summers I used the Library's resources for a full year. The State Library of Austria was also useful for non-Russian materials from the eighteenth century. The Austrian State Archives were also consulted for the despatches from Russia. My appreciations go also to Central Washington University which granted me a sabbatical in 1975/76 to do the research and much of the writing at the University of Helsinki. I also owe a debt of gratitude to Mrs. Tony Peterson who patiently typed the final copy which involved the difficult task of typing the footnotes which were in languages completely unfamiliar to her.

CONTENTS

INTRODUCTION

absolutism

Enlightened despotism, the political movement which accompanied the intellectual enlightenment of the 18th century, is a movement difficult to define and study since it occurred in several countries and took on varying forms. Generally, in view of the political realities, it was enlightened ideas enacted by all-powerful rulers in a period in which most of the European states were ruled by absolute monarchs. The movement did not really become a feature of the European scene until after approximately 1750 when the ideas of the philosophes became widespread and a part of the major intellectual stream of European thought.

The despotic side of the movement, or better, the interference of the government to further the enlightened development of the state, has its roots in sources other than the enlightenment itself. One of these is to be found in the activities of such figures as Peter the Great (1689-1725) who subsequently became one of the heroes of the philosophes. His use of autocratic power, traditional with the Russian rulers, to drive out what he considered "barbaric" traits in Russia set an example for other rulers. His attitude towards the state, in which he viewed himself as the first servant of the state, and his feeling that it was his destiny to bring Russia into the mainstream of European politics was taken to prove this. Of course, involved in this was his well known effort to "westernize" his backward country.

One can cite the activities of other rulers such as Louis XIV during the periods of peace in his country when he also introduced reforms. But for the purposes of this book the most important source are the ideas first generated in

9

England in the late 17th century which were transferred to France--then the intellectual center of the European world--where they became the accepted norm. Reason was applied to social and political institutions to determine if they were "rational". In determining what was actually "rational", a large measure of sujectivism naturally occurred as in most human situations. In France the movement started as a criticism of society by Montesquieu, to an attack upon the Church and social distinctions and finally culminated in the radical phases of the French Revolution. In the process hardly any of the major European states were not affected by one or more of the phases of this movement.

Until recently it has been generally held that enlightened despotism only flowered in Russia in the reign of Catherine the Great (1762-1796), but her actions have given historians some serious problems. A patron of the philosophes, fluent in French and issuing her famous Nakaz of 1767 to reform the law codes of the Russian empire which was often taken directly from the writings of the philosophes, are noted as examples of her enlightenment. On the other hand the historian can hardly ignore the deplorable state of the majority of her subjects who were mere slaves. Whatever her intentions, she did nothing substantial to improve their lot. In fact it worsened during her reign in which she enslaved the Ukraine and gave its people as serfs to her favorites. Although the owners of serfs were not allowed by law to kill the serfs, they had complete power over them otherwise. When one of her enlightened friends pointed out to her the inconsistency in her policy she could only reply that they wrote on paper, but that she had to write on human skin which was infinitely more sensitive. Her contribution to education is also noted, but doubt can be thrown upn her real contribution since no institutions of higher learning were established during her entire reign of approximately thirty-four years with the minor exception of the school at Smolny.

This situation caused a re-examination of the problem by Russian historians just before the war and Revolution. These historians had started to take a closer look at the activities of her predecessors, and started reaching interesting conclusions. But the trend was interrupted by the Revolution and only in exile did it continue. The historian, A. Kizevetter, writing in France, made the generalization that the groundwork for all the famous actions of Catherine had been prepared in the previous reign of Elisabeth Petrovna but had been done so with so little attempt at publicity that they had been previously overlooked.[1] More recently this same thesis was reaffirmed by S.O. Shmidt. In his words: "en réalité, ce qu'on appelle 'le siècle de Catherine' à commencé bien avant l'événement de La Tsarine".[2]

The traditional approach to the history of Russia in the 18the century after the death of Peter the Great is to view it as the age of the "gynecocracy" when the country was subjected to the dark rule of a series of weak women with low morals. This predominate trend indicates that the reigns of Anna (1730-1740), that of Elisabeth (1741-1762) and to a lesser degree Catherine the Great were periods in which the country was terribly misgoverned, that the rulers were dominated by favorites seeking their own personal greedy ends, and that the only redeeming feature was to be found in the enlightenment of Catherine the Great and even this only to a limited degree. Much of the explanation for this attitude is to be found in two sources. Men were writing the history and simply had a double standard. A male ruler was permitted much which was condemned in a woman. If women had written the history of the period, the picture would have been vastly different. The second factor which contributed to this image

11

was the fact that most of the historians had no use for the institution of monarchy and thus were seeking means of discrediting it. One of the easiest ways to achieve this would be through darkening the historical record of the dynasty as much as possible. Hence, it is not surprising to discover liberal and revolutionary historians picking the 18th century as one of their chief periods for down-grading the monarchy by spending a great deal of time considering the loose morals of the court to prove that monarchs and rulers are not selected by God, but merely by chance.

With this as a background it is not surprising that when critical history was first permitted after the death of Nicholas I in 1855, the leading historian of the period, the liberal V.S. Eshevskii, a professor at Moscow University, was allowed to lecture and write about the 18th century in the following terms:

> The idea of reforms [initiated by Peter the Great] started to reappear again only under Catherine II [the Great], and it may be stated that the legal successor of the great reformer, successor in spirit, if not blood, was Catherine the Great. The intermediary period was some sort of interregnum.[3]

With some notable exceptions this became the line for historians until a genuine re-evaluation was undertaken.

There exist other factors which allowed the image of the reigns of Anna and Elisabeth to be painted in dark colors. Anna had little claim to the throne. Elisabeth was born out of wedlock and subsequently legitimatized by her father, Peter the Great. Her mother was an illiterate peasant woman from Lithuania. During the 18th century, starting with Peter himself, Russia underwent a thorough

12

westernization which called forth a reaction on the part of some of the more critical nobles in Russia. Also, the continued use of Peter's method of determining promotion on merit rather than birth, which diminished with time, caused nobles, Russians and foreigners, to look down upon the Russian court. An example of this is the work of Prince M. Shcherbatov, a leading figure of the period. In 1859 a manuscript which he wrote for his own use and not publication, was issued from the press of Alexander Herzen in London. The work entitled *On the Corruption of Morals in Russia* reflects a most terrible picture of the court with which the author was associated.[4] While some accept the book as fully accurate, there is good reason to question this since Shcherbatov took only the negative aspects of court life and ignored the positive. He also tended uncritically to accept stories which darkened the court. many of these have become accepted. Yet in some cases his story teller has been proven a liar by the archives.

A similar problem exists with materials published outside Russia by foreigners, who, viewing Russia as thought it was still the barbarian state it supposedly had been before Peter the Great and approaching the situation with a noble's attitude, allowed western ethnocentrism to form their image of Russia and the court. An example of this is to be found in Adolf Wilhelm von Helbig's *Rüssiche Günstlinge* published in 1802. From the author's title it is clear that he was or claimed to be a noble. For him the court of Elisabeth--and the entire government for that matter-- was in the hands of servants, cooks and lackys, who, showered with honors and awards which they did not deserve, arrogantly managed affairs.[5] A curious book published in 1736 is very critical of Russia. The author, Locatelli, viewed Russia as still the way it had been before the Battle of Narva in 1700 and, upon one major defeat, it would give up its holdings in the Baltic region and revert to Moscovite ways.[6]

These attitudes were not limited to individuals. Often the ambassadors to St. Petersburg believed them as well. In 1741 both the British ambassador--a friendly power--and the French special envoy viewed the situation as being very fragile and with the slightest shock it would collapse with Russia reverting back to the pre-Petrine times.[7] Even the home governments were capable of believing these stories as in the case of England.[8]

With these considerations it can be anticipated that treatments of the reign of Elisabeth would tend to be highly critical and often simply erroneous. Perhaps the most outstanding of these occurs in the introduction to Christopher Marsden's *Palmyra of the North. The First Days of St. Petersburg.* The introduction was written by Sacheverell Stitwell, apparently after the death of Marsden. "The empress Elisabeth was illiterate like her peasant mother".[9] In addition to the fluent use of Russian both spoken and written, Elisabeth was also fluent in French and German. When a new ambassador was received at court he was informed that the official reception by the empress could either be in a language both understood or they could use an interpreter. Marsden himself stated:

> Indeed, as queens go, they [Anna and Elisabeth] rank fairly low. From her cerebral heights, Catherine could look back with something of a sneer at the simple ladies into whose outsized but dressy slippers she had stepped.[10]

A perusal of the *Memoirs* of Catherine the Great themselves indicate that she had a very high respect of the empress Elisabeth and her sharp mind despite the differing Weltanschauung between the two which was very great.[11]

But these are matters of court intrigue. The main purpose of this book will be directed to the operation of the state, changes in policies and economic growth .

There is one ironic note to the histories written about the reign of Elisabeth. All of these have concentrated almost exclusively on the court life and most have ignored the internal development of the country. In 1757 Elisabeth contacted Voltaire in order to induce the most famous writer in the western world to prepare a biography of her father whom she idealized so greatly. Voltaire readily agreed, but he warned his patroness that the book should not be a biography but rather a history of Russia during the reign of Peter.[12] Thus, he stated it would be possible to avoid certain aspects of the reign--mainly about court affairs--which would not reflect too well on her father. In other words he suggested that his history be selective. When the book appeared it was entitled *Russia During the Reign of Peter the Great.* With a few exceptions people writing on the reign of Elisabeth have done just the opposite--written histories of court life many of which were not accurate.

NOTES

1. A. Kizevetter, "From Catherine I to Catherine II: The Nobility's New Role," *History of Russia. Volume Two. The Successors of Peter the Great-- From Catherine I to the Reign of Nicholas I.* Miliukov, Seignobos, and Eisenmann. Translated by Charles Lam Markmann (Funk & Wagnalls, New York, 1968), 42-43.

2. S.O. Shmidt, "La politique interieure du Tzarisme au milieu de XVIII-é Siècle", *Annales* (janvier-février), 1966, 110.

3. S.V. Eshevskii, "Ocherk Tsarstvovanyia Elizavety Petrovny," *Otechesvenyia Zapiski,* CLXXVIII, **5,** May, 1868, 23.

4. M. Shcherbatov. *On the Corruption of Morals in Russia by M.M. Shcherbatov.* Translated and edited by Professor Lentin. Cambridge, 1969. Shcherbatov believed that the Empress Elisabeth thought that England was connected to the mainland. His source was a Senate clerk who also assured him that he himself, the clerk, had written the manifesto granting liberty to the nobles from state service inorder to assist the Emperor Peter III in his love life for one night. The archives have proven this last claim to be untrue. Hence, this casts doubt on his statement about the supposed ignorance of the Empress. Impressed by her knowledge of the geography of Finland the German historian Mediger also called this claim into question. Walter Mediger, *Moskaus Weg nach Europa. Der Aufstieg Russlands zum europäischen Machstadt im Zeitalter Friedrichs des Grossen* (Braunschweig: George Westermann verlag, 1952), 239.

5. Adolf Wilhelm von Helbig, *Rüssiche Güstlinge* (Tü-

16

bingen: J.G. Cottalsche Buchhandlung, 1802), 209. "Unsere Leser werden am Schlusse dieses Buchs die Bemerking machen, dass es unter keiner Regierung in Russland so viel Gemeine und so ganz verworfene Günstlinge, die Schlechterdings auf keinen Vorzug der Seele Anspruch machten konnten, gegeben hat, als unter Kaiserin Elisabeth. Am Hofe dieser Prinzessin wimmeltes von Bauren, Stallknechten, Kutschern, Soldaten and Bedienten, die zwar, weil sie Selbsgefühl hatten, sich wegen ihrer Staatsämtern anstellen liessen, aber dock ansehnliche Hofchargen bekleideten, Ordensbändern bekamen, und vorzügliche ganz unverdienter Weise, die ungeheursten Richthümer erhielten". The chief "Günstling" was Alexis Rasumovsky who came from a lower class Ukrainian family, but secretly he was married to the empress. His younger brother, Kyrill, was well educated, married into nobility and had a remarkable family. It was one of his sons who commissioned the quartets from Beethoven which bear the family name. Otherwise the charge bears little or no reality. But it circulated widely at the time and caused the English government considerable concern.

6   Locatelli. *Lettres moscovites*. Paris[?]: La Compagnie, 1736.

7   "Doneseniia Markiza de-la-Shtardi frantskomu pravitel'stvu i otvety Ministerstva, 1740 (oct 21)-1741 (9 mai)", *Sbornik imperatorskago russkago istoricheskago Obshchestva,* Vol. 92 (St. Petersburg, 1894), 526-27. Le Marquis de la Chétardie à m. Amelot.St. Petersburg, 2 mai 1741. In the future this item will be referred to as *SIRIO* which is standard usage. "Doneseniia i drugiia Bumagii angliiskikh Poslov, Poslannikov i Rezidentov pri russkom Dvore s 7 marta 1741g. po 16 iiulia 1747g," *Ibid*.vol. 91 (St.Petersburg, 1894),

17

111. No. 24 Ed. Finch to the honourable Lord Harrington, St. Petersburg, June 2, 1741. The English ambassador noted: "After all the pains, which have been taken to bring the country into its present shape, by which it is so greatly connected with the rest of Europe, and has so great a weight in the affairs of it, I must confess that I can yet see it in no other light, than as a rough model of something meant to be perfected hereafter, in which the several parts do neither fit nor join, nor are well glewed together, but have been only kept so first by one great peg [Peter the Great] and now by another driven through the whole [Count Ostermann], which peg pulled out, the whole machine immediately falls to peices". When the "peg" was removed the machinery continued to function normally.

8 "Colonel Buy Dickens to the duke of Newcastle". No. 213. 28th of January, 1752, *SIRIO,* Vol.   148, 322.

9 Christopher Marsden, *Palmyra of the North. The First Days of St. Petersburg* (London: Faber   and Faber Limited, 1943), 7. In the reign of Elisabeth's mother, Catherine I (1725-27), Elisabeth read official papers to her mother and signed them since her mother was actually illiterate and of peasant origin.

10 *Ibid.,* 21.

11 *The Memoirs of Catherine the Great,* ed.   by Dominique Maroger. New York: Collier Books, 1961.

12 "Copie de la response de M-r Voltaire a M-r Wesselovskoy de Morion [Ivan Shuvalov] du 19 février 1757 ", *Arkhiv Kniazia Vorontsova,*Vol. III (Moscow: Grachev, 1871), 270-71. Voltaire's letter .concludes: "NB. Il paroit important de ne point inti-

tuler cet ouvrage Histoire de la vie de Pierre
1-r; un tel titre engage necessairement l'his-
torien à ne rien suprimer. Il est forcé alors de
dire des verités odieuses, et s'il ne les dit
pas, il se deshonore sans faire honneur à ceux
qui l'emploient. Il faudroit donc prendre pour
titre, ainsi que pour suject, la Russie sous
Pierre 1-r. Un telle avance écarte toutes les
anecdotes de la vie privée du Czar, qui pour-
roient diminuer sa gloire, et n'admet que celles,
qui sont lié aux grandes choses qu'il a com-
mencées, et qu'on a continuées depuis lui".

CHAPTER ONE

THE SEIZURE OF POWER

illigitimate

Elisabeth Petrovna born in 1709, shortly after the Battle of Poltava had shifted the Balance of Power in eastern Europe for good, was known officially as the "cooks daughter" since her mother had not yet married Peter. After Peter had disinherited (and probably executed) his first son he decided that he needed more security for his own family since he himself was the product of the second marriage of his father and several half sisters still remained from the first marriage of Tsar Alexis. Hence, he married his mistress, Catherine, had her annointed Empress and declared his children by the second marriage legitimate. From this marriage two daughters survived whose main purpose, as Peter saw it, was to find well-placed husbands in the West. This explains the care he took in teaching them foreign languages. The first did marry into the Holstein family and delivered a son shortly before her premature death. The efforts to find a husband for the second daughter, Elisabeth, failed for various reasons--chiefly his strong desire for a French husband which was not acceptable to the French on the basis of her origin and religion. Hence, on the death of Peter his second daughter was still unmarried. Elisabeth aided her mother, Catherine I, during her short reign and then started drifting away from court affairs during the reign of the grandson of Peter by his first marriage, Peter II. When he died at the age of 15 in 1730 the will of Catherine I was ignored by a clique of leading nobles who selected as the new ruler one of the daughters of Peter's half brother Ivan, Anna of Courland, with the stipulaton that real power rest in the hands of the Supreme Secret Council. Soon Anna gained full power and destroyed the Council ruling for ten years as autocrat (1730-1740). During this period Elisabeth was allowed to retain her own court at the expense of the state and bore the title Princess. The best legal claim to the throne belonged to her nephew living then in Holstein who was a Lutheran.

The reign of Anna Ivanovna has been little studied and is considered to be the real "dark age" in Russian history. But when examined more carefully it becomes clear that Anna was not intelligent but generally had good intentions. [1] Her marriage to the Kürfurst of Courland had been arranged by Peter and before she could even reach that country she was widowed. Here she ruled alone with the help of the German, Biron or Bühren, with whom she is suspected of having a close liaison. One of the stipulations which the Council had placed on her was the Biron be left behind in Courland, but soon he appeared at the Russian court alongside the new Empress.

As was the case in most of the reigns, war followed war and Russia, as in the time of Peter the Great, could ill afford to support long war efforts since its economy was so backward. In the ten year period of her reign two long wars were fought, one over the Polish Succession and the other against Turkey. The government needed every source of income and all taxes had to be paid as rapidly as possible. The chief tax was the so-called "soul" tax on all male serfs of 70 copeecks a year. The method used to collect this tax was one that Peter had used but had been dropped by his successors--direct collection by the military in place of collection by local authorities which allowed for the build-up of large arrears. Under the newly adopted measure the landowner who possessed serfs could in turn be held responsible if his serfs did not pay. Thus, in practice many estates came into the possession of the government. In this situation the heavy burden fell upon the service gentry who had to serve the government for twenty-five years and were also responsible for the taxes owed by their serfs. In addition special burdens were placed upon the serfs besides providing recruits. They had to supply forage for the needs of the army, etc. The result of this situation was great resentment against the government and led to many nobles being sent into exile.

Pressure was also brought to bear upon the Church as in the time of Peter to support the war effort. The lands of the Church were placed under direct control of the state to insure that the miximum revenue could be obtained from them. Resisting clergy were jailed. Like the nobles the churchmen began to feel that these pressures were coming from the "forces around the throne". Since Biron was German and had imported many Germans to work for the Russian state resentment turned against them. Did not the state take Church lands in Lutheran countries? Was not Biron Lutheran?

But in this matter it is easy to miss some of the positive aspects of the reign. In 1733 a general crop failure hit Russia and the government tried to help, but the news arrived too late.[2] The Treasury was authorized to loan money directly to the nobles for three years at a modest interest rate to help feed the serfs. The need for a general survey in the land was also noted in view of the local battles among the landlords. Most important perhaps was Anasim Maslov, the Ober-procurator of the Senate until 1735, who correctly blamed the landlords for the poor conditions exisiting among the serfs and called for lifting of pressure on serfs so their general condition could be improved.[3] His advice went unheaded largely due to the wars, but at least a person could voice such concerns and die a natural death. His indirect influence was felt later in 1737 when, during war preparations, the government banned distilling of vodka in regions designated for collection of grain and forage.[4] In addition, Marshal Münnich induced the Empress to open a Cadets Corp school for sons of nobles to provide them a liberal education. This proved to be one of the most lasting reforms of the reign.

Despite the often overlooked positive aspects, the reign was repressive in most aspects and often crude. A clerk could be sent to Siberia for making a slight error in the name of the empress. Punishments for crimes were cruel and too severe. But worst of all in the eyes of many was the "terrible" influence of the "nemtsy" or Germans on the government. Indeed, Biron took most of the blame for this situation as it developed. Having no love for Russia (since he was from Courland) he took little interest in the vital needs of the state while at the same time taking a most active interest in furthering the Germans and their demands. Many were gathering in Russia in anticipation of material gains. Biron was probably taking gifts from these Germans and bribes. The resulting corruption became very great and the court a scandal. The most infamous example of this was nearly complete monopoly in the iron trade given to one Shömberg for the payment of a generous bribe. In 1742 it was discovered the Shömberg had taken illegally from the Russian government over one hundred thousand rubles by selling iron directly to English merchants without paying the customs duty on it.[5] Even Russians like Demidov, from the famous industrialists family of serf origin ennobled in 1727, had to make his "contribution" to Biron to keep the family mines.

Hence, on the surface it appeared that the government was under the control of greedy German-speaking people whose chief aim was to gain as much as possible from Russia. The problem was somewhat different in the military. The Russian army had only two Marshals both of whom were viewed as "Germans". One, Marshal Münnich, was actually German and the other, Marshal Lacy, was Irish by origin who had risen from low to the highest rank in the Russian army by merit during the time of Peter the Great. Münnich had a grand reputation for his military abilities in the West whereas Lacy was less well known.

Münnich had entered Russian service considerably later than Lacy and had, by his behavior, gained the general hatred of the Russian soldier and officers. He had a condescending attitude towards those with less education than himself which meant then most of the Russian officers. He showed little concern for the needs of the lower ranks and was accused of causing the unnecessary deaths of thousands of Russian soldiers. Also, apparently he was not well mentally balanced since he enjoyed the imposition of cruel and unusual punishment and actually attended while they were being carried out to satisfy his sadistic desires. One such punishment involved the cutting of slashes in the back of a man, filling them with gunpowder, letting it dry and then watching when it was ignited.[6]

In contrast, Lacy, coming from a modest background (he had fought with the losing side at the battle of the Bougne at the age of thirteen) and having served long with Russian soldiers, could sympathize with them. In fact, even those historians trying to re-examine the reign of Ann in a more favorable light admit that he was the soldiers' favorite.[7] He complained repeatedly about the poor supplies or lack of them for the army, but this never seemed to annoy Münnich who took what he could obtain without a guilty conscience. It is easy, on this ground, to understand why Lacy survived the anti-German rising and why Münnich spent the reign of Elisabeth in exile.

More difficult to understand was the position of the expert diplomat, Ostermann, who was one of Peter's discoveries. He had worked his way up under Peter from an interpreter to the head of the Foreign College. He managed to be ill whenever there was a crisis at court so that he would not be forced to share the blame. But for some reason this did not save him from being one of the "hated" Germans. If anyone deserved punishment less it was the aging Ostermann. But his name was German and he had been in St. Petersburg (but not at the meeting) when Elisabeth had been passed over in favor of Anna in 1730.

This growth of resentment in Russia against "German" rule was noted by some foreign observers. The above mentioned Locatelli - not related to the composer or opera manager - in his book critical of Russia as early as 1736 noted that the Russians were suspicious and hostile towards all foreigners and that he anticipated a Sicilian Vespers Russian style in the near future.[8] He was somewhat unreliable since he had been held as a prisoner and mistreated before being expelled from Russia. Hence came his bitterness. A better source was a Danish theology student, Peter von Haven, who took a break from his university studies to see a little of the world before starting his career. Arriving in Russia in 1736 he took a position as a secretary and chaplain for a Danish captain and crew in Russian service against the Truks. In the process he learned enough Russian to make himself understood. Thus, with an open mind and a shaky knowledge of the language he traveled about the country before leaving. He discovered that the nobles did not hate foreigners or western ways, but that they showed a natural resentment concerning the condescending attitude people from the west took towards Russians--again a case of western ethnocentrism.[9] The fact was resented that more foreigners did not learn Russian but expected the Russians to know their languages. Thus, we have two contrasting viewpoints. An embittered exprisoner and an open-minded university student. Haven subsequently completed his studies and became the Lutheran minister for one of the two churches of that denomination in St. Petersburg where he evidently acquired a good knowledge of Russian.

While this feeling was widespread there was one important, yet controversial figure in the government, Artemii Petrovich Volynskii (1689-1740), who came to symbolize the opposition. Of the old nobility, he had risen rapidly during the reign of Peter. Although he formed no special circle he did have many friends including Elisabeth with whom he exchanged books or held discussions. His large library was famous in Russia. He was also given to writing projects for the improvement of Russia. He wanted to up-grade the lower nobility and increase education in the country.[10] He became one of the most important figures in the Russian government responsible only to the empress. However, he was caught in a fight between Ostermann and Biron which proved his undoing. His apparent aim was to reduce the power of the German element in the government which he planned to do by abolishing the powerful Cabinet (with all Russian members--but subject to the influence of Biron) and increasing the power of the Senate which was more strongly pro-Russian. But in the process he criticized Ostermann which Biron took as directed against himself. Hence, Biron told the empress that she must decide between Volynskii and himself. The empress then made the fatal decision to proceed against Volynskii using torture and a picked court of Russians who were certain to find him guilty. As a consequence Volynskii and two of his friends were executed despite the weakness of the evidence.[11] Hardly was the body of Volynskii cold when the empress Anna followed him to the grave in October of 1740. Anna wanted to insure that her branch of the Romanov family would continue to occupy the throne instead of the Petrine line. As a consequence she willed the throne to the newly born son of her niece who was married to a German. Suddenly the throne was occupied by a six month old child - little John - with Biron as regent for 15 years. Anna could not have made a worse mistake if she really wanted to keep her family in control. Biron was universally hated and was overthrown within a few months. But his ouster did not end the control of the line of Anna. Little John was still the theoretical ruler with his mother as regent.

The strongest claimant to the throne was Peter the Great's grandson to whom Anna had referred as "the little devil living in Holstein."[12] His aunt was Elisabeth Petrovna living then under the careful watch of the court which feared intrigue on her part. She was very popular with the guard units in St. Petersburg,   not only as the daughter of Peter, but also as a result of her charity towards these soldiers. She was clearly the candidate of the Russian party. When Biron was overthrown many of the guards thought that they were placing Elisabeth on the throne. The "Germans" still ruled. It is estimated that upwards to 20,000 people had been exiled and many others executed during the "bironshchina".[13] Thus, to say the least, in 1741 the stage was set for another coup.

At this point international politics came into the picture to play an important role. Russia, as most other states, had agreed to honor the so-called Pragmatic Sanction which insured the Hapsburg lands to the daughter of Charles VI, Maria Theresa. In diplomatic dealings Ostermann indicated that Russia, unlike most of the other states, planned to join England in supporting it. Prussia and France were especially concerned that Russia would come to the aid of Austria in 1740 after the death of Charles VI. The states of Europe, with noted exceptions, wanted to take advantage of the young Maria Teresa and divide up her empire. With the "German" party in office it seemed certain that Russia would enter the fray. But Anna and the father of Frederich the Great died in the same year as Charles. The death of Anna and the weak changing regency temporarily paralized the Russian government although it received requests for assistance from both Austria and England, another court upholding the Pragmatic Sanction.

Typical French diplomacy was called into action at this point. The special French ambassador in St. Petersburg was the Marquis de la Chétardie, a man who overjudged his own ability as a diplomat. The French government decided to put their support on the person they considered a sure winner, Elisabeth Petrovna, whom they correctly viewed as the only real contender to unseat the "Germans". The French drew the Swedish ambassador, Nolken, into the plot. Elisabeth received two thousand ducats from the

French.[14] Then the Swedish government was induced to declare war on Russia to unseat the "German" party and insure the neutrality of Russia in the War of the Austrian Succession. For this support strong conditions were forced upon Elisabeth. She was (a) to pay the costs of the transportation of Swedish troops to Finland for the war, (b) to give Sweden subsidies for the rest of her life, (c) to give Sweden the same most-favored-nation trading rights then enjoyed by England, (d) to renounce all the treaties with England and Austria replacing them with similar treaties with France and Sweden, and finally (e) to keep always in mind the economic interests of Sweden while keeping secret from the Russians certain of the terms of this agreement. To this Elisabeth wilingly agreed adding her own additional small gifts.[15] But later to the horror of both the French and Swedish ambassadors she would give only verbal, not written assurances, that she would carry them out. She had no intention of honoring them which France and Sweden realized only too late. In short she had defeated France and Sweden at their own game of intrigue.

Thus, with a weak regency supported by Münnich and Ostermann the Russian government received the declaration of war from Sweden in the summer of 1741 stating that the aim of the war was to put the nephew of Elisabeth on the Russian throne!

Under these circumstances it took just a little push to overthrow the government. The tradition of coup d'Etat was deeply intermeshed in the Russian system by then. Also the regent was considering putting Elisabeth in a convent which was the last fate she wanted, given her lifestyle. On the evening of the 24th of November, 1741 it was learned that the guards regiments, among which the influence of Elisabeth was greatest, were to be moved to Finland for purposes of the war. Elisabeth leading the soldiers seized power with ease and arrested the majority of the members of the deposed government.[16] Münnich,

Ostermann and others were tried for "crimes" against Elisabeth, but in reality to satisfy the anti-German feelings of the nobles.[17] Sentenced to death all eventually found themselves in exile until death (Ostermann) or the reign of Catherine II (Münnich). Biron stayed in exile and was soon joined by the ex-regent and her family.

While the revolution might have been anti-German as it appears to have been, it was not anti-foreigner as far as the new ruler and the upper classes were concerned. It marked the ascendancy of French culture and language over German, but it was not a lasting victory from the standpoint of France itself since direct French influence was shortlived. Chétardie learned of the coup only after it had taken place, although he later claimed otherwise. This is one of the clearest proof that it was not just French and Swedish influence plus the popularity of Elisabeth which account for the success of the change in government.[18] Yet Chétardie remained in favor until 1743 when he wrote indiscreet secret despatches about Russia and the empress which led to his expulsion and three years later to full diplomatic break. The engineer of this split was the brilliant, but vain and greedy chancellor, Restuzhev-Riumin, who was pro-English.

There exists a significance to this coup which was not apparent at the time. By her coup Elisabeth had freed Russia for good upon heavy reliance upon foreigners which, after Narva, had been one of the main goals of her father. It is true that the Russian state continued to employ foreigners long after this event, but the most famous of the "bourgeoisie" historians, S.M. Sovovev, in his twenty-nine volume history of Russia which starts from the earliest times and ends in the middle of the reign of Catherine the Great, attributes much greater importance to the reign. He viewed the reign of Elisabeth as a direct continuation of that of her father and made the significant generalization that it was in this period that Russia "became herself".[19] He noted that foreigners were used only if there were no Russians prepared for a given position.

However, there was a degree of xenophobia among the lower classes which was disturbing to foreigners of all nationalities. This, in addition to the treatment of Münnich and Ostermann, caused a large number of foreigners to leave the country in fear of their safety. While the war with Sweden continued the government was very hesitant to allow them to leave. When it ended in 1743 many Germans and Englishmen announced in the official journal, *Sankt Petersburgskiia Vedomosti*, that they were winding down their affairs and leaving the country as seemed to be customary for business people about to depart. Euler, the genius of the Academy of Sciences in mathematics, left Russia and was not induced to return to the country until the reign of Catherine although he maintained his membership in the Academy. However, one of the most important persons who was German and nearly indispensible to the Academy, G. Müller, remained and continued his varied services for the Russian state.

Many of the military officers, especially those of German origin, left to the great detriment of the Russian state. Of those remaining two were outstanding--Marshal Lacy and General Keith. Both played key roles in the war with Sweden which followed.

The Swedes and French then tried to gain what had been promised them by the empress before her victory and found to their horror that she was not ready to give them even one centimeter of the land Peter had gained. Thus, Chétardie discovered that the woman with whom he was dealing was not the weak individual he had thought. And the war continued as if nothing had happened although negotiations continued. Lacy, who was awakened the night of the coup and asked which party he supported replied "the ruling party," was left in command of the troops with the Scotish Jacobite Keith as second in command.

They attracked the Swedish army, or better, started chasing it in 1742 finally trapping it in Helsinki. The Swedish army put up no resistence and the commander, when allowed to return to Stockholm by the empress, was shortened by a head. The Russian army then occupied Finland.

The plight of Sweden was so desperate on land and sea that the new empress could very easily have kept Finland and seriously considered doing so. Keith was placed in charge of the country and told to treat the local inhabitants well which indicated intentions in this direction. But dynastic considerations prevailed, and since the ruling line in Sweden was about to die out, Elisabeth selected the Bishop of Lübeck to be his successor because her nephew in Holstein had the best claim on the Swedish as well as the Russian thrones and she wanted to insure her family would retain control in Russia.[20] After much negotiation the Swedes were forced to accept the Russian proposal by which they received back most of Finland and accepted the "Russian" candidate as their next ruler. The French/Swedish plan was thus a total failure and in the future it was Russia that dictated to Sweden and not the reverse.

NOTES

1 V.T. Stroev. *Bironovshchina i Katinet Ministrov. Ocherk vnutrenei Politiki Imperatritsy Anny.* Moscow: Moskovskii Universitet, 1909. V.N. Bondarenko. "Ocherk finansovoi Politiki Kabineta Ministrov Anny Ioannovny ", *Zapiski imperatorskago arkheologicheskago moskovoskago Instituta imeni Imperator Nikolaia II,* Vol. XXIX, Moscow, 1913. For more recent attempts in English see A. Lipskii, "A Reexamination of the 'Dark Era' of Anna Ioannovna," *American and East European Review,* XV (1956), No. 4, 477-88. Ibid., "Some Aspects of Russia's Westernization during the Reign of Anna Ioannovna, 1730-1740," *American Slavic and East European Review,* XVIII (1959), No.1, 1-44.

2 P. Bezobrazov, "Neuroshai proshlago Veka", *Russkoe Obozrenie,* 1892, Vol. I, 693-749. The year of the appearance of this article was the second famine year in a row in Russia and apparently subsequent installments of the article were suppressed.

3 Bondarenko, 206,16.

4 Stroev, 134.

5 Roger Portal, *L'Oural au XVIII-e siècle* (Paris: Institut d'Etudes Slaves, 1950), 118.

6 Peter von Haven, *Reise in Russland aus dem Däischen in Deutsch übersetzt von H.A.R.*(Coppenhagen: Gabriel Christian Rothe, 1744), 233-36.

7 Bondarenko, 328-35. *Dictionary of National Biography.* Vol. XXXI (London: Smith, Elder & Co., 1892), 385-87. "Lacy, Count Peter. (1678-1751)". "Complaints against Münnich's severities and mismanagement were now so loud that the Czarina

asked Lacy to undertake the investigation of his colleague's conduct. Lacy declined the invidious task; but Münnich appears to have accused him of detraction, and a violent scene ensued, in which the Marshals drew on each other their swords ...."

8 Locatelli, 112.

9 Haven, 403-04.

10 A.D. Korsakov, "Artemii Petrovich Volynskii i ego 'Konfidenty' ", *Russkaia Starina,*LXVIII, October, 1885, 17-54. Iu.V. Got'e, "Proekt o Popravlenii gosudarstvennykh Del Artemiia Petrovich Volynskogo," *Dela i Dni,* III, 1922, 1-31.

11 S.M. Solovev, *Istoriia Rossii s drevneishkh Vremen,* X (Moscow: "Mysl'," 1963), 670-686. He was judged by Russians and his estate given to Nepliuev, later the famous governor to Orenburg. From 1960-66 *The History of Russia* by Solovev has been reprinted in the USSR with two volumes printed in one book. In the book the number for the old volumes will be given for the new edition.

12 *Ibid.,* 21, 99.

13 N.N. Firsov, *Vstuplenia na Prestol Imperatrtsy Elizavety Petrovny* (Kazan: Kazan Universitet, 1887), 72. This work is the best for the seizure of power by Elisabeth.

14 "No. 69. Le Marquis de la Chétardie à m. Amelot. St. Petersburg, 2 septembre 1741", *SIRIO,* Vol. 96 (St. Petersburg, 1896), 354.

15 "No. 60. Le Marquis de la Chétardie à m. Amelot. St. Petersburg, 10 août 1741". *Ibid.,* 294.

16 The reader is referred to Firsov's book mentioned above for more details. For the best account in

English see Robert Nisbet Bain,*The Daughter of Peter the Great* (Westminister: Archibald Constable & Co. 1899), 50-65.

17 As is known Elisabeth was the first modern ruler not to use the death penalty which explains the relatively mild treatment of her "enemies". She could still be unjust in her selection of victims. Biographies of the leading "victims" appeared in the next few years. Christian-Fredrich Hempel. *Merchwürdigs Leben und trauriger Fall des weltberufenen russischen, Staats-Ministers, Andrei Grafen von Ostermann*. Bremen: N. Saurmann, 1742. The same author wrote a similar book for Biron in 1742 and one for Münnich in 1743. As could be expected he praised the fallen persons and condemned their treatment. The fact that this series was issued indicates the interest then in Europe for Russia and the lingering ethnocentrism directed against that "dark and barbarous state".

18 A recent writer takes a greatly differing view on the situation. Frances ley, *Le Maréchal de Münnich et la Russia aux XVIII-e siècle* (Paris: Plon, 1959), 200. "La prise du pouvoir d'Elisabeth, en conclusion, apparaît comme une victoire purement personelle de la fille de Pierre le Grand, favorisée par les evenéments, et appuyé par le parti franco-suedois de Saint-péterbourg". The difference between the two points of view resides in the attitude toward Münnich. It was to the advantage of Ley to make Münnich appear in as favorable light as possible. Thus, he chose to minimize or ignore the supposed negative sides of the Münnich affair.

19 Solovev, 23 (Moscow: "Mysl'," 1964), 638-39.

20 M. Borodkin, *Istoriia Finliandii. Vremia Elizavety Petrovny* (St. Petersburg: Gosudarstvennaia tipografiia, 1910), 21-243.

CHAPTER TWO

GOVERNING RUSSIA

Once the Russian party had come to power the question was posed: How should the governmental form be organized? There was no challenge to the concept of the autocratic power of the new ruler for by this time it was accepted as part of the political structure. But this autocratic power needed to be implemented in some manner. In 1711 Peter had instituted the Ruling Senate which had two main functions: (1) to oversee the implementation of the Ukazes of the ruler judging on minor points concerning the intent (thus it had a judicial function), (2) it was to act in the place of the Tsar or his successors when the "imperial presence" was out of the country. On rare occasions it acted on its own as when it gave Peter the title "emperor" and "Great".Upon Peter's death the importance of the Senate was lessened and its chief function became judicial. In the reign of Catherine I in February of 1726 a new governmental body was created to assist the inexperienced ruler to carry out her functions--Supreme Privy Council. This Council actually issued laws and took upon itself much of the more important functions of the Senate. Initially the Council was selected by Catherine and Menshikov and besides themselves included Ostermann, Golitsyn, the Herzog of Holstein, the husband of Catherine's oldest daughter, Ann, and eventually members of the leading Dolgorukii family were included. Upon the death of Catherine I in 1727 the Herzog of Holstein was forced to leave the country and return to his own country. With the young Peter II as ruler the Supreme Privy Council took on more importance and the leading families started gaining greater control. Elisabeth had no influence upon the course of events and soon Menshikov was removed from the scene as well. This left the Council a clique of the leading families of Russia having no representatives of the service nobility which Peter had pushed to the forefront.

The sudden death of Peter II in 1730 gave the Supreme Privy Council the power to ignore the will of Catherine I and make its own choice. As noted above the throne and the autocratic power went to Anna of Courland. Anna soon destroyed the Supreme Privy Council and sent its members into exile with the exception of the cautious Ostermann. She replaced it with a Cabinet of Ministers which served as her executive throughout her reign and lasted briefly into the regencies which followed.

Through this period the Senate remained and,briefly,at the beginning of Anna's reign regained much of its importance before the creation of the Cabinet.[1] Once Elisabeth had taken the power the situation was once more open. With eleven chief advisors Elisabeth then proceeded to reconstruct the government. Elisabeth, like the new service nobility, felt a very strong bond with her father and what he had done to reform the country. Hence, on the 3rd of December a few days after coming to power it was decided that the Senate be given its old powers and become the chief ruling power in the country. Russia was not to see another cabinet until the start of the Seven Years' War in 1756.[2] There were certain areas in which the Senate did not have any authority such as foreign affairs, the Ukraine, religious matters which were under the control of the Holy Synode, the secret police, and personal matters concerning the ruler such as her private estates, gold and silver mines and a few other minor exceptions.

The Senate was officially restored to its old powers by an Ukaz of the 12th of December, 1741.[3] Several of the members of the inner council of the initial take-over period were added to the Senate. Never before or after

38

was the Senate to have so much power. It was one of the few Petrine institutions which survived until destroyed by the Bolshevik Revolution in 1917 and its last act was a condemnation of that Revolution.

The empress announced her intention of attending the meetings of the Senate which, along with those of the Foreign Office, were to be held in her palace. But after a few visits her attendance was rare and the meetings held in the traditional buildings. The Senate was comanded to consider only matters which she ordered it to consider,but soon, as a result of her inactivity, the Senate ignored this order and became a sort of legislature.[4] For the first few years of the reign the Senate had difficulty finding its role in the system since it had been so little used during the previous reigns, but it did regain at once its powers over the Colleges and local administration. Throughout the period it gradually extended its range of activities handling nearly all matters relating to the internal ordering of the state except for those specifically exempt from its authority like the Synode. Starting December 12, 1741, the Senate was given the impossible task of examining all the laws issued since the death of Elisabeth's father in 1725 to determine if these laws conformed to the "spirit" of the reforms of her father.[5] Given the rate with which the Senate proceeded with this task it would have taken a hundred years to finish. Eventually this hopeless enterprise was abandoned for a full codification of the laws. Automatically all laws issued since the death of Anna Ioanovna during the regencies were declared void and all books mentioning Anna's nephew, little John, were to be changed. Only with difficulty did the Senate persuade her not to cancel all awards and honors given during the two regencies of Biron and the mother of little John. In addition, the Senate was given the unpleasant ordeal of the judicial trial of members of the "German" party such as Ostermann and Münnich.

As will be recalled Elisabeth inherited a war started to place her nephew on the Russian throne and refused to stop the fighting when she came to power. It became the duty of the Senate to oversee the war. Hence, the Senate had to provide forage to support the horses in the Finnish campaign, feed and pay the troops, as well as keeping the forts in readiness in case of attack. A typical order of this nature was sent to the governor of Revel, Avram Petrovich Gannibal, to prepare for an attack by the Swedish fleet and to keep an especially close watch for Swedish spies.[6] Lacy and Keith reported the activities of the army directly to the Senate in the year 1742 when Finland was overrun. The start of the campaign was marked by a total lack of respect for the Finns who, according to reports received and approved by the Senate, were cut down like grain even if they offered no resistence.[7] When the fighting stopped and peace negotiations started, after the occupation of nearly all of Finland, the Senate had the responsibility, in conjunction with the army, of administering the region until peace was concluded and most of the region returned to Sweden. The peace negotiations leading to the Treaty of Åbo (Turku) were under the exclusive control of the Foreign Office and no reference to them appears in the published *Senatskii Archiv*.

The Senate had control of local administration. The existing system had been inherited from Peter the Great. Starting in 1708 Peter formed the Gubernias as the chief large administrative unit of the country. He used large Gubernias on the assumption that he could find enough honest people to keep them running correctly. By the time of his death there were fourteen of these units but not the same number of honest officials. The Gubernia were subdivided into units called provinces which in turn were divided into uezdy. Each of the Gubernias had a governor as its head while the Provinces were headed by officials bearing the old Moscovite title voevoda. Each of these regions originally had special officers attached to them existing outside the official structure named procurators whose job it was to insure the honest management of affairs. These had been dropped soon after Peter's death, but they were revived on the Gubernia level by Elisabeth. Actually they seem to have been ineffective and in any case they were responsible to the secret police.

In the reign of Elisabeth the Senate had to concern itself with sixteen Gubernias: Archangel, Belgorod, Kiev, Moscow, Novgorod, Petersburg (formerly Ingermanland), Riga, Astrakhan, Voronezh, Smolensk, Kazan, Nizhnyi-Novgorod, Revel, Siberia, Orenburg and Vybourg.[8] The latter two were formed in 1744 from territories recently acquired by the Russian state. Siberia was a special case. The Gubernias were normally named after the largest city which acted as the capital. But the governor of Siberia lived in Tobolsk not too far from European Russia and his assistant, the vice-governor, in Irkutsk.

Of equal importance to the local government was the control of the central bureaucracy. Using various foreign models Peter the Great drastically changed the form of the central administration. In place of the old numerous Prikazy which had been created according to need, he established fixed institutions with defined powers misleadingly called Colleges.The Shtats-College was charged with disbursing funds for the entire territory, the Commerce College handled the foreign trade, the Treasury College collected funds, the Justice College was charged with legal matters, the Estates College was charged with recording the estates of nobles and handling disputes over them, the Foreign Office or College, the War College, the Admiralty, the Manufacture College to encourage industrial production, the Mining College to search for and exploit mineral deposits (which was closed during the reign of Anna but immediately reopened by Elisabeth), and lastly the city administrator called the Chief

41

Magistrate.[9] These were to be operated through a system of Collegial responsibility to reduce the chance of corruption. The Foreign Office had been separated from the control of the Senate as a consequence of its great importance. These Colleges and offices had tended to drift from under the control of the Senate when the Supreme Privy Council and its successor, the Cabinet, were in existence. It was during this period that the functions of the Senate were chiefly judicial. But with the re-establishment of the Senate as Peter had empowered it caused the Senate to take nearly full control of the Colleges which in turn could send orders to the local administration concerning matters within their competence.

The functioning of the Colleges--especially those of lesser importance--was indeed poor. In 1744 the Commerce College complained that its employees came to work late or not at all. Thus, it was unable to function. In October of that same year a soldier was sent from the Senate to the Justice College with a message and did not find one person there.[10] This loaded more and more of the routine work on the already overworked Senate. On New Year's Day of 1756 the Senate issued a sharp reprimand to the Commerce College because it was receiving the regular business of that college.[11] The Senate had to order the officials of both the central and regional administration to be on time for work or lose a day's pay for one hour's tardiness and a month's for an unexcused day's absence.[12] It is doubtful if this had any real effect since the officials tended to protect each other.

The situation of the remuneration of the selected officials for both the central and local administration was confusing and somewhat contradictory. Peter had instituted an unequal system for paying his officials. Foreigners in the service of the Russian state were paid more since they were considered more likely to be honest and also the desire of the government to retain their services. There is

42

little doubt that this caused resentment among the Russians and contributed to the downfall of the "German" party. In addition, Peter ordered that the pay of those in military service be twice that of those in the bureaucracy. Thus, when we consider the pay scale of governmental officials in 1755, a year for which the information is available, the variances are great. The members of the Foreign Office received the highest salaries. The Chancellor who also headed the Foreign College received 7,000 rubles a year and the vice Chancellor 6,000. The President of the Mining College, a Russian with serfs, was paid 1,800 rubles per year while his assistant, a foreigner without the right to hold serfs, received 2,400 rubles. The picture of the Manufacture College is likewise striking. The President, a member of the wealthy Saltykov family with a large number of serfs, was paid only 529 rubles whereas his assistant, a German, received 2,400 rubles. The ambassadors were the only persons truly well paid. The ambassador to Vienna received 15,000 rubles a year. [13] The Chancellor for most of the reign, Bestuzhev-Riumin, was notorious for his bribe taking, but he took them only from friendly powers. But in all justice to him, given his post of importance, his salary was simply inadequate and had often to be supplemented by gifts from the empress and her favorites. On the other hand, the ruble was a strong monetary unit in a period of virtually no inflation when 700 rubles could purchase a comfortable estate with a significant serf-labor force for those having the right to own serfs.

The pay for the local administrators was also low. This was especially noticeable among the governors whose salaries varied greatly depending upon the sensitivity of the post. The governor of the bordering province of Orenburg which had just been raised to the level of a Gubernia in 1744 received 4,188 rubles a year while the lowest paid governor received only 809 rubles--a level low enough to encourage corruption. Alongside each governor was a procurator whose sole job was to insure the honest operation of the governors. The pay levels for the procurators is not known. The voevodas would normally at least rank eight on the table of ranks (College Assessors) which meant that they were hereditary nobles with the right to own serfs and insured a salary of 300 rubles a year.[4]

The Soviet historian, S.M. Troitskii, in his excellent book on the relationship of absolutism to the nobility in Russia, has discovered much interesting information concerning the composition of the bureaucracy. He concluded that in the higher levels of the government there tended to be more members of the higher-ranked nobles than in the lower and that, therefore, the rich nobles had a disportionate influence in the policy making process.[15] This is not surprising. However, in the lower levels of the system a different picture emerges. The raznochintsy become much more important. An inquiry was made in 1753 concerning the social origins of this lower bureaucracy and partial returns were received. These replies indicated that of the civil servants only 21.5 percent were hereditary nobles while a large majority of 78.5 percent were raznochintsy.[16] This information tends to run counter to what had been previously suspected since the Universal Service State remained in tact, it was assumed that the percentage of nobles in the government would be very high. The raznochintsy--people without ranks--were clearly already a strong and growing force in Russian society which up to now have been underrated by historians. The bureaucracy could not function without them and their creation was a post-Petrine phenomenon which developed very rapidly. This assists in providing an explanation for the previously little understood governmental orders to people without the serf-holding right to sell their serfs or lose them to the state. The raznochintsy were social climbers seeking to work their way up through the system to a rank which would give them and their family hereditary nobility. This was countered by the government and finally made illegal.

Directly connected to this was the staffing problem of the governmental offices. This was a problem which was partially solved by the freeing of the gentry in 1762, but it was a severe problem of many years standing. Since the government wanted as many nobles as possible in local and state systems it would seem curious that the double standard for pay was maintained since the military career offered more to the nobles than the civil. There was a chronic problem of finding people for the civil service which was true even in the large cities with the high concentration of nobles. In 1739 the important offices of the Moscow and St. Petersburg governors provide examples. In Moscow the set staffing level was 128, but the governor had a staff of only 65. In 1754 even the Justice College had to request the Senate to find fifteen chancellary clerks for it.[17]

Having covered the structure and staffing of the Senate, the central government and local government, the question poses itself as to how they actually functioned and the types of problems which occupied them. The Senate would be the natural first choice since, next to the empress, it was the most important political body in the country. While it was trying to find a clear role in the system the Senate tended to become involved in matters which seemed petty. Perhaps it was its limited role in the past which accounted for this. A clear example was its initial concern with the supply rhubarb roots then considered an important medicine.[18] Nearly a third of the time of the Senate before 1753 was taken by this one problem. During Peter's reign the government had a monoply of this root product which came from China. Agents were placed in various centers to sell it for the government. After Peter the trade in it was freed for a large portion of the period, but in 1741 in the face of falling prices for it, the government again resumed its monoply role in the control of rhubarb root sales. Yet it was possible to purchase approximately a kilogram for 2.30 rubles and sell it abroad for 17.46 silver rubles for a profit of 765 percent.[19] This was a period before the development of extensive silver mines and Russia was dependent upon imported silver. The high profit margin was conducive to smuggling which in turn was followed by strict laws governing the control of rhubarb root supplies. Finally in 1760, with the price very low, the Senate permitted an individual to purchase rhubarb roots at the low rate of 6.10 rubles for a kilo.[20] The continued talk about rhubarb was probably enough to drive the empress away from the meetings of the Senate by itself.

The Senate continued to act as a last court of appeals (with the exception of the empress herself) and handled both criminal and civil cases outside the jurisdiction of the Synode. For criminal cases, especially those involving governmental officials, special commissions were established which were normally so slow that the person under investigation was dead or the charge had lost its meaning with a new reign.[21]

As a civil court the Senate often handled trivial affairs which at the time seemed important. A good example of this was the contribution of the German born Müller, the leading editor for the Academy of Sciences, of a history of Russia in which he did not link the ruling Romanovs as with the legendray founder of the Russian state, Rurik. Other members of the Academy of Sciences disagreed and the problem was presented to the Senate which established a committee of three Academy members, Lomonsov, Trediakovskii and Struve, to decide. Of course, they "proved" that the Romanovs were descended from Rurik on both sides of the family.[22] In another case a smithy from the Aleksandro-Nevskii monastery complained to the Senate that the monks there would not provide him with the necessary funds to construct a perpetual motion machine. This time the Senate ignored the Academy of Sciences and gave him the requested funds.[23] Hence, the all-powerful Ruling Senate could lose itself and its valuable time in trivialities.

Yet it did have very serious issues come before it. Just before the seizure of power the empress had vowed that nobody would be executed in Russia during her reign--a promise which she kept. The death penalty was not abolished by Ukaz, but it was done rather by careful neglect. The empress ordered that all cases involving capital punishment be reported to her where they remained. In an age in which the death penalty was accepted without question this horrified the Senate which was helpless to take action to restore it. In 1744 the Senate made a direct request of the empress concerning what action should be taken in these cases.[24] By then the prisons were beginning to be filled with convicted criminals who normally were destined for the most cruel and unusual deaths. Receiving no reply the Senate acted on an order she had given to Lacy during the Swedish war to "execute" them by burning the sign VOR for thief on their foreheads, putting them in chains for good and then assigning them to some governmental project "eternally".[25] This marked change in policy was perhaps the most sensational of the reign and made Russia the first country to abolish capital punishment. The contrast with the previous reigns including that of her father could not have been greater. For the murder of a husband or wife the guilty party was buried in the ground with just their head exposed and left to die. In 1759 there were in Omsk alone, on their way to the silver mines, twenty-four women convicted of killin their husbands, ten for killing their children and one for killing her father.[26] At first these people were sent to the ship-building yards near Revel and then later to Siberia to work the silver mines as these were discovered. Throughout her reign the Senate tried unsuccessfully to induce her to reverse her decision.

It was the task of the Senate to insure that no dangerous disease broke out in Russia. Of course, some like smallpox were always there. But when a disease was reported in a neighboring country the Senate at once ordered the border closed and threatened that anyone trying to cross would be shot. When disease was reported and trade was still desirable, quarantine posts were established where arriving foreigners with merchandise or money could be kept for weeks under strict observation. This quarantine was so strict that it was often suspected that the Russian government was using the quarantine to the disadvantage of foreign merchants.[27] The Senate acted with great rapidity when a suspected disease was reported. Many cases could be cited but one will be used as an example. On July 6th, 1747 it was reported that four men had died on an estate near Moscow of a violent disease in a few hours. From the description it appears to have been a case of food poisoning. Doctors were rushed to the region and reported to the Senate on the 21st of July that if it was actually a disease it was not spreading and therefore not dangerous.[28]

The Hoof and Mouth disease had made its appearance in Russia in the previous reign and was another serious problem which the Senate handled. A serious outbreak in 1743 took up much of the time of the Senate and continued to do so as the disease did not let up.[29] Horses and horned cattle were the chief victims of this frequently fatal ailment. This posed especially serious problems since the horse constituted the only fast communication and transportation system in the country. The state owned and operated a postal and transportation system based on post-stations. Soon it was discovered that the number of horses had fallen so greatly in certain regions that the rates had to be raised to compensate the serfs who ran the system. The methods used by the Senate against the disease are similar to those in use today. Quarantine was strictly enforced in the affected regions, and the importa-

tation of animals from regions reporting it was strictly illegal. These countries were listed in the bi-weekly official
Sankt Peterburgskiia Vedmosti and enforced at the
customs posts. Animals dying from the disease were to be
burned or buried so deeply in the earth that wild animals
could not reach them. Under no circumstances were the
skins to be taken from the dead animals.[30] About the
only major difference in today's treatment of this disease
is that bleeding is no longer used as a means of treating
dying animals.

One of the most important functions of the Senate in view
of the needs of the state was the use of governors and
local authorities to monitor events in neighboring
countries. This function was performed for the Foreign
Office and reports went to it through the Senate. The governors were to insure that no sudden attack could come
from a country neighboring a given Gubernia. Although no
actual war broke out until 1756 and then not with a neighbor, there were near wars with the Ottoman Empire,
Persia, the Central Asian states, Sweden and even China.
For example in the early forties the governor of
Astrakhan and foremost historian of his time, Tatishchev,
repeatedly reported threatening developments in Persia
and was constantly answering inquiries by the Senate
about the situation.[31] The governor of Smolensk kept the
Senate informed about events in Poland, the governor of
Kiev sent in reports about Poland and the Ottomans while
the Siberian governor had to observe the entire boundary
with Central Asia and China. When Orenburg became a
Gubernia in 1744 its governor had to watch carefully the
peoples of the plaines who were constantly restive. Likewise when Vybourg was elevated to a Gubernia in the
same year its governor was warned to watch for plots and
spies from Sweden.[32]

The voevodas at the provincial level were subordinate to
the governors in most matters except the "soul" tax. The

collection of taxes to support the army and recruits to fill its ranks were functions which the forty-four voevodas were directly responsible to the Senate. The collection of the taxes had been a serious problem over the years ever since Peter's system of 70 copeecks per male "soul" had gone into effect. The collecting agency had varied with the needs of the state. In time of war when the need was great, troops accompanied the local officials on their rounds to the various estates to collect the taxes. It will be recalled what a crushing burden this had been in the previous reign with its prolonged wars and very short periods of peace. The landowners themselves could be held responsible for the payment of the tax. The local officials maintained the records from one census to another. It was according to these records that the taxes were collected. Thus, a typical situation of collection during the reign of Elisabeth would be the following: the uezd official would receive an order for the yearly collection of the tax. Accompanied by a clerk and if necessary police or soldiers (normally police to protect the collected monies from robbers) the local official would visit each village and ask for the taxes. If the village paid it was so recorded in the clerks records. If a village could not pay this was also recorded and the village could fall years into arrears. Upon completion of the round the local official would then forward the records and money to the voevoda who had the right to retain a limited amount for local needs. The remainder would go to the treasury for use by the government especially the army. The collection of taxes was so lightly handled in comparison to other periods that the historian Kliuchevsky stated that the reign of Elisabeth rested most lightly upon Russia.[33]

The voevodas were also responsible for the "state serfs" who belonged directly to the government and had no duties to the landowners. As shall be indicated these were the people having the best lot among the serfs.

The local authorities had the duty of acting as both police and courts of first instance. Minor crimes could be handled by the landowner or the elders in the commune. More serious crimes were handled first by the uezd authorities and if of sufficient severity by the voevoda who maintained a prison and court. Hence, law and order rested with the local authorities, but if matters really became difficult it was traditional for the governor to maintain a force of soldiers in readiness especially in troubled regions.

The government undertook special measures to try to upgrade the local authorities. In a special law the size of the houses of the voevodas were made uniform differing little from those of the governor.[34] The house of the governor was to have eight rooms, a stable for twelve horses, winter and summer storage areas, a bath, and sufficient offices including a detached stone building for keeping records. The voevodas were allowed five rooms (or four if in a city), a barn and one storage area. These were to be paid for by money taken from the "soul" tax. Attempts were made to establish levels of employees for each gubernia (30), for the provincial (15) and personally for the voevodas (10).[35] The shortage of potential officials made this impossible until after the freeing of the nobility from the Universal Service State in 1762. After this event Catherine set the levels at 34, 13 and 11.[36]

Bribe taking and arbitrary rule were serious problems facing the government. The problem was not new nor was it to be solved quickly. Peter had made it a serious crime to take bribes, but many of his associates still broke the law. Despite the fact that by the end of the 1740's three-fourths of the voevodas were between 50 and 70 years of age and that 61.2 percent of them owned fifty serfs or more, the bribe taking continued.[37]

The governors were appointed for the term which the

ruler set which could be indefinite. One manner in which it was possible to fight corruption was to shift the voevodas about in short periods of time so that they could not really entrench themselves. In 1730 the government set the term for the voevodas at an unreasonably short two years.[38] In 1744 the term was made indefinite as long as there were no complaints, but this made the situation worse since it was noted that the poorer and honest voevodas were kept from the management of their estates by their jobs while the greedy and dishonest officials built up fortunes and did not have to worry about their estates. [39] In 1760 the Senate again set a definite term of five years for a voevoda which could be exended for another five if in the last year of their five years favorable petitions concerning them were received from the localities. [40] One of the main sources of the trouble in this situation was simply the limited number of persons legally capable of holding high office since most of the nobles were in state service and those remaining were ill, wounded or elderly.

A few examples of the corruption and the fight against it would help expose the magnitude of the problem. Protection in high places helped. One General Procurator of Senate lost his position as a result of a scandal he had helped suppress several years before. In 1758 the government sent one Krylov to Irkutsk to collect the new tax on strong drinks which had just gone into effect. Since Irkutsk is isolated (or was then) by distance from St. Petersburg it was possible for Krylov to seal the region off and keep control despite the existence of a vice-governor. He tortured the population by forcing wealthy merchants to pay outrageous taxes, he violated the women at will and even killed persons he felt could be paying him more. Repeated efforts failed to alert the central government, but the protection of Senator Glebov saved him. Finally he overstepped even the brutal bounds existing in Siberia and was arrested by the vice-governor. But the "memory of Krylov lingered long in Irkutsk" and his protector was made head of the Senate before his connection with the incident was uncovered.[41] Nepliuev, the honest governor of Orenburg, had a highly dishonest official working under his jurisdiction. With a great deal of trouble, patience and hard work Nepliuev was successful in the dismissal and trial of the official. The dismissed official pretended to be insane and when he encountered a high official he said with some justice: "A little thief greets a big thief".[42] In 1760 he was reinstated. Even Tatishchev, the above—mentioned governor of Astrakhan and historian took bribes. Peter himself accused him of it and his reply was that the apostles had taken gifts to continue their work. He was exiled finally in the reign of Elisabeth to his estate and found not guilty just before his death.

Despite the above the government did have a few honest persons it could depend upon. It is interesting to note that the empress herself was active in rooting out corruption which she attempted to achieve by promoting those known to be honest. Thus, Prince Shakhovskoi, the head of the Holy Synode for a number of years was appointed in 1760 to be the General Procurator of the Senate with orders to clean up the entire structure. Nepliuev from Orenburg was shifted from his position as governor of Orenburg to the Senate to assist in the attempted reform from above and during the reign of Catherine was used as a special advisor on ways and means of improving the bureaucracy. Neither was very bright or original.

In conclusion to this chapter it can be noted that the general theme in the ordering of the structure and functioning of the governmental apparatus was based mainly on the model of Peter the Great. The nature of many of the problems had changed, but the main thrust of the government, or the empress more specifically, was to re-establish the "pure" system established by her father.

Like her father, she lacked the necessary educated people to make the machinery work as intended. But the process was underway to develop such people and subsequent reigns benefited by the seeds sown from Peter's time on.

imp. pt.: didn't succeed; but started ball rolling

NOTES

1 A. Filippov, "Doklad Impertritse Elizavete
Petrovne o Vostanovlenii Vlasti 'Pravitel'
stvuiutsago Senate", *Zhurnal Ministerstva narodnago
Proveshchenii,* February, 1897, 279.

2 *Ibid.,* 285-91.

3 *Polne Sobranie Zakonov rossiiskoi Imperii,* Vol. XI
(St. Petersburg: Tipografiia II Otdeleniia Sobst-
vennoi ego imperatorskago Velichestva Kantseliarii, 1830), No. 8480. Personal. December 12,
1741. Hereafter this important collection of Russian laws will be referred to simply as *PZS.* The
volume and number of the law will be provided, but
the page will not be. The source of the law
will also be given so the reader will be able to
determine if the law was ordered directly by the
empress or the Senate. Finally the date of the law
will be provided. This is one of the most important sources for the history of Russia after
1649 since the most important laws are printed in
it.

4 In the last half of the 19th century and up to the
revolutions of 1917 the old regime was doing an
excellent job of publishing much of the archival
materials of importance. The 148 volumes of the
SIRIO are a good example of this. In addition portions of the minutes of the Senate were also
published. *Senatskii Arkhiv.*St. Petersburg: Senatskaia Tipografiia, 1892-1904. Volumes 5-12 cover
the period under consideration and these tend to
be very long. Despite the length, on the basis of
the studies Soviet and non-Soviet historians who
have used the actual archives, a very large
portion was, indeed ,not published. Waliszewski, who

claimed to have used the archives at the end of the 19th century, lists actions of the Senate on days when no meetings are listed in the printed archives. This indicates that the Senate must have been heavily utilized and overworked. Unfortunately for the reign of Elisabeth with few exceptions, the members in attendance are not listed as they had been in the previous reigns.

5 A.E. Presniakov, *Istoriia pravitelstvuiushchago Senate za dvesti Let, 1711-1911.* Vol. II. *Pravitelstvuiushchii Senat V Tsarstvovaniia Elisavety Petronvy i Petra Feodorovicha,* (St. Petersburg: Senatskaia Tipografiia, 1911), 6. This is one of the best works on the period. It was written as a team project by a number of famous historians. Hence, it is listed normally without the author. But in this case the author--an outstanding historian--wrote the section on the reign of Elisabeth.

6 *Senatskii Arkhiv,* V, 357-65. June 24 and July 7, 1742. Gannibal or Hannibal was a member of the "Russian" party who had sufferred during the previous reign. Peter the Great had received him as a black slave, converted him to the Orthodox religion, acted as his God-father, and, in view of his excellent mind, sent him to Paris to study. In the Orthodox religion the God-father relation is nearly the same as blood relation. Hence, Elisabeth treated him very well. He served the state throughout the reign and retired as a full General with an estate near Pskov and 569 serfs. He was the great-grandfather of Russia's greatest poet, Pushkin, who himself had traces of his black ancestry and was extremely proud of it. D.M. Khmyrov, "Avraam Petrovich Gannibal. (Biograficheskii Ocherk po Dokumentam)", *Istoricheskiia Stati M.D. Khmyrova* (St. Petersburg: Pechatkin, 1873), 1-66.

7 Senatskii Arkhiv, 334-35. March 29, 1742. One officer "proudly" reported that he had burned 97
Finnish villages with all their grain killing in
the process 300 people and taking only four
prisoners. Soon the government decided it would
annex Finland so they started to treat the Finns
very well.

8 "Ropis' Guberniiam, Provintsiiam, Gorodam,
Krepostiam i drugim dostopamiatnym Mestam v rossiiskoi Impreii nakhodiashchimsia",*Ezhemesiachnyia
Sochineniia k Pol'ze i Uveseleniiu Sluzhashchiia*
(St. Petersburg: Akademiia Nauk), January, 1757,
3-49; February, 1757, 99-125; March, 1757,
195-223. Hereafter this periodical will be
referred to by its shortened title *Ezhemesiachnyia*
... With the exception of 1759 this was the only
monthly learned journal in the country. It was
semi-official being printed by the Academy of
Sciences.

9 B.B. Kafengauz, N.I. Pavlenko, *Ocherki Istorii
SSSR. Period Feodalizma. Rossiia v pervoi Chet-
verti XVIIIv. Preobrazovaniia Petra I* (Moscow:
Akademiia Nauk, 1954), 303.

10 Solov'ev, 21, 249-50.

11 *PSZ,* XIV, No. 10,495. Senate. January 1, 1756.

12 *Ibid.,* XIV, No. 10,657. Senate. November 26,
1756. *Ibid.,* XV, No. 11, 169. Senate. December
15, 1760.

13 S.M. Troitskii, *Russkii Absolutizm i Dvorianstvo
v XVIII veke. Formirovania Biurokratii* (Moscow:
Nauk, 1974), 258-59. This book is one of the best
studies of the bureaucracy yet to appear for the
18th Century in any language. The fact that much
of it concerns the reign of Elisabeth makes it
doubly valuable for this study. Troitskii noted

in addition that the General-Procurator of the Senate was likewise paid a low 3,000 rubles for his important position. Apparently in April of 1761 the General-Procurator of the Senate, Shakhovskoi, raised the whole issue of governmental salaries, 265.

14 Iu. Got'e [Greuthier], *Istoriia oblastnogo Upravleniia v Rossii ot Petra I do Ekateriny II*. Vol. 1 (Moscow: Moskovskii Universtet, 1913), 187.

15 Troitskii, 179.

16 *Ibid.*, 366.

17 Got'e, 287-90.

18 Brokhauz I Efrom, *Entsiklopedicheskii Slovar* (Liepiz, 1899), Vol. 51, 420.

19 V.K. Andreevich, *Istoricheskii Ocherk Sibirii.Tom III. Period ot 1742 do 1762 goda* (Tomsk,1887),120.

20 *PSZ,* XV, No. 11,118. Senate. October 11, 1760.

21 Got'e, 252.

22 *Senatskii Arkhiv,* VII, 182-86; 238-39. July and December of 1747.

23 Presiankov, 205.

24 *Senatskii Arkhiv,* VI, 62-63. May 11, 1744. *PSZ,* XII, No. 8944. Senate. Max 7 [sic], 1744.

25 Senatskii Arkhiv, VI, 642-43. March 17, 1746.

26 Andreevich, 60.

27 Jonas Hanway, *An Historical Account of the British Trade over the Caspian Sea with the Author's Journal of the Travels from England into Persia, and Back through Russia, Germany and Holland ... The Second Edition Revised and Corrected* (London: J. Sewell, 1754), Vol. I, 221.

28 *Senatskii Arkhiv,* VII, 166; 175-76. July 6, 1747-July 21, 1747.

29 *Ibid.,* V, 608-09. July 14, 1743.

30 *PSZ,* XII, No. 9130. Senate. March 27, 1745.

31 *Senatskii Arkhiv,* V, 485-87. November 23-26, 1742.

32 *Ibid.,* VI, 286-88. December 7, 1744.

33 V.O. Kliuchevsky, *Sochineniia.* Vol. IV. *Kurs Russkoi Istorii'.* Part 4 (Moscow: Sots Ekon. Lit., 1958), 339-40.

34 *PSZ,* XIII, No. 9662. Senate. September 1, 1749.

35 *Ibid.,* XIV, No. 10,473. Senate. October 11, 1755.

36 Got'e, 149-50.

37 *Ibid.,* 217.

38 *Ibid.,* 149-50.

39 *Ibid.,* 152-53.

40 *PSZ,* XV, No. 11,131. Senate. October 26, 1760.

41 P. Golovachev, *Irkustskoe Likholet'e. 1758-1760gg.* (Moscow: Kas'ianov, 1904), 3-45.

42 V.N. Vitevskii, *I.I. Nepliuev i orenburgskii Krai v Prezhem ego Sostave do 1758g, istoricheskaia Monografiia* (Kazan: Kliuchnikov, 1987), I, 201-15.

CHAPTER THREE

SERFDOM

The lowest position as is known in Russian society in this period was occupied by the serfs or "human cattle" as many foreigner observers called them. Of all the developments of the post-Mongol period it is the general consensus that the institution of serfdom had the dubious distinction of retarding the growth of Russia as a modern state. Indeed, traces of serfdom's effects still existed in backward rural Russia after emancipation in 1861. There were a few hundred thousand "free" people like the nobles, merchants, and raznochintsy living lives which contrasted greatly to those of the millions of "taxable" serfs living in miserable poverty, owned by the nobles, the Orthodox Church, merchants, the imperial court and the state itself. These people were true slaves in the full sense of the word especially those belonging to the nobles, Church or merchants. While the reign of Catherine the Great is normally considered the worst period for the serfs, the reigns of Anna and Elisabeth were likewise terrible. It is often noted that even at the beginning of the reign of Elisabeth they were "dehumanized" by being explicitly excluded from taking the oath of allegiance to the new empress which was the duty of the "free" classes. But in this case a note of caution is necessary. Upon the death of Anna in late 1740 the serfs had been required to take an oath to the regent, Biron. Soon after he was overthrown and they had to take an oath to the mother of the infant John,Anna. Now within months a new ruler had seized the throne. It was confusing enough for foreigners to follow the events much less the serfs or "plowing peasants" as they were called in the decree.[1]

As noted before Elisabeth retained many of the aspects of the Universal Service State created by her father while retaining at the same time some subsequent modifications of Anna such as the abolition of the entailment law which required that the whole estate of a noble go to only one son as well as the limit of 25 years obligatory service for the nobles introduced by Anna in 1736. Any justification of serfdom ended with the abolition of service by the nobles by Peter III in 1762. Yet their condition continued to decline in the reign of Catherine despite her views on the subject.

The power of the landowner over his serfs and their possessions was almost unlimited. However, they were not permitted to put serfs to death possibly on the religious grounds that the serfs were Orthodox and still did have souls which could be lost if killed. Practically any form of torture was permitted as long as it did not result in the death of serfs. Questionable cases were tried near the end of the reign in which tortured serfs died. If a noble was found guilty of really wanting to induce death by torture he or she could lose title of nobility and be shipped to Siberia "eternally". If there existed the least doubt the noble was forced to do church penance and be completely freed of guilt.[2] The most notorious case of the reign, and historically the most renowned, was that of the noble woman, Saltykova, who personally ordered the torturing of serfs to death for her own amusement over a period of several years. Repeated petitions bought no results until the reign of Catherine the Great when the demented Saltykova was found guilty in the deaths of over seventy-seven serfs, stripped of her title of nobility and placed under guard in a convent for the rest of her life. Her serfs whom she had forced to torture other serfs were given bodily punishment and sent to Siberia.[3]

These facts are well known and accepted by historians. But there also exist misconceptions concerning the serf situation during the reign of Elisabeth. For one thing the government did not encourage the selling of individual serfs although the practice was accepted. Some say that advertisements appeared in every issue of the official journal, *Sankt Peterburgskiia Vedomosti*. This is incorrect since only estates with serfs on them were advertised for sale.[4] It was clear that the government was attempting to retain Peter the Great's concept that the serfs be linked with the land. There were advertisements for black slaves, parrots and even a ten ruble reward was offered for the return of a lost dog.[5] Another problem involved the actual value of the serfs sold. The sale of estates took place on a regular basis. These give us some concept of the actual value of the serfs. It has been accepted on the basis of the work of S.M. Semevskii that the average price of a male "soul" in 1760 was thirty rubles.[6] In reality it was about one-third of the price he placed upon it. An advertisement in the official journal, *Sankt Petersburgskiia Vedomosti,* in 1760 offered a large amount of land (81.94 hectars or 241.7 acres) with forty-four male "souls" and forty women serfs for a minimum of 610 rubles.[7] Not taking into account the value of the land, but just that of the men and women the average price of a serf would be 7.26 rubles which means that the true average was approximately five rubles. Another sale in 1756 involved fifteen males and sixteen women with "much land" near St. Petersburg indicated an average price of 10.48 rubles per person not taking land into account.[8] When the government bank for the nobles opened in 1756, it allowed the use of male "souls" as collateral and set a value of ten rubles. Since the bank required collateral worth one and a half times the value of the loan, this indicates that the government itself valued a male serf at fifteen rubles. The cost of the land was never considered.

Another source for the value of serfs exists. The Kursk Archives, recording the sales of serfs between 1689 and

1838, provides us with more information on the subject. As all sales had to be recorded with the local clerk and eventually with the Krepostnyi Kontor through the clerk, it is surprising that more information does not exist on this subject. According to the Kursk Archive, the lowest prices for serfs were in the reigns of Anna and Elisabeth. There were 34 individual transactions in which women sold for about two to three rubles whereas men sold for five to ten rubles. In some cases in this period a whole family could be purchased for ten rubles.[9] In another province three small girls were sold for a ruble each.[10] In the Kursk sales, one thing is marked--women outsold men. Of the thirty-four sales twenty-three were women.[11] While some were purchased as wives for other serfs, the system was open to clear abuse.

*****

Much has been written concerning the terrible conditions among the serfs in the XVIII century. Foreigners resident in the country or visiting it were usually appalled by the situation often comparing conditions among the serfs with those of the slaves in the American colonies. Winch, the British Ambassador, noted shortly after Elisabeth's coup that the nobles would prefer to " ... live at their villages at their ease and to tyrannize over their boors [serfs], who are the greatest slaves in the world".[12] Hanway traveled 200 kilometers from Moscow growing ever more disgusted by the large number of poor serfs living on rich land oppressed by rich nobles who refused to consider helping them.[13] Haven found the serfs were already using the saying that there was no hope in this world because "God is high above and the Tsar faraway" (Bog vysoko i Tsar daleko).[14] In contrast it is remarkable what an impression the free Cossacks made upon both Hanway (an English merchant) and Haven. The Cossacks were enterprising; they had much better villages and Haven, himself a theology student, was impressed by their priests who apparently had been trained in Kiev some even knowing Latin.[15] The state of the Cossacks was an indication of what a different fate the serfs would have had if freed and allowed to operate their own farms.

Several groups had the legal right to own serfs the chief of these being the nobles holding the rank of eight or above on Peter's scale of fourteen. The merchants engaged in mining or manufacture also owned serfs although in the reigns of Anna and Elisabeth this right was being slowly withdrawn by stages. For example, the merchants were regulated in the number of serfs they could own for various activities. Any excess in the allowed number had to be turned over to the government for its on mines and factories.[16] Under no circumstances could the merchants own serfs for working the land only. These serfs were often permitted to work land of their own during the summer and then work in factories and mines in the winter.

The Orthodox Church also had the right to hold serfs. Monasteries, convents, bishops and sometimes important churchmen were permitted to hold serfs. One small group also had this right. This was the border militia called the Onehouseholders who normally owned no serfs and were themselves endangered by local landlords. But it was legal for them to have a few serfs. The Onehouseholders appear to have been descendents of nobles who had lost nearly everything but the special rights. There was one other group who held serfs illegally. This group was the social climbing raznochintsy who, working in isolated offices, were often able to purchase a small estate illegally out of their salaries and bribes. Their aim was to work up to step eight on the scale so that they could become hereditary nobles with the right to pass the title on to their own children. The government constantly threatened them with confiscation and apparently did actually seize and sell their estates. In April of 1761 an advertisement appeared in *Sanktpeterburgskiia*

Vedomosti that the Chancellary of Confiscation was selling "the immovable property and people" of a person named as a "secretary".[17] Nearly all the secretaries were below the rank of nine, or, in other words, non-nobles. Such illegal ownership continued throughout later reigns although Peter III made a concerted effort to limit such upwards movement by not allowing clerks to move up to step eight.

As a part of the government on the local level or provincial, a clerk was designated to register the sales and transfers of serfs. While the government frowned upon the sale of serfs apart from the land, individual sales of one or a few serfs had to be registered with the clerk for a small fee, reported to the Krepostnyi Kontor in Moscow after which the sale was considered final if both parties had the legal right to own serfs (Kreposnoe pravo).[18]

The question then arises as to the number of persons concerned. Fortunately for the historian (but not for the serfs) Peter the Great reformed the state on a new basis which involved periodic censuses. These were required to determine the resources for purposes of taxation and selection of recruits for the military forces. These censuses were initiated about every twenty years the first being started in 1719 took about six years to complete. The first census started in 1719 revealed a population of 15,578,000 people in Russia (probably excluding the nobles) of whom 5,737,272 were in the "soul" tax category. Peter set the tax at 70 kopeecks for each male serf, but placed no special duties upon the women since they could not serve in the military. The census which ended in 1747 indicated an increase to 18,206,000 persons with 6,666,284 in the taxable category. The third census began in 1761 by Elisabeth and completed in 1768 revealed a surprising rise in population to 23,236,000 persons with 7,865,002 required to pay the tax.[19] That the growth rate during the reign of Elisabeth was high can probably be explained by the absence of serious famines like the one in 1733/34 or serious epidemics. Also, Elisabeth had only one really major war whereas Anna was at war throughout most of her reign.[20]

On the basis of the census of 1747 Elisabeth's government should have been receiving 4,666,398 rubles a year from the tax on males. This tax was collected by the provincial authorities twice yearly based upon the copies of the census retained for this purpose. It will be recalled that the reign of Anna had been a harsh one as a consequence of the two long wars she fought, and that her government had applied special levies in addition to the regular taxes. This was a heavy burden upon the serfs and the land-owners held responsible for payment of these dues. Hence, the arrears developed to 2,534,008 rubles for the period between 1719 and 1747--a figure which appears to be rather small when compared with the sums collected. In any case, in 1752 as a Christmas gift to the nation the empress cancelled all arrears up to 1747.[21] This was as much an act of charity as pragmatic necessity. Other arrears like the providing of horses were cancelled subsequently.[22] While, as mentioned before, these measures are explainable by necessity, it is more likely that given the character of the empress the main inspiration was enlightened Christian charity.

But there was no effort to hinder the recruitment of men from the countryside and city for the military. This was a duty far more difficult for those "selected" than the taxes since it meant twenty years service and removed a man from his village permanently. Thus, the selected individuals were considered much the same as those who died. To modernize the country Peter had adopted this method to replace the old weak armies and streltsy. The nobles still served in the military or civil service for twenty-five years. If in the army it was assumed that they would hold the position of officers. The ranks were filled by the "select" unlucky few. For the serfs owned by the landowners (54 %) this represented a real curse as is clear from Radishchev's *Journey From St. Petersburg to Moscow*.[23] The census records were used to determine the number of "souls" to be selected from a given region. The War College determined the number of recruits needed at a given time and informed the Senate. The Senate then ordered the calling up of a given number of serfs per hundred of "souls" in the various regions of

the country. The recruit had to be 1.6 meters high, between 20-35 years old and in good health.[24] On the
private estates the landowners or their agents had the
power to select the recruits and naturally used this as a
means of ridding themselves of the drunkards, trouble
makers, lazy, etc. State owned serfs, to be discussed
below, had elected elders who made the decision. It was in
this function that much bribe taking and illegal transactions took place. The serfs fixed to the factories could
evade duty if their owners paid a flat fee.

In the reign of Elisabeth there were approximately eight
demands for recruits issuing from the Senate. In 1743 the
order was for one "soul" from each 330 revision serfs; in
1747 one for each 121; in 1748 one per 190; in 1756 with
the Seven Years' War starting, one for each 135; in 1757
one for each 194; and in 1759 one for 128.[25] In 1759 a
yearly scheme was introduced for one from about 116, but
the country had fallen into such a state of anarchy that it
is doubtful if the local officials were obtaining many.[26]
This is why no precise number of call-ups can be given.
Horses were also necessary for war and each region had
requisitions for a number of horses based upon the souls in
that region. Given the necessity of the horse for agriculture and the Hoof and Mouth disease, the arrears in the
number of horses provided tended to be great.

If the duties of the serfs to the state were not enough
they had duties to their owners as well. This included the
serfs belonging to individuals (54 %) and the Church
(14.1%) whose obligations to their owners were sufficient
in themselves to overburden these serfs.[27] As is accepted,the westerninzing trend started by the predecessors of
Peter the Great and much accelerated by him,caused the
wealthy nobles to acquire expensive tastes for foreign
goods which came largely from the West. In Moscow, for
example, a bottle of champagne cost 1.30 rubles, or more
than the cost of a small girl.[28] It was accepted practice

that a noble lady attending a function at the court was expected to wear jewels valued at ten to twelve thousand rubles.[29] The vice-chancellor from 1742 and chancellor from 1758, M.L. Vorontsov, serves as an example of the problem facing a man of his high position. He owned 5,805 serfs which according to accepted belief should have earned him a ruble a year for each.[30] He was paid 6,000 rubles as vice chancellor and 7,000 as chancellor. But we have his budget for the years 1753-54 in part which belies the theory of his real income. In 1753 he earned 3,224 rubles from his estate and in the year of a relatively poor harvest (1754) only 1,831 rubles. His expenditures for 1753 were 30,668 rubles which is not a high figure when it is realized that he was the third most important figure in the empire at the time. He was forced to sell some of his estates to maintain his official lifestyle. In addition to his salary he received gifts from persons like A. Razumovsky, the secret husband of the empress and a generous man, and his wealthy brother, R.L. Vorontsov. He even resorted to the state bank when it opened borrowing 1,000 rubles silver.[31] Under the circumstances it is not surprising that the nobles attempted to obtain as much as possible from their serfs. So the serfs had felt heavy pressure from their owners and the government.

The nobles used all possible means to obtain the maximum income from their serfs. Since until 1762 most of them had to serve the government for twenty-five years, they could hardly directly manage their own estates. Hence, they hired or selected persons to handle the affairs of the estates who were called "prikazchiki" or "upraviteli". Normally these individuals were literate, drawn from either the serfs themselves or from the rapidly expanding pool of raznochintsy and were given extensive power over the management of the estate.[32] True, they were responsible to the owners. But the system had a serious disadvantage since these hired people often were concerned more with their own aggrandizement than to the interest in the welfare of the serfs or of their master.

The prikazchiki on private and Church lands gained a very bad reputation which those on the lands of the nobles retained down to the emancipation of the serfs. One of the most famous memorists of the time, A.T. Bolotov, a noble estate owner who participated in the Seven Years' War presented himself as a person annoyed by the violence and ignorance around and portrayed himself as a humane, sober person.[33] Yet in his treatment of the serfs he differed little from the rest of the nobles and prikazchiki. To force serfs to give up hidden money and goods he applied various "refined" methods such as forcing people into very hot water, feeding them salted fish but no water, etc.[34] He was considered enlightened for his day!

The serfs of the various branches of the Church (14.1 %) lived in worse conditions than those of the landowners since they had more people to support and had the full duties towards the state as well. They strongly desired to become state serfs who, as we shall see, had a much better position. The empress Elisabeth broke with her predecessor and accepted petitions presented to her personally.[35] The various Colleges and local officials were ordered to accept petitions and on occasion these came directly to the empress herself. This was fortunate since for all her other faults the empress herself was honest. According to Soviet historians who have studied the imperial archives, an extraordinary number of these came from the Church serfs complaining about the intolerable conditions of their lives. These started to accumulate until 1758 according to the Soviet historians, or 1760 if we are to believe the pre-revolutionary expert on the serf question, Semevskii, when the empress established a special committee to study the problem of the serfs of the Church.[36] The result was the secularization of the Church lands and the changing of the status of these serfs into state serfs in 1762.

Another category of oppressed serfs were the so-called possessional serfs fixed to factories or mines totaling 87,253 according to the second census of 1747.[37] Fixed to the mines and factories by Peter the Great to speed the industrialization of the country, these serfs belonged to the government, merchants and nobles engaged in production. Although not significant numerically these serfs were most heavily exploited. Usually they belonged to the owner of an enterprise and were fixed to it for life as were their off-spring. Sometimes whole villages were assigned to a given enterprise but allowed to work their own land during the summer.

Another category of serfs were the persons fixed to the service of the house of a noble to undertake the daily needs of the noble family as a consequence of which they were called household serfs and had no land to support them. Their position was not too bad in the sense that they were normally guaranteed enough worldly goods to survive since they were fully supported by their owners.

The court serfs were the personal property of members of the imperial family assigned to undertake specific tasks related to the needs of the court. Often they maintained palaces for the rulers, kept hawks for hunting, etc. They represented an insignificant portion of the population.

A much larger group of serfs (22.1 %) were designated state serfs and maintained a better situation in life than the rest. These were the state serfs belonging directly to the government itself. The state serfs had only to pay their "soul" tax and provide recruits until the Seven Years' War in 1760 when their "soul" tax was raised by one ruble.[38] Often they were delegated the power to run their own communes with some interference of the state authorities. This provided them with a degree of independence not enjoyed by other serfs which in turn made them more enterprising and affluent. The most famous example of a successful state serf was the famous genius Lomonsov who, living in northern Russia, traveled great distances on his father's prosperous business. He learned to read which opened many new potential avenues for advancement. But most of the state serfs, like the other serfs, could not read. It was the relatively desirable status of the state serfs which induced the Church serfs to desire strongly to obtain the same status which was acheived in 1762. It was very dangerous to attempt to alter the status of state serfs because they would fight to their deaths to maintain their slightly advantageous situation.

Certain regions were spared serfdom. The Cossacks have been mentioned. In the reign of Elisabeth the Ukrainians were also left free since her husband was from that region. They were to suffer the fate of their Russian brothers in the reign of Catherine. Fortunately, serfdom never spread to Siberia, although the taxes did. The Russians paid the "soul" tax and provided recruits while the aborigines paid a tax called the "iasak" or a tax in furs which gradually became very burdensome as the valuable sable grew scarce.

With the minor exceptions noted above, the vast majority of the people in European Russia were virtual slaves, as a consequence of which a vicious cycle developed. The serfs knew that if they worked harder and produced more, they would lose it to the state, landowner or prikazchiki. This does not include the state serfs. Hence, the "owned" serfs did as little work as possible to survive. The landlords or their prikazchiki replied with brutal violence to force them to produce more. From this sad situation contemporaries derived the misconceived stereotype of the Russian serf as lazy and capable of enduring inhuman physical torture. It is surprising how bitterly conscious these serfs were of their condition.

The question poses itself as to the reaction of the serfs to this seemingly hopeless situation. Since service in the military was equated with death, it was the first thing to be avoided. Some serfs would seriously injure themselves so as to be ineligible for service. Flights across nearby borders presented the government with an especially serious problem when a call-up was announced. The Polish border was the favorite since it was relatively open and easy to cross. When making one call-up the Senate requested that it be provided with a map of the Polish border to hinder flights; it was discovered that the Foreign Office did not have a copy of the map from the Treaty of Andrussovo of 1667. Next the Senate turned to the governor of Smolensk from which most of the serfs were fleeing to determine if he had a map. Despite the fact that these flights were ruining the nobility of that region, he likewise did not have an accurate map. Finally in desperation the Senate ordered the army to carry out a secret survey of the border so that Poland would not learn of this and take land away from Russia. The whole matter took nearly one and a half years, and it is not certain if the Senate got the map or not.[39] Since the border posts were separated by long distances it was easy to slip across the border by night. According to Semevsky in 1766, at one point fifty families crossed the border knowing that they would be welcomed by the Polish nobility who needed more people.[40] These flights continued and were one of the reasons for the first partition of Poland.

In other parts of Russia it was more difficult for the serfs to escape, but many did despite the difficulty. In the north the flight was into Swedish controlled Finland or into the Baltic states where treatment was better despite the fact that they were ruled by Russia. In 1743-44 a special commission was established to return those fleeing into the Baltic states. In ten years of existence the commission returned a total of 1,125 serfs and went out of existence since it was so manifestly a failure.[41] Repeated laws and manifestos issued by the government guaranteed returnees good treatment, but since these were so often repeated it is apparent that the former serfs who had escaped were not at all inclined to return to what was almost certain to be trickery on the part of the authorities.[42]

There were a number of other possible regions for movement to find better conditions. Siberia was not the most favored place since so many criminals were exiled there, and the authorities, the most corrupt and brutal of all. Yet in the face of the need for settlers in the region the Senate ordered in 1759 that state serfs could settle in the regions of Nerchinsk or Irkutsk and be free.[43] The serfs of landowners and the Church were allowed to be exiled there later also when the economic need for them was very great. Often fleeing serfs headed south and east into the developing Orenburg region where the governor, Nepliuev, had a reputation for honesty and humanity.[44] He ignored orders to return such serfs who discovered that all they had to do to remain was to tell the authorities that they could not remember where they had come from or that they were born out of wedlock. Many fled to the Don Cossacks who greeted runaways and refused repeated governmental orders to return them. For the Cossacks these runaways played a major role in their economies. So-called khutors were maintained some distance from the Cossack villages for the storage of forage which was cut in the region and stored there for winter use. These khutors were natural places for the runaway serfs to find shelter since they could be used to cut the grass for the Cossacks and guard the forage. In return for this service they were left alone and not returned. Later these people were to be enserfed by the Cossack Starshina (Elders). [45]

There were other more violent reactions on the part of the serfs than simply voting with their feet. On several occasions whole estates or villages would unite if an effort was made to change their status for the worse. An example of this took place in 1744 on an estate which had just been confiscated by the government and the owner declared a criminal. The serfs now considered themselves to be state serfs and were determined not to return to their old status of "owned" serfs. This estate, in the Pskov region, had 8,074 serfs and heavy arrears which the serfs hoped to retire now that they did not owe anything to the former owner. The Senate viewed matters differently and judged that these serfs should continue their old payments as they had to their owner. Eighteen soldiers were sent in June to force them to continue their "regular" payments, but they were forced to retreat in the face of an organized force of two thousand angry serfs. In August a much larger group of soldiers came very heavily armed and attacked the villages killing fifty-five serfs and destroying most of the homes of those in revolt.[46] Less serious incidents of this nature were frequent.

But it was the shifting of the status of serfs from that of state serfs to possessional serfs which encountered the greatest resistence. In 1751 Nikita Demidov, a leading member of a serf family which, in 1727, had been ennobled for its entrepreneurial activities, bought an estate from the government near Tula to attach to his factories. The serfs refused outright to accept the change in status and forced the local authorities to declare them serfs of the court. The unhappy Senate sent a force of five hundred soldiers to force the serfs to accept the change, but the force was defeated by the serfs, the commanders captured with thirty soldiers of the rank at the cost of fifty-nine dead serfs. The serfs were well armed. A much larger force was then dispatched to pacify the uprising which it succeeded in so doing.[47] In 1752 a merchant in the Tula region had requested troops to bring his workers back to obedience.[48] These events touched off a wave of similar disorders.

Resistance to the call-up or a change in status for the

worst could also cause organized reactions of a different nature--the development of robber bands. When a male serf realized that he was about to be selected to "serve" in the military he could react by accepting his fate or by flight as noted. Many of those fleeing were not in border regions and found it difficult to travel long distances since they needed passports issued by their local authorities at the request of their owners. Often they would take to the woods to hide and find others there in a similar situation. They had to live so they often became robber bands. These robber bands became a serious problem for the government especially when the army was on campaign and unable to control the situation. Robber bands were especially active during the Swedish war (1741-44). Prince Khovanskii and Major General Sheremetev reported that their estates had been robbed and looted in 1744.[49] The census was another stimulus to flight and the growth of robber activity. Special troops had to be deployed to control these robbers and keep the all-important trade link of the Volga safe for travel and merchants. In 1747 the large call-up of men issued then and in the next year caused the robbers to start robbing even the churches. Often these groups started with simple protests and rapidly developed into fully armed robbers bands.[50]

The departure of the army for the Seven Years' War induced another serious outbreak of banditry in which estates were looted, governmental local offices were "relieved" of their cash while the Senate was unable to stem the tide. Special troops were sent to the Moscow and Novgorod regions to regain control, but soon the trouble spread to the factories, many estates and especially to the Church lands where the discontent was most serious.[51] The war really threw the countryside into chaos which was a forewarning of the Pugachev rising under Catherine with similar conditions of war and the absence of the army.

The vast majority of the serfs had no choice but to stay on the land and hope that they would be able to survive with their families. Escape was not possible for most of them with large families and much work to do simply to survive. They had to pray for good weather and the good will of their owner if they belonged to nobles, merchants or the Church.

Some of these serfs showed great ingenuity in attempting to better their terrible position. Traditionally the peasants were very clever in making small items needed for home consumption. Usually a family or individual in a village concentrated on a single item such as shoes, plows, pans, etc. They would either barter these goods or sell them for money which they would then attempt to conceal from their owners. Generally the serfs were very resistant to innovation, but during the long winter nights they worked in their huts producing goods. In some villages, such as in the iron-rich region around Tula and in the village of Pavlov in Nizhnyi-Novgorod Gubernia, serfs actually developed complex systems for producing muskets based upon a division of labor and interchangeable parts.[52] This had been a long tradition since they had been supplying the army in the time of Peter the Great.

The government was placed in a dilemma concerning these serfs engaged in manufacturing and trade. On the one hand it was to the advantage of the nobles and the country to allow these activities since the serfs could better pay their state taxes and obligations to their owners. Yet, on the other hand, these serfs were harming the interests of the merchants and even of those nobles engaged in manufacture and trade whose direct interests ran against those of the serfs when it came to the production and sale of certain goods. Hanway observed that the serfs, as a consequence of the above, disliked merchants whether Russian or foreign.[53] In 1745 the Kammer College attempted to solve the problem by keeping the serfs out of the towns and city markets while allowing them to sell goods along the road of a nature necessary for travelers.[54] In 1758 the Senate limited the serf trade to a region of approximately five kilometers (verst is nearly a kilometer) and outright forbad any trade with foreign ships.[55]

Yet the Senate could contradict itself on the issue of serf trading. The region around St. Petersburg developed very rapidly economically as the importance of the port grew. The serfs in a few of the surrounding villages showed great initiative and on occasion had their status altered from state serfs to merchants. Such was the case of the village of Ostashkov near St. Petersburg which had 589 state serfs who were elevated to the lower guild of merchants in 1752 by an act of the Senate.[56] These were the lucky few.

Another general concern for the serfs were famines. It will be recalled that in 1733/34 a very serious famine had affected much of Russia. No such famine repeated itself during the reign of Elisabeth, although there were minor often localized famines. In 1749 a famine was reported in the Belgorod Gubernia--late as usual. The immediate order went out that the local officials check the real grain supply to insure enough for survival and seed in the next year. Speculation was outlawed and the Governors were authroized to spend 5,000 rubles to insure the supply of grain.[57] In 1754 another famine was reported in the Voronezh Gubernia. In this case Peter Shuvalov, the leading member of the Senate at that time, carried the enlightened measure through the Senate that the owners of the serfs were responsible for their welfare, fixed the price of grain so that no profits over 10 percent were allowed, again allocated 5,000 rubles to obtain grain from less affected regions, and ordered the governors to be more careful in the future in watching the crops in their regions.[58] Shuvalov was also the author of the scheme to abolish the "soul" tax by raising the taxes on vodka and salt which will be considered below.

In conclusion it is clear that the status of the serf worsened slightly during the reign of Elisabeth. The cancelation of the arrears in 1752 and the attempt to introduce indirect taxes to replace the "soul" tax can be viewed either as enlightened or necessary measures on the part of the government. However, Elisabeth maintained the Universal Service State in a strict fashion which explains the plight of the serfs. Indeed, while the power of the nobles was growing, Elisabeth fought this trend by retaining service requirements for the nobles. That explains in part the enthusiasm of the nobles in 1762 when they were freed from twenty-five years of service. So the linkage between nobles' service and serfdom retained some outward appearances of validity.

To contrast this, serfdom in Russia can be compared to serfdom in other European countries where steps were being taken to assist serfs. Maria Theresa in Austria ordered the courts in the German speaking areas to protect the serfs from their owners. In Prussia it was forbidden to sell serfs apart from the land. In the 1770's Maria Theresa limited the amount of work a serf could be forced to do on his master's estate to three days.[59] In contrast the Russian serfs lost the right to petition the colleges against their landowners in 1768. Hence, the general trend in Russia was to make serfdom more severe.

79

1 *PSZ,* XI, No. 8474. Senate. November 25, 1741. The identification of this law as coming from the Senate is an error since the Senate was not restored to its full power until the 12th of December. It came from the conference of advisers to the empress who probably realized how confused the lower classes would be if they swore to uphold three people within a year and had to retract two of their oaths.

2 *Ibid.,* XV, No. 11,291. Senate. July 10, 1761. In this case the noble underwent church penance after a Senate trial.

3 G.I. Studenkin, "Saltychikha, 1730-1801gg. Istoricheskii Ocherk". *Russkaia Starina,*June, 1874, 497-546.

4 For the years 1743, 1746, 1748, 1749-54, 1756-61 as checked by the author. Also. A. Romonovich-Sla-vatatinskii, *Dvorianstvo v Russii ot Nachala XVIII Veka do Otmeny Krepostnogo Prava,* (2nd ed.; Kiev: Iakovleva, 1912), 347.

5 *Sanktpeterburgskiia Vedomosti,* No. 72, Friday, September 8, 1760.

6 V.I. Semevskii, *Krest'iane v Tsarstvovanie Imperatritsy Ekaterny II* (St. Petersburg: Stasiulevich, 1903), Vol. I, 171.

7 *Sanktpeterburgskiia Vedomosti,* No. 47, Tuesday, June 13, 1760.

8 *Ibid.,* No. 45, Friday, June 6, 1756.

9 S. Efremenko, "Dvizhenie Tsen na kres'ianskie Dushi i na Khleb s 1689. Po arkhivym Dokumentam ",

*Izvestiia Kurskogo Obshchestva Kraevedeniia,*1928, 3(9),29.

10 "Prodazha Liudei",1760g. *Russkaia Starina,*II,February, 1875, 399.

11 Efremenko, 29.

12 "No. 70 C. Winch to the right honourable lord Carteret. Moscow, December 15, 1742", *SIRIO,* Vol. 99, 180.

13 Hanway, I, 63.

14 Haven, 326.

15 *Ibid.,* 312-13.

16 *PSZ,* XIII, No. 10,137. Senate. August 12, 1752.

17 *Sanktpeterburgskiia Vedomosti,* No. 38, Tuesday, April 17, 1761.

18 *PSZ,* XII, No. 9,317. Justice College after a Personal Ukaz in 1744. August 12, 1746.

19 V.M. Kabuzan, *Narodnaselenie Rossii v XVIII-pervoi Polovine XIXv. (Po Materialom Revizii)*(Moscow: Akademiia Nauk, Institut Istorii, 1963), 56-66.

20 I. Patlaevskii, *Denezhnyi Rynok v Rossii ot 1700 do 1762 Goda* (Odessa, 1866), 276-79.

21 *PSZ,* XIII, No. 10,061. Personal All Merciful Manifesto. December 15, 1752.

22 *PSZ,* XIV, No. 10,230. Personal. May 13, 1754. Also the arrears in the military call-ups were cancelled by this law.

23 A.N. Radishchev. *A Journey from St. Petersburg to Moscow.* Translation by Leo Wiener edited with notes by R.P. Thaler, Harvard University Press, Cambridge, Massachusetts, 1966.

24 *PSZ,* No. 8,730. Personal. February 11, 1743. This would be a height of about 5 feet 6 inches.

25 *PSZ,* XII, No. 9,366. Personal. January 27, 1747. *Ibid.,* XII, No. 9,652. Personal. December 14, 1748. *Ibid.,* XIV, No. 10,613. Personal. October 2, 1956. *Ibid.,* XIV, No. 10,785. Personal. December 23, 1757. *Ibid.,* XV, No. 10,990. Personal. September 18, 1759.

26 *PSZ,* No. 10,786. General Regulation. December 23, 1757. This was an attempt by Peter Shuvalov to regularize the call-ups. But the 1759 call-up indicates that it was not working well. Much pressure was then being placed on local authorities to conform with the laws, but few were probably coming into the service since the previous call-ups had been so heavy.

27 Alefirenko, 155. 22.1 % were state serfs. *Ibid.,* 215.

28 Solov'ev, 23,165. The price is for Moscow.

29 Vladimir Osippovich Mikhnevich, "Semistvo Skrovronskikh", *Istorichechskii Vestnik,*Vol. XXVI, March, 1885, 570.

30 "Prikhodoraskhodnyia Knizhki gosudarstvennago Kantsler Graf Mikhail Larionvicha Vorontsova, 1753-1754 Godov", *Arkhiv Kniazia Vorontsova,* Vol. XXXIII (Moscow: Katkov, 1887), 31-64.

31 *Ibid.*

32 For a consideration of these prikazchiks see: Michael Confino, *Domaines et Seigneurs en Russia vers la Fin du XIIIe Siècle.* Collection historique de l'Institut d'Etudes slaves, Tom XVIII. Paris: Institut d'Etudes slaves, 1963.

33 Andrei Timofeevich Bolotov, *Zaspiski Andreia Timofeevicha Bolotova.*St. Petersburg: Semevskii, 1871-1875. IV Vols.

34 *Ocherki Istorii voronezhshogo Kraia s drevnei-shikh Vremen do velikoi oktiar'skoi sotsialisti-choi Revoliutsii,* (Voronezh) Voronezhskii Un-versitet, 1961), 139.

35 *PSZ,* XI, No. 8,497. Personal. January 15, 1742. Petitions were to be signed and would be received only on Tuesdays. There is no indication as to how this worked.

36 P.K. Alefirenko, *Krest'ianskoi Dvizhenie i krest' ianskii Vopross v Rossii v 30-50 Godakh XVIII Veka,* (Moscow: Akademiia Nauk, 1958), 194. Semevskii, II, 222-23.

37 Semevskii, II, 304. The figure is for the second census after which the number of these serfs grew rapidly.

38 *PSZ,* XV, No. 11,120. Senate. October 12, 1760.

39 *Senatskii Arkhiv,* VII, 534-535; 578; 612-614; VIII, 76-79; 223-225. Most of this activity was in the years 1749-1950 after two call-ups. It was especially intense May 19, 1749-October 26, 1749 which meant that flights across the Polish border were high at that point.

40 Semevskii, I, 401.

41 *Ibid.,* 399.

42 *PSZ,* XV, No. 10,865. Senate. July 24, 1758. Punish those trying to flee to Poland. *Ibid.,* No 10,889. Manifesto. October 16, 1758. Return from Poland before September 1, 1760 and all will be forgiven. *Ibid.,* No. 10,896. Senate. October 31, 1758. Return those fleeing to Latvia and Estonia. *Ibid.,* No. 11,007. Manifesto. November 5, 1759. Deserters can go freely to Riga to build fortica-tions and be forgiven. *Ibid.,*No. 11,179. Manifesto January 2, 1761. Return before September 1, 1761 and be forgiven. *Ibid.,* No. 11,350. Personal.

October 31, 1761. Persons of the Greek Orthodox faith found in Poland and Prussia are to be taken into the army. *Ibid.*, No. 11,387. Personal. December 21, 1761. Runaways and deserters have until May of 1762 to return and be forgiven. This Ukaz was the last "personal" law issued in the reign of Elisabeth.

43 *PSZ,* XV, No. 10,974. Senate. July 7, 1759.

44 Vitevskii, 101-215.

45 A.P. Pronshtein, *Zemlia donskaia v XVIII Veke,*(Rostov-on-the-Don: Rostovskii Universitet, 1961), 47-52.

46 Alefirenko, 145-146.

47 "Delo o Volnenii Krestian statskogo Sovetnika Demidova i Assessor Goncharova fabrichnykh Liudei v kalushskoi Gubernia 1752 Goda ", *Chteniia v imperatorskom Obshchestve Istorii i Drevnosti Rossiikikh pri moskovskom Universitet,* 1863, Vol. II, 17-44.

48 Solov'ev, 23, 102-104.

49 Got'e, I, 335-338.

50 Solov'ev, 22, 507.

51 *Ibid.*

52 K.N. Shchepetov, *Iz Zhinzni krepostnykh Krest'ian Rossii XVII-XIX Vekov. Po Materialam sheremetistikh Votchin,* (Moscow: Uchpedgiz, 1963), 29.

53 Hanway, I, 56.

54 *PSZ,* XII, No. 9,210. Senate. August 19, 1745.

55 *Ibid.,* XV, No. 10,862. Senate. July 21, 1745. This law was issued in part to keep serfs out of contact with foreigners.

56 I.R. Klokman, *Ocherki sotsial'no-ekonomicheskoi Istorii Gorodov severo-zapada Rossii v Seredine*

XVIIIv, (Moscow: Akademiia Nauk, 1969), 144.

57 *PSZ,* XIII, No. 9,590. Senate. March 17, 1749.*Ibid,* No. 9,709. Senate. February 9, 1750. The Gubernii affected by the famine were Moscow, Belgorod, Smolensk, Kazan, Novgorod, Voronezh, Archangel and Nizhny-Novgorod. It was accepted procedure to ban the distillation of strong spirits until sufficient grain supplies were available.

58 *Ibid.,* XIV, No. 10,299. Senate. September 2, 1754.

59 Semevskii, I, 138 and 234.

CHAPTER FOUR

THE "FREE CLASSES" AND THE DEVELOPMENT
OF RUSSIAN CULTURE

It is difficult in the reign of Elisabeth, as in those of her predecessors, to state that anyone other than the ruler was truly free since all had direct or indirect obligations to the state. For purposes of convenience the classes having some degree of "rights" will be considered in this chapter and their contribution to Russian culture considered. The nobility, merchants, raznochintsy and a curious group called Onehouseholders constituted the groups living "freely". The Cossacks were a special case. As is generally recognized the power of the nobles increased throughout the eighteenth century after the death of Peter the Great. They "selected" rulers, slowly undercut the Universal Service State until 1762 when they ended it for themselves. Still under Anna and Elisabeth the nobles had to serve the government for twenty-five years either in the military or civil sections.

For a select group of the most wealthy nobles no other group underwent a more marked change in the reign. At the start of the reign the vast majority of the nobles, no matter how wealthy, just longed to return to their estates and remain there torturing their serfs for their own gain. By the end of the reign there were a significant number of younger nobles looking to Paris and France with longing and not so worried about their estates. It was the age of the victory of French culture in Russia.

The attitudes of foreigners varied in their respective views of the Russian nobility which was often colored by ethnocentrism of persons from countries economically and socially more developed. An example of this was the remark quoted above by the British ambassador about the lazy attitudes of the nobles or like the embittered Locatelli. However, these were before the reign of Elisabeth. The Austrian archives contain materials very derogatory in relation to the Russian nobility written in 1761 by the ambassador from that country, Mercy Argenteau. Writing in 1761 to Kaunitz he stated that all the Russian nobles were corrupt and greedy. He called the honest General Procurator of the Senate (Shakhovskoi) the worst usurer in Russia when a bank had long been in operation making loans at 6 percent. While it was noted that there was a great deal of corruption, the letter is far too negative. In fact the letter is so vicious in its tone concerning Russia that one must conclude the author was prejudiced.[1] The Swiss jewelier, Gremie Pauzié, found them to be unreliable in paying for their jewelry, nevertheless in the reign of Catherine II he was allowed to return to Switzerland a wealthy man. He did have great respect for individuals from the nobility.[2]

Von Haven whose contacts were chiefly with the members of the higher nobility had a more positive attitude towards them probably explainable by his age, lack of prejudices and his knowledge of Russian:

> The Russian nobility applies itself more to
> its history than any other field of know-
> ledge, however, I cannot but admit, that in-
> deed, more effort is applied to holding
> facts, than to making judgements upon them to
> see if they cannot make from them as great a
> use and discover as much as others have out
> of this study ....

> And I must say without flattery that the no-
> bility is generally very well brought up and
> educated.[3]

The nobles accepting the reforms of Peter and the westernization were ordered, if they had the money, to construct houses in St. Petersburg to help populate the new capital. At first the nobles had followed the old traditional Moscovite manner of building houses with the servants (household serfs) quarter on the ground floor and the master's on the second.[4] Soon the style changed with the coming of Rasteralli and later his son. The Italian rococo became popular then and remained so until the death of Empress Elisabeth. Hanway noted about St. Petersburg: "I was extremely pleased to find a city so open, airy, regularly built in many places, with very good houses in the Italian taste".[5] But the poorer nobles either took apartments, stayed in Moscow or on their estates when not in state service.

Tradition being as strong as it was in Russia there still existed a significant number of nobles not accepting the reforms of Peter the Great who remained in hiding on their estates, dressed in the old style manner and took the long naps after the large noon dinner.[6] These people were outlaws as far as the state was concerned. The heraldic Office was placed in charge of matter concerning the nobles or their estates. It clearly had trouble enforcing the order of Peter that all the children of the nobles be educated since as late as the convening of Catherine's law commission many of the provincial nobles signed the instructions to their delegates with an "X" since they had had no education. Orders repeating that of Peter the Great were issued by the Senate concerning the education of the children of the nobles. The governors and the voevodas were given the task of capturing the nobles who failed to appear before the governor at ages seven and twelve (for males) to insure that they were being educated.[7] These laws were repeated throughout the reign the last being in 1760 when the governors were again ordered to find and punish nobles living according to their own will (prazdno).[8] There was the possibility of disgrace if these laws were not observed, although in a burst of charity the Synod set a fine of ten rubles on a family failing to educate its children which fine was to be used to purchase books for the newly opened Slavic-Greek-Latin Academy in Moscow which had the duty of training priests.[9]

The favorite method of educating wealthy young noblemen was hiring a foreign tutor to live with the family. Since languages were so important many adventures came from France and German - often with inadequate training - since many of them could find no employment in their native lands. This situation forced the government in 1757 to order all tutors to report either to the Academy of Sciences in St. Petersburg or Moscow University to determine if they were really qualified.[10]

The wealthy nobles in the city often retained an educated person as a city counterpart for the prikazchik. This person acted as a secretary, legal advisor and very often as an interpreter for those not knowing foreign languages.[11] It is highly likely that most of these people were raznochintsy by origin and perhaps they played a double role by acting as tutors for the children of the nobles.

The policy of the government towards the nobles as a class was ambivalent. On the one hand the Universal Service State with its modifications was maintained and the nobles were forced to serve. On the other hand the nobility was gradually increasing its power and gaining advantages which it did not previously have. Much of this is explicable by the policy of the empress herself who, in trying to maintain her father's system, treated the nobles with the old severity combined with occasional bursts of mercy.[12] The other was the influence of the Senate and the service nobility whose power by then was very great and growing. By inaction the empress often allowed the Senate to take steps which clearly enhanced the economic and social position of the noble class. An example of this took place took place in 1755 when the Senate took away from the merchants the right to distill strong drink to be sold to the government at a good profit and made it an exclusive right of the nobles many of whom were deeply engaged in business themselves. Later the Senate granted to the higher ranking nobles the "right" to distill 1,000 barrels (vedro) of vodka a year (34 liters per day) for their own personal use tax free.[13] A number of other examples could be cited. Perhaps this right to distill vodka freely explains a curious law which was not included in the collection of laws. This law stated that people (nobles attached to the court) were required to behave themselves in the presence of the empress and in church. Punishment for failure to observe this rule was that the guilty party had to have a gold box chained to them for a fixed period of time so all would know that they had violated the rules.[14]

Nobles were subject to the law for their actions.[15] However, with the growth of the power of the nobles it became rare for one of them to suffer for something they had done of a serious nature since nobles would be sitting in judgment over them. It was a crime to murder a serf since that represented the possible destruction of a Christian soul. When a noble was punished his or her family normally retained the estate while the guilty party had to suffer prison or exile. Elisabeth could be severe when the nobles transgressed the boundaries of what was acceptable to her. That is one of the reasons, among others, that the nobles proposed building a golden statue of Peter III when he freed them from all state duty in 1762. Their victory was then complete.

Next in importance as a "free" class came the merchantry (kupechestvo) which class in most cases was far behind their counterparts in such advanced countries as England, France or Holland. The westernization had reached them slowly. For example, Russia did not have a significant merchant fleet worthy of consideration. But as in most other cases Peter had tried to push the merchants into the modern age with limited success. Their position was further undermined by the trade of the serfs and more especially the nobles, who in Russia were often deeply engaged in manufacture and trade, in contrast to England and France.

Peter had tried to introduce a form of self government into the cities among the merchants. He had formed guilds for production of goods and established a means for running a city free from the control of the greedy governors. Using the western model he created the position of Magistrate selected by the big (wealthy) merchants who was assisted in the larger cities by two burmister and four ratsmen.[16] The craftsmen were in theory divided into guilds which apparently never function- ed as planned. It was the duty of the Magistrate and other officials in the city to insure the payment of taxes and the securing of recruits for the army. In 1727 these were abolished and power given to governors and voevodas. In 1743 Elisabeth, trying to re-establish the system of her father again, re-established the Petrine structure, but power again drifted back into the hands of the local authorities. Despite this the Senate still held them responsible for taxation and recruit functions. In 1744 they were effective agencies, but by 1751 when a case involv- ing the Investigation Department came before a local court--which should have been handled by the Magistrate in the first place--the Moscow Magistrate did not even take the time to send an observer as required by law.[17] This loss of jurisdiction over cases involving merchants and business affairs probably explains the curious law of 1754 calling upon the merchants to elect two of the members in each community to act as a court of honor in their mat- ters.[18].

The merchant class, as was the case of the craftsmen, were hereditary as was common at the time. The wealthy merchants seemed to have been able to more than hold their own despite the fact that the nobles used the right to build factories, open mines and trade in competition with them. But the craftsmen tended to slip from their positions with time to the lower level of the city population. The lower class called the "podlyi liudi" made up the great bulk of the city population and had difficulty paying their 1.10 ruble a year tax. The Soviet historian, Idova, claims that in Moscow there were only 787 members in the higher merchantry 9.7 percent of whom were manufacturers with a total capital 1,175,800 rubles.[19] These wealthy merchants were free from the "soul" tax but by the middle of the XVIII century they were paying a one percent tax on their business.[20]

Like the nobles the merchants were allowed to travel abroad. This was a rare right in old Russia where the lower class was kept in Russia as if it were a prison and could leave only illegally. To cross the border the merchants had to clearly establish their identity and business. Despite the strong competition of the nobles and serfs the position of the merchant was not difficult. They enjoyed a great deal of personal freedom and could participate in the cultural life of the country if their monetary status permitted.

Another group of "free" persons in Russia were the raznochintsy (singular--raznochintsev) who formed a social class unto themselves and owed nothing to the government until 1760 when some were placed under the tax system.[21] The raznochintsy were already mentioned in their relation to the development of the lower levels of the bureaucracy. The origins of the raznochintsy varied greatly although a majority were the sons of priests not wishing to follow their father's profession and according to church law they could not be forced to do so. Others were of serf origin who claimed that they could not remember their owners and subsequently obtained some degree of education. Some were former household serfs freed through the generosity of a humane owner. The origin of the genius, Lomonosov, is indicative of this. He was a state serf by origin who obtained an education by claiming to be the son of a priest. When the opportunity arose he turned to secular studies, attended western universities eventually becoming a professor in the Academy of Sciences which gave him personal nobility but not hereditary. After being shifted from religious to secular studies he would have been considered a raznochintsev.

The raznochintsy could move about the country freely and engage in certain professions such as a secretary in governmental offices, as prikazchiks, as tutors or the above mentioned secretaries to the nobles. They were not allowed to engage in trade, own serfs or land or factories. Education was therefore very important to them as a result since all the jobs which were open to them required it. There also existed the tempting possibility of obtaining noble status through governmental service in the civil service. Probably because the government was so dependent upon these raznochintsy for the staffing of civil service offices that it protected them and gave them a special status.[22] On the other hand, the government was so alarmed at their social ambitions that efforts were made to make the position of secretary hereditary.[23] As mentioned previously raznochintsy often purchased land and people without the right to do so and the government fought this trend vigorously but without much success.[24]

*****

These three groups or social classes had the largest percentage of literate persons in Russia and therefore as could be expected they were the cultural leaders of the country. Peter the Great and his father, Alexis, had started to place greater stress upon change and western ideas. To achieve this Peter the Great founded the Academy of Sciences which did not really become operative until after his death. Its purpose was, at first, to import foreign specialists to train Russians in various fields of science. Unlike the other similar academies in the West it paid fixed salaries to the staff, it was able to obtain some outstanding people, who, for a reasonable salary were willing to move to St. Petersburg and in effect work for the Russian government. The Academy had already undertaken a number of expeditions in all parts of the empire to study the geography, botany, history and other fields of interest for an understanding of Russia. In 1745 it published an excellent atlas of the Russian empire.

For a number of years before the reign of Elisabeth there were only four presses in operation in Russia. The chief of these belonged to the Synode and the Academy of Sciences. In the space of the twenty year reign six new presses were established bringing the total to about ten.[25] The most important press was that of the Academy of Sciences which produced a very large output of works in Russian. Starting in 1727 it published the only newspaper in Russia, *Sanktpeterburgskiia Vedomosti,* which appeared bi-weekly. In 1727 a German edition was added and in 1756 it appeared also in French.[26] Thus both Russian and foreigner could learn quickly of the latest news from the world and court. This was a great contrast to the previous century when foreign news was kept out of The reach of the literate public with the foreign office preparing a hand wirtten journal called *Currans* for the Tsar and the Boyar Duma. Of course, the gate to general knowledge remained closed to the serfs. The press of the Academy of Sciences also printed much of the materials produced by its members chiefly in Latin for international use, but also on occasion as a supplement to *Sanktpeterburgskiia Vedomosti.* These latter became rare after 1742.[27]

In 1754 G. Müller, one of the leading figures in the Academy, suggested that a special monthly periodical be established to replace these supplements and to carry useful information to the literate society of Russia. After some debate the project was approved by the President of the Academy, Kryll Razumovskii, and it was planned to issue 2,000 copies each month. Unfortunately the journal did not prosper in the early period so in 1758 the number printed was dropped to 1,250.[28] The editor was Müller himself assisted by the leading figures in Russia at that time. When Catherine II transferred Müller to Moscow in 1764 the journal ceased publication.

Lomonosov selected the name for the journal, *Ezhemesiachnyia Sochineniia k Pol'ze i Uveseleniiu Sluzhashiia* (The Monthly Journal Serving to Provide Useful Information and Entertainment), and was one of the leading contributors. The journal--the first of its kind in Russia--served a very valuable role in the enlightenment of the country. V.A. Miliutin, writing in an unsigned article in *Sovremennik* in 1851, quoted a contemporary the Metropolitan (a high Church official), Evgenii as making the following statement concerning the importance of the journal:

> All Russia with avidity and satisfaction reads the first Russian monthly, in which are placed the most curious historical, geographical, commercial, learned and other articles.

Miliutin himself a professor provided his evaluation of the journal:

> In this way the "Ezhemesiachnyia Sochineniia" not only accustomed the Russian public to reading, but it also disseminated among it [the public] a large amount of useful information and more closely acquainted it with

past and contemporary conditions of Russia, but in addition it likewise laid a firm basis to national journalism. By their example they [the writers of it] showed the value of periodical publications and awakened other writers likewise to enter the field of journalistic activities [which] up to that time was completely unknown to them.[30]

This statement is overexaggerated since the journal had a limited subscribership.

The contents were both scientific and literary. The famous XVIII century Russian writer, Aleksandr Petrovich Sumorakov (1717-1777), destined to found the first private journal in 1759, provided many poems for the early issues. These were frequently odes to the ruler so common under the ancient regime. While the creative writers such as Sumorakov and Lomonosov were attempting to create a distinctive Russian literary language in their articles and poems in the journal, the majority of the articles were translations, summaries of the materials from foreign journals, to a large number of which the Academy sub-scribed. It was through these translations that people literate only in Russian received their first acquaintance with the writers of the Enlightenment. Voltaire was the most important of these writers to be so introduced. He had been made a corresponding member of the Russian Academy as early as 1746. In the September issue of 1756 Müller published a translation of his short work entitled: "A Talk about Glory with a Chinaman."[31] More important was the translation of his work, Zadig, which appeared in the journal in 1759 after its name had been slightly alter-ed to *Sochineniia i Perevody k Pol'ze i Uveseleniiu Sluzhashchiia* (Compositions and Trans-lations Serving to Provide Useful Information and Enter-tainment). Zadig was a longer novel and thus had to be serialized. Zadig is generally seen as one of the clearest forerunners of the more famous Candide. As in Candide the hero finds that the world is not good as claimed, but that Providence (perhaps Voltaire's agnostic God) really worked against man. This certainly contains the seeds of irreligion and scepticism which for some reason did not annoy the older generation as did some of Voltaire's other works. At various points other enlightened writers such as Bayle and Buffon are mentioned.[32]

It is possible that Müller used the journal as a vehicle for social criticism. One article was translated out of the *Guardian* dealing with cruelty to animals. In it there was a plea for the good treatment of pets and animals in which Montaigne and Locke are cited as opposing any cruel treatment. It takes little imagination to transfer this to the inhuman treatment of the serfs, but it is only possible to make conjectures about his motives.[33]

Many of the articles were simply practical advice or an attempt to spread applied knowledge. A good example of this was the long debate which appeared in the journal over the Turkish/Greek method of preventing smallpox by vaccination with live virus. After six articles, including one against, a writer summed up the discussion by noting that the new system was widely used in England among the upper classes including royalty whereas in France it was not being used and probably accounted for a million deaths there since 1723.[34] Hence, the Russian reader was introduced to vaccination before Catherine had herself and Paul vaccinated to remove any possible taboo from the method.

Other articles dealt with agriculture which made important revelations to the public. In one such article the Russian literate public was informed about a new plant which the English called Potato[e]s and others ground apples (French pomme de terre). It was noted that they tended to grow small in the north which is true, but that the

yield was as high as fifty times the planted potatoes--
which is not accurate. The qualities of the root as food
and the ease of storage were noted and in passing it was
suggested that they had high potential as food in remote
regions like Kamchatka where storing food was a real
problem.[35] The Soviet Encyclopedia states that twenty
to thirty years later potatoes were being used successfully
there.[36] It was not until much later that the serfs
accepted them, in fact, nearly a century although before
the publication of the article individuals such as the
historian/civil servant of Peter's Tatishchev,   had long
used them.

The geographic study of the country and the precise locations of various towns had long been one of the chief
goals of the Academy of Sciences which maintained a
staff of mathematicians, astronomers, geographers, etc.
mainly for the purpose of obtaining as precise a map as
possible of the Russian empire. In 1757 based upon their
work the journal printed a list of the Gubernia with the
towns in them along with the size and locations of these.
In the same year the religious divisions of the Orthodox
Church were given.[37] Thus, the "reading public" received
a fairly accurate concept of the size and nature of Russia.

Since the Monthly Compositions was an official magazine
of the government, it could be anticipated that it would
carry articles furthering the interests of the Russian
state. Probably the best example of this practice relates
to China. By the Treaty of Nerchinsk of 1689, Russian efforts to obtain the Amur Valley (Hei-Lung-Chaing to the
Chinese) to its mouth were thwarted by the Chinese
government, and the Russians were excluded from the
lower portion of the river by force. This made communication with Kamchatka exceedingly difficult. In 1753 the
Senate became interested in obtaining the right to use the
river for communications with Kamchatka with a view to
the future annexation of the entire region. The Foreign

Office warned the Senate that the Chinese were suspicious of Russian intentions in the region and would resist, which, indeed happened.[38] A series of articles appeared in the Monthly Compositions in 1757 entitled: "An Explanation of the Doubtfulness Existing Concerning the Establishments of the Boundaries between the Russian and Chinese Governments in 7197 (1689)." The first article appeared in the April issue of 1757 and the last in October of that year. This article, probably written by Müller who understood Siberia and knew some history, concluded:

> With this we finish the history about the Amur River, but however, it appears that as we have indicated that the tribes [countries] there, presently under Chinese rule, belonged once to the Russian state, that in an unjust fashion by overwhelming force of the enemy [China] the Russians were thrown out and even less justly were forced to give them [the tribes] over to the Chinese by the forced treaty concluded at Nerchinsk.[39]

The merchants were not ignored by the editor. Much material was directed to this particular class. Of course, in another sense it was not just the merchants but also the many nobles engaged in trade and manufacturing. In the August issue of 1755 an article appeared entitled: "Concerning the Gains and Losses of Commerce in England and France."[40] This article drew heavily upon the works of an English minister-economist, Josiah Tucker, whose main book appeared in 1753. It was of such great interest to the economists of the time that none other than Turgot translated it into French. Tucker is placed in the tradition which produced Adam Smith.[41] In September of 1755 a series of articles started appearing on the trade with Siberia. Much information was also provided about the most important fair held yearly at Nizhny-Novgorod. Many other examples could be selected. For example, in the March issue of 1756 an article entitled the "English Merchant" appeared and in 1757 one on the Swedish merchants which was merely a translation but which ended on the following note:

> The merchantry is the mother of wealth and the true source from which governmental strength and force proceed. Trade awakens people from their natural laziness, puts them into useful action, makes handiwork successful ... and finally awards all alike with money, from which not only domestic particular happiness flows, but also a society comes to be known and praised by its own neighbors.[42]

Many minor problems were considered. Articles appeared on the treatment of animals for the Hoof and Mouth disease (blood-letting was suggested), fighting locust infestations, the duties of soldiers and officers, etc. It was easy to see that the journal was indeed dedicated to the three "classes" in Russian society--noble, merchant and by implication, raznochintsy.

These three groups along with the empress herself were responsible for the start of the Russian theater and the opera (which was manily Italian). The Russian theater appeared at approximately the same time in three different locations--St. Petersburg, Jaroslav and Moscow. St. Petersburg, more under western influences, often had visiting groups performing plays and opera. Some of these were German, Italian and French. The best educational institution in Russia was the Cadets' School in St. Petersburg which had been founded by the empress Anna in 1732 on the advice of Münnich for the training of future officers. In addition to being a good military school it also taught the more refined liberal arts and languages. With the example of the visiting players the students on their own initiative started performing plays in 1749 and soon became welcome guests at court.[43]

Feodor Grigorevich Volkov (1729-1768) was the son of a merchant from Jaroslav who received an excellent education for a merchant. He studied for several years in St. Petersburg where he became acquainted with the foreign theater and with that of the Cadets. Returning to Jaroslav he formed a team of actors of which he was the leader. Starting in 1750 regular performances were staged in Jaroslav and became very popular. The leading actor was Volkov himself and he can be considered the true founder of the Russian theater. In 1752 the empress learned of him and ordered that he perform for the court. Very pleased with what she saw she ordered that another theater be established in Moscow.[44] In 1756 Elisabeth decided to make the theater permanent. Hence, the writer, Sumarokov was relieved of all other duties, named its director and started writing his own plays based upon Russian and foreign themes for the entertainment of the court and public.[45] So was founded the theater in St. Petersburg and Moscow. Sumarokov was given a salary of 1000 rubles a year and a budget of 5000 rubles to support his theater. In Moscow the theater, which did not have initial success, was staffed chiefly with raznochintsy many of whom were educated at Moscow University.[46] Thus the three literate classes had a part in the formation of the true Russian theater. The Cadets Corps represented the nobles since all the students came from noble families, the Jaroslav theater was the creation of the merchant class and that in Moscow maintained by the raznochintsy.

A number of opera companies also visited Russia starting in the reign of Anna where they had been well received. Elisabeth became especially fond of the Italian opera and it was said that she learned Italian from the operas. This is doubtful since her sister had been fluent in Italian and the two sisters had the same education. In 1757 one Giovanni Locatelli (?-1785) - no relation to the author of *Lettres moscovitiques* or the composer of the same name -was given 7000 rubles to establish a permanent opera for Russia both in St. Petersburg and Moscow. He was to give two performances a week--one for the court free of charge and the other for the public for which he could charge. Locatelli was commissioned to hire actors and stagehands abroad and to construct a permanent opera house in Moscow. He was also ordered to train Russians with talent to eventually replace the hired foreigners. In 1760 in Moscow University there were nineteen raznochintsy being trained under the supervision of Locatelli for his opera and ten students for the Russian theater.[47] While the theater continued to thrive after the death of Elisabeth (Volkov was ennobled), the opera seems to have had a more difficult fate since Locatelli became poor and had to spend his declining years teaching Italian and Russian in the St. Petersburg Theater School.[48]

The cause of education was greatly furthered during the reign of Elisabeth to an extent often ignored. In this regard the empress was following the wishes of her father. The names most associated with the educational efforts of the period are Lomonosov and Ivan Ivanovich Shuvalov (1727-1797). The Shuvalov family played a significant role in the reign. Ivan had two cousins, Peter and Alexander. Peter Shuvalov was one of the most strongly criticized figures of the reign since his power was based on the fact that his young cousin, Ivan, was the "favorite" of the empress and used his position to promote his greedy goals. Alexander Shuvalov headed the deaded Secret Chancellary which handled investigations involving crimes against the ruler or state. Ivan Shuvalov became the reigning favorite about 1750 and has drawn mixed reaction. To the Austrian Ambassador he was a lazy good-for-nothing.[49] One of the few honest officials working for the empress, Prince Shakhovskoi, disliked Peter Shuvalov greatly and clashed with him on several occasions. Yet his attitude towards Ivan was quite different. On one occasion Peter Shuvalov arranged to draw the wrath of the empress on Shakhovskoi who appealed to Ivan and received an apology in reply.[50] On another instance Ivan arranged an interview between Peter and Shakhovskoi in which the latter sharply criticized Peter for his greed (sometimes unjustly). Ivan seemed to have been amused by the whole scene while Peter was highly angered by it.[51]

Ivan was a highly intelligent young man who was self educated and loved to read books in French, German, Italian and Russian. In his reading he became deeply emersed in the French Enlightenment, reading the works of Voltaire and others. He started a correspondence with Voltaire which was to last for years. He attempted to correspond with Helvétius, whose ideas had been condemned as atheistic, but nothing came of his effort. In the eyes of the higher nobility the Shuvalovs were upstarts since apparently the family had been ennobled by Peter and had become strong mainly because the family had adhered to the "small court" of Elisabeth before she came to power. [52] This caused Ivan to be less class conscious and more open to persons who were non-nobles. Thus, he became a friend of the genius Lomonosov. Lomonosov noted that the Academy of Sciences was not fulfilling adequately the educational role Peter had planned for it.[53] In addition, Moscow was without any type of higher education institution. Thus, in May of 1754 he suggested to Ivan that a new university be founded in Moscow and Ivan agreed. Jointly they worked out the project and created the University which today bears the name of Lomonosov, although the publicity at the time attributed the idea to Shuvalov himself.[54] Ivan was made the Curator of the University which he was not to see himself until the year 1778 after his return from an extended stay abroad. He did guide it through his letters.[55]

The University consisted of several faculties and was to have about ten professors. Two preparatory gimnazii were established, one for the nobles and one for the raznochintsy--a clear indication of their importance for the Russian State. The merchants apparently were to enter the gimnazia for the raznochintsy. Once in the University class distinctions would tend to fade. Serfs were not allowed to enter the University unless they had the permission of their owner, and upon completion of work they became raznochintsy. The University of Moscow was given a building, a set yearly sum of 15,000 rubles which was too little, a supplement of 5,000 rubles to start a library and eventually a printing press.[56] Upon the advice of Shuvalov the press started to issue in 1756 *Moskovskyia Vedomosti*, the second Russian language journal of its kind in Russia.

To insure the maintenance of the concept of the Universal Service State and make certain that nobles would not stay out of the University for fear of losing rank the Senate issued a law stating that those completing studies in the new institutions would receive credit for the time spent studying for seniority in state service.[57] Despite these efforts the University and the gimnazii were moderately successful, but they did start to graduate qualified persons in 1758 who were to become important state servants in later reigns. The ending of obligatory service for the nobles in 1762 caused many of them to drop out of the schools. Perhaps the limited success explains the long lag before similar universities were established in other regions after 1800.

Ivan Shuvalov continued to push for the development of better education facilities in Russia despite the slow start of Moscow University. In 1758 two gimnazii, similar to those in Moscow, were ordered to be opened in Kazan, again one for the nobles and the other for the raznochintsy. They were to be staffed by graduates of Moscow

University and would presumably be raznochintsy. [58] Despite the relative lack of success of these schools to the point that they were closed for a time it can be said that they prepared the groundwork for Kazan University which later was one of the outstanding universities in the world. The most ambitious plan of the reign in the field of education appeared in an Ukaz directly inspired by Ivan Shuvalov in 1760. It called upon the governors and voevodas to prepare plans for primary schools in the provinces and gimnazii in the Gubernia capitals.[59] This had been one of the aims of Peter the Great, but it was too ambitious for his time or that of his immediate successors in the XVIII century, although a few primary schools were opened in the reigns of Elisabeth and Catherine II.

Education alone was not the only field which interested Ivan. He had a love for all cultural matters. It is said that he learned Italian by attending operas and talking to the directors and artists. His tastes extended to the fine arts such as painting and sculpture. In 1757 a law directly attributed to him opened the Academy of Arts with a yearly stipend of 6,000 rubles to hire two French painters to train Russians.[60] It is difficult to determine why the painters had to be French and not Italian since the latter had a better reputation at the time. Perhaps the fact that one of the leading French artists, Tocqué, was visiting Russia to paint protraits of the empress answers the puzzle. Later Ivan spent eight years in Rome chiefly studying art and western culture. His interest in the theater is evident from the fact that in 1761 he wrote a letter to the directors of Moscow University ordering the reopening of the Russian theater which had just closed in that city.[61]

Ivan Shuvalov was one example of a younger person whose world view differed from that of the older generation. The older generation, including the empress, had been mainly trained in religion and was very devout. The wealthy Vorontsov family provided a clear example of this split and how the generation gap developed. There were two brothers, R.L. Vorontsov, one of the wealthiest serf owners in Russia, and M.L. Vorontsov who was the Grand Chancellor at the end of the reign. The children of both were educated together in a secular spirit of the Enlightenment. Alexander R. Vorontsov, the son of M.L. Vorontsov and his cousin, the princess Dashkova-Vorontsova received outstanding training and proved to be excellent pupils. While the aging empress and their parents were worried about such trivia as dirty or unartfully painted icons, they were reading Voltaire, Bayle, the Encyclopédie, and the other works of the Enlightenment. The same was true of the brother of the empress's husband, Kyrill Razumovsky, who had been given an excellent educatior and was later known for his religious scepticism. When the empress had Ivan Shuvalov commission Voltaire to write his history of Russia during the reign of Peter the Great and when it appeared without being checked by Russian authorities, the Chancellor, M.L. Vorontsov, wrote in irritation that the book "...Renfermant les principles le plus pernicieux de materialism et d'irreligion".[62] The complaint was directed to Ivan Shuvalov who did not reply probably because he did not aggree with M.L. Vorontsov.

Alexander Vorontsov was sent to Paris to continue his studies and was astonished by the lines of book stores in the Latin Quarter of Paris. As he himself describes his education:

> There was a theater at the court with a comédie francoise two times a week; my father made us go there into a loge which he had obtained. I make mention of this circumstance because it contributed greatly to giving us in our tender youth [he was born in 1741] a decided penchant for reading literature. My father had bought for us from Holland a very good library which contained

the best French authors and poets and historical books, in such a manner that at the
age of 12 years I had been familiarized with
Voltaire, Racine, Cornelle, Boileau and
other French literary figures.[63]

But unfortunately these young people were still a small
minority in a country with a high rate of illiterate nobles
and backward merchants. But they set the stage for the
upswing which was to take place in the following reigns.

That some of this culture carried over to the merchants
is clear. On the 28th of October, 1748, Prince Gargin announced that he had arranged in his mansion a concert of
songs in Italian, Russian, English and German. Merchants
were specifically invited. However, drunks and women
without escort would not be permitted.[64] It appears to
have been open to raznochintsy even if no mention was
made of them.

*****

The last group to be considered in this chapter were the
curious small numbered peoples called the Onehouseholders who, in theory, were free. In fact some were
even allowed to hold serfs as was previously mentioned.
They had been settled on the border to protect it as the
state expanded. According to the second census there
were 430,219 male "souls" of Onehouseholder or raznochintsy supporting the land militia.[65] Ukrainians had not
yet been enserfed. The Onehouseholders resembled the
raznochitsy in that they lacked a fixed position on
Peter's Table of Ranks.

Unfortunately they were one of the groups most heavily oppressed by the local officials. Frequently they had their land taken from them, and local officials assisted the nobles in their efforts to enserf them. Unlike most of the raznochintsy there were few among them who were literate to write petitions about their terrible conditions. Hence, many of them joined the restive serfs and voted with their feet. It had become so bad that by 1743 10,425 of them had moved from Voronezh and Belgorod Gubernias alone.[66]

The empress took special interest in them and tried to become their protector since many of them were Ukrianians. Once schools were ordered to be opened for them.[67] The government first attempted to stabilize their situation by ordering them to stay on their land or to return to their former homes.[68] Later the Senate issued a special order that if found working in factories they were to be returned to their original place of residence.[69] When the Seven Years' War broke out a strong order went out to them to return immediately to their posts on the border or where they had originally lived if in the interior of the country.[70] In 1759, to emphasize their special status, they were made responsible to the Governors instead of the voevodas. But this measure did not help since the governors were as corrupt as the voevodas in their treatment of them. The governors of Voronezh and Belgorod where the plight was greatest were the worst--a Pushkin and a Saltykov. These governors were given awards by the Senate either through ignorance or corruption which caused the empress to explode since even she knew about their evil actions. She reorganized the Senate as a result and told the Senators in strong terms to clean up the corruption. In 1761 the last law concerning Onehouseholders was issued placing them once again under the control of the voevodas who were ordered to give them as much land as they needed and to leave them alone.[71] The treatment which the central authorities tried to give to these people was unique in that later they retained a special status but were leveled with the state serfs in that they were fixed to the land.[72]

NOTES

1   Austrian State Archives. 11 nov. 1761. "Très grand et Très Puissant Empereur ". Russland Berichte. 1761-1762-X-III. Item #45.

2   Ieremiia Poz'e, "Zapiski pridvornago Brilliansh-chika Ieremiia Poz'e, 1729-1764gg.", *Russkaia Starian,* Vol. 1, 1879, 42-127.

3   Haven, 106-108.

4   A.A. Golubev, *Opinsanie Dokumentov i Bumag', khra-niashchikhsia v moskovskom Arkhive Ministerstva Iutitsii* (Moscow: Snegirev, 1894), Vol. IV, 6-7.

5   Hanway, I, 54.

6   A.T. Bolotov, *Zapiski. 1738-1795* (3rd Edition; Moscow, Russkaia Starina, 1875), 264-324. The author spent one year too long on his estate and nearly failed to obtain an expected promotion in the army. He claimed that it was an error on the part of his deceased father, but since he had pe-titioned unsuccessfully for a delay it was likely his own fault--he just wanted to stay on his estate.

7   *PSZ,* XI, No. 8683. Personal. December 11, 1742.

8   *Ibid.,* XV, No. 11,121. Senate. October 16, 1760.

9   I.S.B., "O ponuditel'nom Obuchenii dvorianskikh Detei v 1743 Godu, *"Russkaia Starina,* 148, Novem-ber, 1911, 343-44. This is a reprint of an order from the Synode to insure that the nobles and cer-tain other groups give their children a religious education.

10 *PSZ,* XIV, No. 10,724. Personal. May 5, 1757.

11 Golubev, IV, 14.

12 Before the Seven Years' War the nobles were assured that they would be forgiven if they reported at once to the authorities from hiding. *PSZ*, XIV, No. 10,234. Personal. May 13, 1754. When the war started the nobles were threatened with the loss of their property for not reporting. *Ibid.*, XV, No. 10,898. Senate. November 2, 1758.

13 *Ibid.*, XV, No. 10,856. Senate. June 7, 1758.

14 Kseniia Polovtsova, "Nakazanie Freilin za'neporiadoshkoe Provedenie'", *Russkaia Starina*, 124, November-December, 1905, 726-29.

15 *PSZ*, XIII, No. 9989. Personal. May 25, 1752. A noble could lose his property for spreading lies and slander or for even maintaining contact with such a person. The property went to the family normally.

16 Solov'ev, 18, 486-87.

17 Golubev, IV, 36-38.

18 *PSZ*, XIV, No 10,222. Senate. May 5, 1754.

19 E.I. Idova, "Rol' dvortsovoi Drevni v Formirovanii Kupechestva", *Istoricheskie Zapiski* (Moscow: Akademiia Nauk, 1961), Vol. 68,207.

20 *Ibid.*, 197.

21 G.N. Vul'fson, "Poniatie 'Raznochintsev' v XVIII-pervoi Polovine XIXV", *Ocherki Istoriia Narodov Povolzh'ia i Priural'ia* (Kazan, 1967) Vol. 1, 107-124. *PSZ*, XIV, No. 11,219. Senate. March 19, 1761.

22 *PSZ*, XIII, No. 10,095. Personal. April 29, 1753. If caught begging they were to be returned to relatives and if this was not possible they were to be sent to work in factories.

23 Got'e, I, 263-270.

24 *PSZ*, XV, No. 10,796. Senate. February 6, 1758. They were given a half a year to sell or have the Office of Confiscation take their property. This law was specifically directed to provincial clerks and lower grade officers.

25 "Pechatnoe Delo", *Entsiklopedicheskii Slovar* (Leipzig: Brokhauz & Efron, 1898) Vol. 46, 528.

26 *Ibid.*

27 P.P. Pekarskii, "Redaktor, Sotrudniki i Tsenzura v russkom Zhurnale, 1755-1766 Godov", *Zapiski imperatorskoi Akademii Nauk,* XII, 1867, Vol. V, 3.

28 *Ibid.*

29 [V.A. Miliutin], "Ocherki russkoi Zhurnalistiki. Preimushchestvenno Staroi. I. Ezhemesiachyia Sochineniia. Zhurnal, 1755-1764 Godov", *Sovremennik,* 1851, Section II, 17. *Sovremennik* was the leading radical journal of its period, and V.A. Miliutin came from a famous family. He was a socialist, involved in the Petrashchevskii circles, a professor at Moscow University and died an early death (1826-1855).

30 *Ibid.*

31 *Ezhemesiachvia Sochineniia,* September, 1756, 303-07.

32 *Ibid.,* October, 1756, 336; January, 1759, 82-95.

33 *Ibid.,* October, 1755, 372-79.

34 *Ibid.,* June, 1756, 510.

35 *Ibid.,* April, 1758, 378-380.

36 *Bol'shaia Sovetskaia Entsiklopediia* (2nd. ed.; Moscow: Gosudarstvennoe nauchnoe Izdatel'stvo, 1953), Vol. 20, 291.

37 *Ezhemesianyia Sochineniia,* January-April, 1757.

38 *Senatskii Arkhiv,* IX, November 17, 1753, 206-217; March 5, 1756, 505-508; April 2, 1756, 532; Vol. X, January 23, 1758, 406-407.

39 *Ezhemesianyia Sochineniia,* October, 1757, 328.

40 "O Pribytakh i Ubytkakh Komertsii v Anglii i Frantsii ", *Ibid.,* August, 1755, 99-216. Tucker also favored the colonies in 1776 and was an early prohibitionist.

41 Dictionary of National Biography, "Josiah Tucker", Vol. LVII (London,1899) 282-284.

42 "Znatnago shvedskago Kuptsa Razmyshleniia o Kommertsii Vobshche", *Ezhemesianyia Sochineniia,* September, 1757, 272.

43 N.V. Drizen, "Liubitel'skii Teatr pri Elisavete Petrovne", *Istoricheskii Vestnik,* LXI, 1895,708.

44 *Ibid.,* 714.

45 *PSZ,* XIV, No. 10,599. Personal. August 30, 1756.

46 Drizen, 714.

47 *Dokymenty i Materialy po Istorii moskovskogo Universiteta vtroi Polovny XVIII Veka* (Moscow: Moskovskii Unversitet, 1960), Vol. I, 323.

48 *Bol'shaia Entsiklopediia* (St. Petersburg, 1903), Vol. 12,288.

49 Austrian Archives, Mercy Argenteau à Kaunitz. September 28, 1761. Russland II Berichte 1761 IV-IX. Item 44.

50 Prince Iakov Petrovich Shakhovskoi,*Zapiski Kniazia Iakova Shakhovskago* (St. Petersburg: Russkaia Starina, 1872), 91.

51 *Ibid.,* 137-143. Shakhovskoi mistakenly thought that the Shuvalovs were brothers--an error which he alone made.

52 I.M. Snegirev, "Ivan Ivanovich Shuvalov", *Zhurnal Ministerstva Narodnago Prosvescheniia,* XV, 1837, 396.

53 In this book the history of the Academy of Sciences will not be covered since it would require a separate volume in itself. For histories of it and Lomonosov see: Alexander Vucinich. *Science in Russian Culture. A History to 1860.*Stanford: Stanford University Press, 1963. K.V. Ostrovitianov (ed). *Istoriia Akademii Nauk SSSR.*Vol. I. (1724 - 1803) Moscow: Akademiia Nauk, 1958. B.N. Menshutin. *Russia's Lomonosov. Chemist, Courtier, Physcists, Poet.* Princeton: Princeton University Press, 1952.

54 *Ezhemesiachyia Sochineniia,*February, 1755, 98-104.

55 *Dokumenty i Materialy ...*

56 *PSZ,* XIV, No. 10,515. Senate. March 5, 1755.

57 *Ibid.,* XV, No. 10,812. Senate. March 20, 1758.

58 *Ibid.,* XV, No. 10,869. Senate. July 21, 1758.

59 *Ibid.,* XV, No. 11,144. Senate. November 15, 1760.

60 *Ibid.,* XIV, No. 10,776. Senate. November 6, 1757. See also: E.I. Gavrilov, "Lomonosov i Osnovanie Akademii Khudozhest", *Russkoe Iskusstvo XVIII Veka* (Moscow: Nauka, 1973), 66-75.

61 *Dokumenty i Materialy,* 232-33. The fate of Shuvalov after the death of the empress is of interest. He supported Peter III and incurred the wrath of Catherine the Great. In a letter to Stanislas Poniatowski she described him as "the most vile and mean-spirited of men." "Deux lettres de l'Empératricé Catherine à Stanislas Poniatowski. 2 août 1762", *Arkhiv Kiazia Vorontsova*(Moscow: Katkov, 1882), XXV, 422-23. Ivan had not been greedy like his cousin so his only holding was a house worth 12,000 rubles. He had turned down

offers of estates from the empress. Romanovich-Slavatinskii, 164. Hence, he found Russia
"unhealthy" and started traveling visiting Paris,
London and Rome. In 1773 he visited his old pen-
partner, Voltaire, who, jokingly referred to him
as the "Ex-emperor of Russia". After meeting him
Voltaire wrote to D'Alambert: "We have with us now
at Ferney Shuvalov; he is one of the best educated
and most curious people I have ever seen ..." Petr
Bartenev, *Biografiia I. I. Shuvalov* (Moscow: Semen, 1857), 35-40; 64. After spending eight years
in Rome and making contact with such figures as
the Pope and the future tragic Emperor Joseph II,
Catherine started to reconsider her attitude towards the Shuvalovs which had been hostile before
her victory. Ivan was greatly interested in art as
was Catherine. Soon she was sending him money to
purchase paintings. In 1777 he returned to Russia
and received a warm welcome from Catherine. It is
easy to determine from the daily record of the
empress (Kammer-Furer) that Ivan was probably the
most welcome guest. He rarely missed a day at the
palace. Once Catherine remarked to him: "Ivan
Ivanovich, I know that thou are not rich" to which
Shuvalov replied: "Reputation (Slava) has already
made me wealthy". Snegirev, 402. He lived a modest
life never getting married and open to people from
various social classes such as the raznochintsy.
Such was the influence of a "young favorite" upon
the cultural development of Russia. In a sense he
was the founder of the famous Hermitage collection
of art.

62 *Arkhiv Kniazia Vorontsova* (Moscow, 1873), Vol. VI,
311.

63 "Notice sur ma vie et les événements différents
qui se sont passés tant en Russia qu'en Europe
pendant ce temps-là", *Ibid*. (Moscow: Got'e, 1872),

12-13. This quote appears in slightly different words in Vucinich.

64 *Sanktpeterburgskiia Vedomosti,* No. 87. Friday the 28th day of October, 1748.

65 Semevskii, II, 728.

66 *Ocherki Istorii voronezhskogo Kraia...,* 159.

67 *PSZ,* XIII, No. 9972. Senate. April 13, 1752. This law applied to Ukrianian Onehouseholders.

68 *Ibid.,* XII, No. 9421. Senate. July 15, 1747.

69 *Ibid.,* No. 10, 256. Senate. July 11, 1754.

70 *Ibid.,* XIV, No. 10,701. Senate. March 10, 1757.

71 *Ibid.,* XV, No. 11,185. Senate. July 6, 1761.

72 Semevskii, II, 735-37.

CHAPTER FIVE

RELIGIOUS AND NATIONALITY POLICIES

The second darkest aspect of the reign was religious intolerance which reflected itself into the policies of the government. Only serfdom was worse. In handling the nationalities the government's record was not as bad as in the case of the treatment of the Old Believers and the Moslems. Of course, to a degree there was a correlation between the religious and nationalities policy since the smaller national groups were often Moslem, Buddhists or pagans. There are interesting parallels between the development of the Austrian Empire under Maria Theresa and Russia under Elisabeth. Both were religious fanatics and saw the unity of religion as a means of strengthening the state. But with Maria Theresa it was the Greek Orthodox and Protestants who suffered whereas Elisabeth was not interested in Catholics or Protestants, but of dissenters from the Russian Church and peoples of completely differing religions. This religious intolerance was typical of the pre-Enlightenment policies of such persons as Louis XIV in France, the English established church towards the Catholics and the Polish Catholic Church towards those of the Orthodox faith. The people of the Enlightenment were often critical of established religions and hence tolerant of those dissenting, or of differing religions. In fact, the monotheism of Islam was much admired by the more radical thinkers of the Enlightenment. Examples of such enlightened rulers would be Joseph II of Austria, Frederick the Great of Prussia and perhaps Catherine the Great. In individual cases these new people could be very religious in their private lives but still tolerant.

Elisabeth was most likely educated in religion and the Russian language by an Orthodox priest trained himself in the pre-Petrine period. We do not know who this individual was but the fact that Elisabeth tended to lapse occasionally into using letters in Russian abolished by her father in his simplification of Russian would tend to support this hypothesis.[1] About the year 1755, the policy of the government started becoming more moderate.

The Russian Orthodox Church itself was governed by the "Most Holy" Synode created in 1721 by Peter the Great with jurisdiction over matters relating to the Church and religion in general. It was placed on a level with the Senate and therefore was not subject to the Senate in matters falling into fields of its competence. By this step the Great Reformer reduced the power of the Church by abolishing the position of Patriarch and consequently increasing the authority of the state over the Church. The Synode, like the Senate, consisted of persons selected by the ruler on consultation with leading members of the Church. The Ober-Procurator of the Synode was not a clergyman, but he was a direct appointee of the ruler. The person holding this position from 1742-1753 was the honest, well-intentioned Prince Iakov Petrovich Shakhovskoi later promoted to war procurements controller and eventually the Senate itself. Unfortunately Shakhovskoi was limited in his mental abilities which made him a pliable tool for carrying the persecution of non-Christians and Old Believers. Relations within the Synode were not always harmonious and the members of the Synode once voted to stop payment of the salary of Shakhovskoi, but the empress intervened with an order that the money be paid.[2]

Since the Synode, like the Foreign Office and the Secret Chancellary, was not under the jurisdiction of the Senate disputes of a jurisdictional nature were frequent. The Senate wanted information on the monasteries in order to determine how many veterans could be supported by the Church. Such requests were simply ignored unless the empress intervened.

The most important task of the Synode was the appointment of bishops and the superiors of larger religious establishments while attempting to insure that previous appointees were acting properly.[3] It also heard important cases of a criminal nature concerning the clergy or persons under its jurisdiction. Certain types of cases, like sacrilege, were generally under its control as well. However, political cases involving the government were handled by the Secret Chancellary alone whether the individual was a noble or clergyman.

The monasteries and converts were likewise under the control of the Synode. In 1750 there were about 726 monasteries and 240 convents.[4] As noted above the Church was a large serf holder the bulk of these (782,736) belonged to the monastic institutions while 116,376 were the property of bishops. The largest and most important for the development of the Moscow state, the Trinity Monastery, had 187 monks and 105,761 serfs.[5] Probably to avoid receiving persons merely trying to escape serfdom or the army the pious empress put a limit on the number of monks at the Trinity Monastery.[6]

There were also paying "guests" at the monasteries and convents. who did not join the order. These were apparently people of modest means such as the elderly men and widows with no place to live. The Synode resisted the repeated efforts of the empress and the Senate to force them to take wounded, cripled and aged soldiers no longer capable of service. This was a mistake since it was one of the reasons used when Church lands were secularized.

With the outbreak of the Seven Years' War the government tried to limit the persons becoming clergy and the servants of the clergy to obtain men for the army. In 1757 the empress ordered that officers not suitable for military service living near religious institutions in the countryside take supervision of these to obtain funds needed for the war.[7] There were not enough such officers so the Ukaz had no effect except that it was another warning of the impending secularization of Church lands. In the first part of the reign the empress had abolished the "Economic College" established by Anna to oversee the Church properties and collect revenue from them. She did this as a pious act, but she herself a few years later tried to gain similar control. Of course, the serfs of the Church paid their taxes to the government while supporting the clergy. The clergy themselves were exempt from taxes as were a set number of their servants such as Deacons.

The Synode had other tasks in addition to these. It encouraged the education of the parish clergy, but its efforts were not well rewarded in this regard. Most of the priests were themselves the sons of priests and had the right to marry. The burden of maintaining a family made it difficult for them to afford the burden of an education although the church schools were free for them.[8] Most had to learn the Church service from their fathers by memory as a consequence. There existed a fine institution in Kiev called the Slavic-Greek-Latin School which prepared priests for that region where contact with Roman Catholicism was great. Such a school was established also in Moscow and monasteries often had schools of their own. But the superior education of the Ukrianian clergy probably explains the sudden rule that only Great Russians could obtain important posts. When the relatively free Ukrianian Cossacks tried to select their own bishop for Periaslav the Synode in St. Petersburg simply placed its own candidate in the position in 1753.[9]

Among the most important contributions of the Synode in this reign was to complete a new printed version of the

Bible which, when printed, was considered the best prepared book of the century in Russian. At a cost of five rubles it should have been good. Peter the Great had ordered its preparation and when issued it possessed the authority among the Russian Orthodox similar to that of the King James version among the English Protestants until recently.[10]

The Synode was the agency handling relations with people of other faiths and the Old Believers. The treatment of peoples of other faiths varied. For the non-Russian Christians the tradition of Peter was generally followed. They could practice their own religion freely as long as no attempt was made to convert the Orthodox. It was not until the dark age of Probedonostsev in the XIX century that this policy was changed. In the cosmopolitan city of St. Petersburg there were three German Lutheran Churches and one Swedish which held services in Swedish and Finnish. In addition the Roman Catholics had their church there also. There were Calvinist and Roman Catholic churches in Archangel, Moscow and the very cosmopolitan Astrakhan. The Catholic churches alone had the right to use bells. Of course, these were only accessable to foreigners living in Russia or persons from the Protestant regions of the empire.[11]

In the Baltic states of Livonia and Estonia where the prevelant religion was Lutheran the churches and their pastors were protected by the government. To try to win the confidence of the Finnish peoples in the newly acquired regions the people and the churches were very well treated despite the prejudice of the Great Russians against the Finns. The traveler and writer, Anton Büsching, himself a German Protestant, was impressed with the toleration of the churches in those regions when he visited them.[12]

Often the Lutherans were treated with more respect than the Orthodox by some of the bishops. An extreme case was the Bishop of Tambovsk, Pakhomii, appointed in 1758 to the position. He was greedy for money, used bodily punishment of a severe nature on the priests, took their sons and daughters selling them to friendly landowners as serfs. He was so severe that he undermined the authority of the Orthodox Church in the region causing many to secretly leave it. Upon repeated complaints he was removed to another region in 1766 where he continued his activities.[13] If the Synode had really been functioning as it was designed he would have been sent to a monastery as a plain monk.

One of the most fiercely persecuted groups was one closest to the Orthodox Church. This group which consisted of a large portion of the Great Russians (but far from the majority) were called schismatics by the Church, but they referred to themselves as Old Believers or Old Ritualists. In 1667 they had split from the Church when a meeting of Patriarchs accepted some changes in the Russian ritual to make it conform more closely to the Greek. The split in the Church resembles the Protestant Reformation in the West except that the reformers were the Church itself and the state which supported it. The Old Believers splintered in numerous groups as in the Protestant Reformation and many of these still exist. One group caused the government special concern because as a form of protest to official policy they would burn themselves and refused to take oaths to support the government. These people would often gather together in a community with a large building, and when the authorities approached or when the "spirit" moved them, they would gather, pray and then burn down the building killing themselves in the process saying that they would rather burn in this world than the next. The last such burnings took place in 1823. The oppressive nature of the regime, and the growing unpleasantness of serfdom drove many Orthodox people to join them. This was one of the means of escaping the authorities albeit not the best. In the face of persecution their numbers actually appeared to have increased.

The ignorance and often unreligious behavior of the clergy, widespread among all classes at that time, was another stimulus for the spread of the Old Believers and for the terrible consequence of self-immolation.

As is known, Peter the Great had forced the shaving of the beards of the upper classes save for the clergy. This the Old Believers considered to be the worst of sins since man was created in the image of God, and He had a beard. Peter placed a special tax on the beards of the Old Believers, which, if paid let them function freely. Anna Ioanovna was a religious fanatic like her successor Elisabeth, and Anna's persecution of the Old Believers was harsh (many of them attributed it to the German influence which was incorrect). During the reign of Elisabeth they suffered terribly although the government did as much as possible to stop the self-immolations. From the collected laws of the empire it is clear that they were scattered over the entire empire except, perhaps, for Kamchatka. When the second census was started in 1743 the crisis broke for the Old Believers since they had to declare their faith and pay extra taxes as a result. The old law of Peter about the tax on the beards was repeated, which caused them to desert the land and seek refuge.[14] One of the first groups appeared in the north near Archangel. With a leader, a large number of them moved into the wilderness to escape persecution. The authorities learned of the location of their main building and sent troops with a false manifesto telling them that they would not be hurt, but with secret orders to arrest them and put them in chains probably for shipment to Siberia. Upon receiving false promises and correctly guessing what faced them 75 persons burned themselves before the troops. Further operations in the region led to 17 more persons being burned.[15] The wave of burning spread throughout the empire. In 1749 Sylvester Glovatsky was named Metropolitan of Tobolsk. There had been burnings before in the region, but this totally unsympathic, or one would have to say un-Christian, man really started the fires. In 1751 189 burned themselves at one time. In April of that year a family of 33 burned themselves. So it continued. In other towns and villages than Tobolsk, the capital of Siberia 72, 64, 39, 6 and 25 burned themselves in separate incidents. [16] It is impossible to give a total figure for the reign but the historian Kostomorov who was not unsympathetic to Elisabeth, claimed that in one incident alone which he did not identify, 6,000 persons burned themselves to death. [17] He claimed that this was the worst reign for self-immolations.

The Synode was totally ineffective in dealing with the situation and indeed seemed to be ignorant of the causes. In 1749 it authorized the funds for the transportation of Old Believers to labor or exile.[18] While this was one case, it set the precedent. Families were broken up when shipped. A special investigation commission using torture was established in 1746 to try to determine the origins of the schism, but most of the people taken in for investigation "died in prison".[19] Under the circumstances it is no surprise that they became entirely estranged from the government and refused any oaths except derrogatory ones for the ruler and her favorites.

With the reign of Peter III came toleration although self-immolations did continue. As memory of the events faded, some of them developed the story that Elisabeth had been a virgin who had given birth to a son, Peter III. After Catherine killed Peter III they believed that he had retired to Siberia someday to return to the ringing of church bells. When Pugachev appeared along the Volga among the Volga Cossacks the church bells started ringing. [20] In 1752 another Christian "heresy" was discovered near Moscow which was called the "Kvaker" heresy. It had first been discovered in the previous reign among merchants having contacts with British and perhaps even American merchants. Since there is no "q" in the Russian language, it is easy to identify this as Quaker. The movement involved 415 people and in contrast to the Old Believers they were treated with moderation. Only a few were sent to Siberia most undergoing just bodily punishment and were then freed. In passing it is interesting to note that one of the charges against them was the ritual murder of babies--a charge which reppears many times in history.[21]

One other group of Christians underwent mild persecution for no clear reason. This was the Armenians many of whom resided legally in Russia. They had their own churches in Moscow and Astrakhan and had permission to construct one in St. Petersburg.[22] Elisabeth took away this right and closed their church in Moscow leaving only the one in Astrakhan open. Upon petition they were informed by the Synode that they could hold their services legally in private homes.[23] However, in other respects they were unmolested. They seemed to even have special rights when it came to trading.

The Armenians are the last Christian group to be considered. The empress had an especially notorious aversion to the Jewish religion with which she had never had any contact. Since 1727 the government had repeated laws forbidding anyone of the Jewish faith to enter or reside in Russia and if any were there they were to leave at once. This law had been repeated by Anna just before her death when it was reported that people of the Jewish religion were living in the Ukraine. Elisabeth hastened to make her notorious remark: "I do not wish profits from the enemies of Christ".[24] However, her orientation was purely religious since she said that former Jewish people were as welcome as any others in Russia if they embraced the Orthodox faith. The "enlightened" Voltaire with his sceptical views of religion was also anti-Semitic, and it would have to be stated that his form was based on race rather than religion which is far worse. Hence, in the reign of Elisabeth there were no Jewish people living legally in Russia.

After the Old Believers, the religious group which gave the government the greatest concern was the Islamic community. The Tatars in the region around Kazan had converted to Islam before the conversion of the Rus' in 988 and with the conquest of the region by Ivan the Terrible they had mixed with the Christian settlers, and little friction had developed between them. Usually the two religious groups lived in separate villages, but on occasion there were mixed villages with the church and the mosque. While the Islamic people did not send out missionaries like the Orthodox they presented the government with a real problem since many pagan people lived in the region and Islam had a strong attraction for them. These pagan people in the region of Kazan were mainly Finnish like the Mordva, the Cheremis and the Chuvash. The conquest of Siberia added large numbers of pagan peoples to the list of potential converts.

The movement of the Russian state into the Orenburg region, which as mentioned above, was turned into a Guberniia in 1744 brought the Russians into closer contact with the religiously advanced plains people like the ever-discontent Bashkir people and the Kirgiz both of the Moslem faith. In addition the Kalmyks, of the Buddhist Laminist faith, were camped on the border of the empire and assisted the Russian government in time of war.

The Synode and ruler had a serious problem in handling the peoples following these higher religions and their relation to the pagans. This was especially acute in the Kazan, Orenburg and Siberia gubernias. To try to reverse the trend to Islam in Kazan the Empress Anna had created the Bureau for the Newly Converted (Kontor Novokreshchago Dela) which was a strange effort to "purchase" souls of the non-Orthodox. The Bureau was funded, and it was announced that any non-Christian desiring to enter the Orthodox Church could appear at the office of the Bureau, be baptised and afterwards receive a monetary reward. There were "fringe" benefits for the newly converted as well. If a non-Christian was selected for the army and chose to be baptised he was freed from service. In addition, if a newly converted person was a serf belonging to a person who was not Orthodox he was freed, although this benefit was probably little used since as a rule only the Orthodox were allowed to hold serfs except in the Baltic states. A Moslem convicted of a serious crime meriting the death penalty could be freed upon conversion.[25] The Bureau was active for the years 1740-1764 during which time it paid out approximately 150,000 rubles.[26] The total of converts for the period 1743-1760 was 409,864.[27] According to the regulations the Bureau was to pay one ruble for each convert, but the figures provided indicate that the rule was not being followed since most apparently received nothing but a little water. The selectiveness of the system is revealed by the fact that important converts could receive up to 600 rubles.[28] The worst period of the persecution of people of other faiths was 1743-1747 when more than half (217,258) the converts were made.[29] No figures are given of the previous religious affiliation of the newly converted probably because they would show the strength of Islam. For example, in 1745 the pagan Barabinskii Tatars accepted Islamic law in the midst of the campaign by the Orthodox.[30]

Many of the new converts did not really understand what was happening which was in violation of Orthodox canon law. The persons doing the work in the field were often fanatics who lacked tact in dealing with potential converts. An example of this was one missionary sent to convert the Mordva people who were known for their peaceful mannerisms. He proceeded to destroy their graveyard which to them was holy, and they responded by threatening the life of the missionary who then turned to the civil authorities for assistance. Troops called in the name of the Prince of Peace killed 35 Mordva, wounded 31 captured 136. In disgust a Christian Mordva tore off the cross he was wearing, an act punishable by death.[31] This incident should have alerted the Synode that something was unlawful in his activities, but he continued to force conversions on the unwilling. Before he was transfered out of the region he had "converted" 50,430 and constructed 83 churches.[32]

In such regions with large pagan populations the Senate and empress ordered the opening of schools for the children of The newly converted so they could in turn serve as missionaries.[33] The parents of the Chuvash children in these schools called them "houses of death" since such a large number of the students were exposed to disease and died.[34]

The fate of the newly converted was not very good. They could move to Christian regions where officials mistreated them and provided them with inferior land or they could stay in the pagan village and be harrassed by their neighbors who had to pay their taxes and serve in the army for them.

Since Islam was so strong it presented especialy difficult problems, and the fanatical empress ordered a study of the locations of mosques in regions with Christians especially Kazan, Astrakhan, Voronezh and Siberia to insure that there were no newly converted Christians or Christians in villages with mosques. If there were such people, the mosques were to be destroyed.[35] This unwise law was applied to the restless Bashkirs in the Oreburg region in 1744.[36] From official reports of 1756 government admitted that of the 536 mosques in the Kazan region where the Moslems were numerous 418 had been destroyed in accordance with the orders.[37]

Religious matters were the sole concern of the Synode, but the situation which developed out of its policy or lack of policy soon brought the whole matter to the   attention of the Senate. In 1748 the Senate was informed by the civil authorities that an anonymous letter had been received in Kazan stating that the Moslem Tatars there planned a major uprising in the spring and that troops were needed in case the letter was correct.[38] The letter, which was probably a clever trick of the Moslems to gain toleration, threw the Senate into panic. Special troops were sent into the region and, of course, the rising did not take place. Instead it was a summer of mysterious fires which seemed to concentrate upon the cities with oppressed peoples like Kazan. The Synode was informed but did nothing to stop the oppression and fanatical policies of its missionaries even with Shakhovskoi then heading it.

The crisis point was finally reached in relations with Islam in the case of the Metropolitan of Tobolsk, the above mentioned Silvester Glovatskii, who was following a foolish policy of forced conversions. He was so certain that his policy would be successful in the region around Tobolsk and Orenburg that he complained about the cutting of trees for factories which, he felt, might be needed for his anticipated new churches.[39] Nepliuev, the pious and honest governor of Orenburg, complained that he was forcing conversion on the nearby Bashkirs who were Moslems. Likewise the General Procurator of Siberia whose task it was to guard against official corruption complained that he was forcefully converting Tatars and merchants from Bukhara.[40] Pre-revolutionary biographical dictionaries have little to say about him since his proceedures were so clearly incorrect and dangerous. The complaints came to the Senate in late 1750 and early 1751 when he had held his position for just a year. The Synode was informed, but the Senate was greatly disturbed since it could do nothing. It is not known if the Senate appealed to the empress who could have forced action by the Synode. The Tatars themselves sent a petitioner to St. Petersburg with a sum of 800 rubles they had collected for the purpose. The fate of the petitioner is unknown.[41]

Forced conversions presented a serious problem to the authorities. For if a person returned to the old religion it was necessary to determine if he had "relapsed" or had been baptised against his will. In the first case he violated the law since a person who was Orthodox would be punished for changing religions, yet forceful conversions were against canon law and had been repeatedly denounced by the Synode even if it took no action to stop them. If it could be proven that a family had "relapsed", the punishment would be especially severe if the unfortunate people were Moslems.[42] One especially interesting case came before the Senate of this nature. A Moslem with some friends was heard shouting in the streets of Tobolsk in Russian that any Islamic person accepting baptism of their own free will were "dogs" - which in Russian is a swear word. In addition they cried that Christians worshipped pictures and bowed down before deamons. The police apprehended one immediately who, upon arrest, requested that he be baptised which would release him from the serious crime of sacreligion. The now confused Silvester turned to the Senate for advise in the disposition of the case.[43] It was clear that the Moslem would accept baptism and immediately move to the Islamic states of Central Asia where he would continue to be a Moslem. The outcome of the case is not given in the Senate archives (printed edition).

Silvester brought the whole problem to a conclusion by his activities among the discontent Bashkir people who revolted against the Russian state on the slightest pretext. Now they had a serious issue in the forced conversions. Hence, in 1755 they declared a holy war, started burning factories which were taking land away from them, but when defeated they fled to the Kirgiz whom they falsely trusted as coreligionists.[44] However, historical differences were more important to the Kirgiz than the religious since the Russian government had treated them relatively well. Nepliuev simply ordered the Kirgiz to keep the women and children of the Bashkirs and return the men.[45] Thus, the revolt was easily crushed. Within a month the Synode ordered the transfer of Silvester to a relatively harmless post and replaced him with a much better individual. The new Metropolitan was appalled by what he discovered-- many of the "converts" did not know that they had been "converted" to Christianity, who Christ was, etc.[46] He had no choice in most cases but to assume illegal forced conversion rather than relapse.

Between 1748 and 1755 the policies of the government became more tolerant or enlightened. Part of this was clearly out of necessity as in the case of the threat of revolt in 1748 and the actual revolt of 1755. The self-immolations of the Old Believers and the alarming reports about these could hardly have left even the most intolerant unmoved.

One other factor seemed to have a large role in this change of policy. Starting in 1755 under the influence of I.I. Shuvalov the Senate issued orders restraining local officials in their investigations of Old Believers and "kvakers". One such law, directed both to civil and clerical authorities, was entitled: "About restraining clergy from forceful measures in investigating cases of schism, for the changing the misled by the spiritual sword, not the civil".[47] By 1756, with war just starting, the last thing the Senate wanted was another rising of major proportions, and, with the Moslem population plus the Old Believers discontent, the Senate had to take steps to appease possible discontent at home. Troops were needed in the foreign campaigns and could not be spared to guard the localities. Therefore, a general order was issued by the Senate allowing the rebuilding of many of the mosques while separating the "newly converted" Christians from the Moslems.[48] Still mosques were not to be constructed unless there were between 200-300 Moslems in a given region, and the mosque could not be inside the village itself.

It is curious to note that Elisabeth's policies became more tolerant as she aged in contrast to Anna's. Perhaps the changing spirit of the age and the Enlightenment explain part of this shift.

To some extent the national groups have been covered in the consideration of the religious policy especially where they were not of the Orthodox religion. This produced a mixed picture of the well-treated Kirgiz to the persecuted Tatars in Kazan and Siberia. There were national groups which did have a more pleasant fate in the reign of Elisabeth among which were the Kalmyks and the Ukrainians. The Kalmyks were Lamanist Buddhists who had fled from China and settled on the border of Russia where, by treaty, they were allowed to remain nomads and practice their religion undisturbed. Indeed, they had a right not allowed to others--they could leave when they so desired; a right they were to exercise in the next reign.[49] They often supported the Russian government in time of war with their troops.

The largest minority in the Empire then as now was that of the Ukrainians. Since they were Orthodox in religion with well trained priests this factor presented no problem although the Great Russians were occupying all the leading positions in the Church as noted previously. The empress herself was favorable to the Ukrainians since her husband came from that region. In the preceeding reign and to some extent even in her reign the rights of the Ukrainians had been eroding. For example the Hetman's post among the Cossacks had been left vacant since 1734 effectively taking away the power to elect their own leader. There were reasons for this erosion. The shift of sides by Mazeppa at Poltava did not help. Also serfdom was starting to put its ugly roots into the region. Big brother, the Great Russians were taking more and more away from them. It was clear that in time given the trend the Ukraine would have become an integral part of the Russian Empire enjoying none of its previous rights and subject to the hardships of Great Russia.

Elisabeth attempted to arrest the process by direct order. She proceeded to issue a series of laws early in the reign oft repeated that under no circumstance could a Ukrainian be enserfed, and she even applied it to Ukrainian women marrying serfs which was against normal usage.[50] In August of 1742 the Ukrainians were given a special grant to "repair" the damage which the war with the Ottoman Empire had caused in the previous reign.[51] This was while the war with Sweden was still a great financial burden upon the government. In 1747 a law was issued announcing that the Hetmanship which had been vacant since 1734 was to be filled again.[52] Care was taken to insure that a candidate suitable to the Russian government be selected and the Cossacks were so glad to regain this lost ground that they elected the brother of the husband of the empress, Kirill Razumovskii, who being educated in St. Petersburg and Europe was too cosmopolitan for the task of protecting the Ukrainians. He preferred St. Petersburg to Kiev which prepared the way for the abolishion of the Hetmanship in 1764 about which, with all his wealth, he seemed indifferent.

But the Ukrainians, peasants or Cossacks, enjoyed a whole series of rights which the Russian nobles alone had otherwise. They could import tax-free goods for their own use, but if these were sent to another area in the Empire they had to pay the normal tax. They had the right to distill vodka for their own use although in Russia this became a monopoly of the nobles after 1755. They were free to move about and trade. This fact is attested to by yearly imports into St. Petersburg of what was called "Cherkass beef" although mention of it stopped in 1754.[53] The Ukraine was under the jurisdiction of the Foreign Office until 1756 when, on the suggestion of Kirill Razumovskii the Hetman, they were placed under the Senate which meant less autonomy for the region.[54] In 1755 they were also included in the uniform tariff for the Russian Empire. Although there were clear signs that the Ukraine was in danger of becoming completely integrated into the Empire, the efforts of Elisabeth to arrest the process were of such a nature that the Ukrainians should errect monuments to her as the last defender of what limited rights they had.

Whereas the Ukrainians represented a distinct ethnic group and rightly belonged on the section dealing with the nationalities, it is more difficult to classify other Cossack groups. They were of the Orthodox religion except where the Old Believers were tolerated. Often such Cossacks as those of the Don had Great Russian, Ukrainian and perhaps some Tatar blood. They also had some rights such as the right to elect the leadership and their priests. It is true that they were becoming more and more dependent upon St. Petersburg, but they were able at least to maintain their autonomy when the Ukrainian Cossacks lost theirs. The elders among the Don Cossacks were gradually increasing their own power at the cost of the run-away serfs who worked for them in maintaining forage supplies. The Cossacks raised little grain and had to import it from the central region which reduced their independence. Finally with the third census in 1764 the soul tax was extended to the Don region for the lower class who thus became serfs again while the upper class became a sort of nobility with the fixed duty of serving the army in time of war.[55] But it must be noted that somewhat as in the Ukraine this social stratification had long been developing and its growth was probably the greatest in the reign of Elisabeth.

Two other groups of Cossacks deserve mention here. These were "planted" Cossacks from other regions one group of whom had been settled along the Volga to try to control the constant robber bands along that river and another on the Orenburg Line named the Iaik Cossacks later to participate in the rising of Pugachev in a significant numbers.[56] These Cossacks were really paid soldiers of

136

the government rather than settled peoples. In addition, their number was small.

Thus we have a picture of the manner in which the government and the empress handled the various religious and national minorities. The pattern appears clear. Inheriting a policy of religious fanaticism, the new empress continued to press heavily upon the Old Believers, increased the persecution of the Moslems who were non-Slavic and in a contrary fashion treated some peoples such as the Kalmyks who were non-Christian with special favor. The shift in policy which gradually started around 1750 was the outcome of the restlessness of the oppressed peoples, the influence of I.I. Shuvalov and the changing mood of the times. Except for the Bashkirs and to an extent the Old Believers, the change in the attitude of the government must have been very noticeable from the oppressive 40's to the more humane and light handed mid-50's. It is true that the role of the empress seems less important in the latter period than in the first. Still a long step had to be taken before anything like modern toleration on the Prussian model would be possible for Russia.

NOTES

1 Esterhasy to Maria Theresa. St. Petersburg. April 22, 176. Austrian State Archives. Russland II Berichte. 1754 IV-1756 VI. Item 37. This message includes a hand written order of the empress to her own Foreign Office commanding it to inform her immediately of any important business relating to Austria. In it, in contrast to her other letters, she lapsed into the use of old letters which her father had removed from the Russian language.

2 Shakhovskoi, 54-58.

3 "Ropis' Restkhiiam vserossiiskoi Imperii, i kakiia Provintsii, Gorody i Uezdy k kazhdoi Eparhii pridnadleshat'", *Ezhemesiaschyia...,*April,1757,291-304. The bishoprics were Krutiskii, Pereslavl, Vladimir, Sudal, Kolomensk, Riazan, Nizhnyi-Novgorod, Rostov, Tver, Kiev, Kostrom, Archangel, Ustiuzh, Vologda, Novgorod, St. Petersburg, Pskov, Smolensk, Chernigov, Pereiaslavl, Belgorod, Voronezh, Kazan, Astrakhan, Viatka, Tobol'sk and Irkutsk.

4 Alefirenko, 154-55.

5 Anton-Friedrich Büsching, *Magazin für neuer Historie und Geographie* (Hamburg: Ritter, 1767), I, 52. This remarkable journal lasted until its author's death in 1793. The author made several visits to Russia at various times, and the data he presents was highly reliable for that age.

6 *PSZ,* XIV, No. 10,177. A Personal Ukaz sent from the Synode. January 20, 1754.

7 *Ibid.,* XIV, No. 10,765. Personal, Promulgated from the Conference of Her Imperial Highness. October 6, 1757.

8 Solov'ev, 23, 254-55.

9 *Akty i Dokumenty, otnosiashchiesia k Istorii kievskoi Akademii. Otdelenie II (1721-1759gg).*Vol. II (1751-1762gg.) with introduction and footnotes by N.I. Petrov (Kiev, 1906), VII-VIII.

10 *Polnoe Sobranie Postanolenii i Rasporiazhnii po Vedomostu pravoslavnago Ispovedaniia rossiskago Imperii. Tom II. 1746-1752gg.* (St.   Petersburg: Synode, 1912), No. 1271, 460. December 23, 1751.

11 Haven, 68-70.

12 Büshching, *Magazin* ... (Hamburg: Ritter,   1770), Vol. IV, 479-86.

13 I.I.Dubasov, *Ocherki iz Istorii tambovskago Kraia* (Moscow: Elisaveta Gerbek, 1883), Issue I, 98-100.

14 *PSZ,* XI, No. 8707. Senate reaffirming previous laws. February 19, 1743.

15 G.V. Esipov, *Liudi starago Veka. Razskazy iz Preobrazhenskago Prikaz i Tainoi Kantseliarii* (St.Petersburg: Suvorin,   1880),   190-201.   G.   Esipov, "Samosozhigateli", *Otechestvennyia Zapiski,* CXLVI, 1863, 605-27.

16 Andreevich, 202-212. D.I.Sapozhnikov, *Samosozhzhenie v russkom Raskole* (Moscow: Moskovskii Universitet, 1891), 83-133.

17 N.I.   Kostomarov,   "Imperatritsa   Elisaveta Petrovna. Istoricheskii Ocherk", *Vestnik Evropy,* III, 1888, 29.

18 *PSZ,* XIII, No. 9582. Senate. February 28, 1749. This involved one case which set a precedence. The initiative came from the Synode.

19 Andreevich, 211-212.

20 Pronshtein, 317.

21 *Senatskii Arkhiv,* VIII, 506-75. April 30, 1752. It is curious that this case came before the Senate since it belonged to the Secret Chancellary or Synode.

22 *PSZ,* XI, No. 8007. Most Highly Affirmed. January 18, 1740.

23 *Ibid.,* XI, No. 8500. Personal following a report of the Synode. January 16, 1742. *Polnoe Sobraine.. Tom III 1746-1752gg* (St. Petersburg: Synode, 1912), No. 1295. May 20, 1752, 777-78.

24 *PSZ,* XI No. 8673. Personal. December 2, 1742. A Protestant or Catholic foreigner in Russian military service was promoted one level if they became Greek Orthodox. *Ibid.,* XII, No. 9305. Senate. July 15, 1746.

25 Andreevich, 219. Anna Leopoldovna passed this decree and Elisabeth accepted it.

26 Alefirenko, 285.

27 Evfim Malov, *O novokreshchenskom Kontore* (Kazan: Kazanskii Universitet, 1878), 203.

28 Vitevskii, II, 545.

29 Malov, 103. Silvester Glovatskii is "credited" with much of that figure before he was appointed Metropolitan of Tobolsk.

30 Andreevich, 222.

31 Malov, 58-59. Solov'ev, 21, 207.

32 Malov, 61.

33 *PSZ,* XI, No. 8792. Most Highly Affirmed Report of the Senate. September 28, 1743.

34 N.G. Apollova, "K Voprosu o Politike Absoliutizma v natsional'nykh Raionakh Rossii v XVIIIv.", *Abso-*

liutizm v Russii (Moscow: Nauka, 1963), 375.

35 PSZ, XI, No. 8664. Senate. November 19, 1742.

36 *Ibid.*, XII, No. 8875. Senate. February 20, 1744.

37 *Ibid.*, XIV, No. 10,597. Senate. August 23, 1756.

38 *Senatskii Arkhiv,* VII, 257-58. February 21, 1748.

39 Andreevich, 217.

40 *Senatskii Arkhiv,* VIII, 285-88. February 21, 1748.

41 Andreevich, 217.

42 *PSZ,* XI, No. 8664. Senate. November 19, 1742.*Ibid.* XII, No. 8978. Senate. June 22, 1744. Forceful conversions were also banned by this law.

43 *Senatskii Arkhiv,* VIII, 482-85. April 6, 1752.

44 Roger Portal, "Les Bachkirs et la gouvernement Russe aux XVIIIe Siècle", *Revue d'Etudes slaves,* I, 1946, 82-104.

45 *Ibid.*

46 Malov, 180. The language barrier appears to have been one of the problems.

47 *PSZ,* XV, No. 11,277. Senate. June 19, 1761.

48 *Ibid.*, XIV, No. 10,597. Senate. August 23, 1756.

49 *Ibid.*, XII, No. 9175. Senate. June 12, 1745. This was a reaffirmation of an old right.

50 *Ibid.*, XI, No. 8555. Personal, promulgated by the Senate. May 21, 1742.

51 D. Bantysh-Kamenskii, *Istoriia Maloi Rossi. Chast' Tret'ia. Ot Izbrannia Mazepa do Unichtozheniia Getmanstva* (Moscow: Stepanov, 1841), 177-78.

52 *PSZ,* XII, No. 9400. Personal. May 5, 1747.

53 *Sanktpeterburgskiia Vedomosti,* Friday, July 1st, 1754, 519. The price of choice cuts of Cherkass beef sold for 4.27 copecks a kilogram. The term Cherkass came to be associated with a type of cattle so it did not have to come from Cherkass although that seems the most probable origin.

54 Presniakov, 275-77.

55 Pronshtein, 161-202.

56 John T. Alexander, *Autocratic Politics in a National Crisis: the Imperial Russian Government and Pugachev's Revolt, 1773-1775* (Bloomington: Indiana University Press, 1969), 46-52. Information on the laik Cossacks and their relation to the revolt of Pugachev is presented.

CHAPTER SIX

THE ECONOMY

Throughout the reign of Elisabeth the mercantilist system, introduced into Russia in the middle of the previous century by Ordyn-Nashcockin and furthered by Peter, prevailed in the economic thinking of the government. This set of concepts was borrowed directly from the advanced trading countries like France, England and Holland. During Elisabeth's reign there were the first vague signs of a change to a more liberal system. In short the mercantilists believed that it was desirable to keep unfinished products in the country to encourage domestic industry. The export of finished products was encouraged under this system and the export of silver and gold discouraged. This policy was difficult in application in Russia since it, like the colonial areas in the New World and elsewhere, was primarily a producer of raw materials such as tar, hemp, timber, thread, furs, grains, etc. Mercantilism was a doctrine flexible enough to permit significant private economic activity if it worked in the direction which the government desired. Often, however, this activity was forced on the community with mixed results. Thus, special trading companies like the English Moscow Company were established to the general good of all parties although there were also simple failures in these ventures like the "bubbles" at the beginning of the century.

Peter the Great had placed great importance upon the economic growth of Russia within the governmental structure which he created. He established special Colleges for Commerce, Mining and even Manufacturing. It will be recalled that these colleges were dependent upon the Senate and the empress alone and that their activity had left much to be desired. Thus, as indicated above much of the work devolved upon the Senate itself which was clearly overworked.[1]

Perhaps the most difficult economic problem which faced the government initially was the coinage system by then in great confusion. Starting in the reign of Peter the Great the government had resorted to the use of copper money for small change. Before this small change had been exclusively in silver in a country which had not yet produced much of that metal. Little slivers of stamped silver called kopeecki had been struck from the time of Ivan the Terrible. Alexis, the father of Peter the Great, had as an emergency measure during the war with Poland over the Ukraine, resorted to the emission of copper coins with a gold or silver value stamped on the face of said coins with the stipulation that they be accepted under the threat of death. The Treaty of Andrusovo had ended the war for Russia successfully in 1667 by which time the economy was ruined by the copper coins. In 1662 there had been the so-called copper riots over the fall in the value of these coins and a number of leading merchants had been ruined. Peter did not issue false copper money, however. Unfortunately he used varying quantities of copper for the coinage depending upon the needs of the state at the time. But the Russian peasant still liked his little silver coins and looked with suspicion upon the copper copecks especially the light five copeck piece they were now required to use. Apparently it was not until the reign of Anna that the government got the little silver coins out of circulation and replaced them with copper. She desired to retire the light five copeck piece and replace it with a larger coin more closely reflecting the true value of the copper content. Peter had struck five copeck pieces at the rate of 1.22 rubles to a kilogram (20 rubles to the pud) and his successor had doubled to 2.44 the amount struck per kilogram (40 rubles to the pud). This rapid emission had the goal of allowing sufficient money to be in circulation to permit the serfs to pay their dues.[2] But this caused inflation and a great distrust among the serfs against the copper money. Anna's best effort was to start striking coins at the rate of .61 copecks from each kilogram (10 rubles to the pud). She also desired to retire the light five copeck piece but was unable to do so since she was almost constantly at war and needed all the silver possible.[3] So Elisabeth inherited a monetary system with many weights of copper money in circulation. The five copeck piece was an especial problem since it was so crudely struck that counterfieting was easy, and the anti-Semitic empress was informed that Jewish persons in Poland were doing just that to obtain Russian silver.[4] Horrified by this prospect she pushed for immediate reform. It was made illegal to import Russian money (as it is today) especially in the form of copper and the value of the five copeck piece was dropped by stages until it was valued at somewhat less than two copecks.[5] The mint (Money Court) was ordered to start the issuance of copper coinage at the rate of 49 copecks from each kilogram (8 rubles per pud) for the smaller coin which made these coins almost full bodied money.[6] As confusing as this sounds it played an important role in Russia's monetary situation. Shcherbatov, always ready to criticize, noted that it hurt the "little people",[7] but it is generally agreed that these measures gave assurances to the masses and merchants that copper money was now safe and from that time on there was no difficulty in inducing them to accept it.[8] The issuance of some 6,846,866 rubles in copper between 1752 and 1761 certainly stimulated commerce and industry without having any significant inflationary effect.[9]

In addition to the issuance of copper money the mint emitted an average of one million rubles in silver money a year.[10] This remained of fixed content until the Seven Years' War caused a slight drop in the silver probe. Silver coins were issued in amounts of one ruble, a half ruble and a quarter of a ruble. Since there were a hundred copecks to the ruble Russia was one of the first European states to use the decimal system. The only exception appears to have been gold coins with irregular value in terms of copper since gold was so valuable and rare at the time. But the government tried to keep the silver content of the ruble coinage the same as the standard Austrian or Dutch Thaler which were known to the Russians as efimki. Many of the early silver rubles were simply foreign coin of fixed value struck over with a Russian stamp leaving signs of the real origin of the coins.[11]

******

The above-mentioned monetary reform was partly the work of the Senate itself and partly that of one of its chief members, Peter Ivanovich Shuvalov (1710-1762), one of the most controversial figures of the reign. A member of the "little court" of Elisabeth before 1741, he gained influence with the empress first by marrying her closest friend and then strengthened it when his cousin, Ivan, became the reigning "favorite" at court around 1750. Himself a Senator from 1744, he was a man filled with ideas for reform. He was often accused of greed in that some claimed his re-forms were only designed to further his own interests. Nevertheless, one of his contemporaries claimed that the rooms in his house had tables covered with schemes to ad-vance the interests of the state and himself.[12]

Shuvalov belonged to a distinct line of Russian reformers which included Maslov, who was Ober Procurator of the Senate until his death in 1735. Maslov had blamed the terrible conditions in the country on the oppression which the serfs received   from their owners. Despite his early death Maslov did influence a number of other people with his desire for reform.[13] The supposed leader of the "Russian party" in the reign of Anna, Volynskii, was also interested in reform and since he was in contact with Elisabeth there is little doubt that he likewise influenced Peter Shuvalov although most of the materials on Volynskii did not survive. One contemporary influence which cannot be ruled out was Lomonosov. However, unlike Ivan Shuvalov, direct contact between the two cannot be clearly established although indirect influence seems certain in view of the fact that Ivan worked so closely with Lomonosov. This is to say that the ideas of Peter Shuvalov were not always original as might be concluded from the manner in which he operated.

As a Senator from 1744 Peter took a special interest in economic, political, social and military affairs—almost exactly the opposite of his cousin, Ivan. The chief problem facing the Senate and the government in general was financial. The finances of the Empire were never orderly. Peter the Great had created institutions like the Treasury (Kamer Kollegiia) to collect taxes and Shtats-Kontor to disburse them. But there was no clear budget until much later. To complicate matters the imperial family had the first right to all income. During periods of war the situation tended to become desperate as in the case of the reign of Anna when there was a yearly chronic deficit of 13-18 percent (estimated).[14] Often in war time the salaries of officers in the army as well as the rank and file were reduced and the civil servants were more severely affected since they did not face direct danger. In 1747 a war with Sweden seemed a possibility as well as Russian intervention in the last stages of the War of the Austrian Succession. The empress called a special conference of all her top advisors to work out a plan of action. It was discovered that the Treasury was reporting collection at 3.5-3.9 million rubles a year while the Senate had placed income at 4-5 million, yet there did not seem to be sufficient money to prepare for a possible war.

At that point the empress ordered a close study of the records for the period 1742-1747 to determine why there was such a difference in the reports. [15] The most likely explanation for the difference was the probability that the Senate was assuming that the "soul" tax had been collected when actually many of the serfs were in arrears. Then there were the expenses of the empress herself about which the Senate was never informed.

Thus, the problem was posed--how to raise the income in order to provide the means in case of a war? Rising to the occasion as he had in 1745 (without success then) Peter Shuvalov who was called the "Cicero" of the Senate for his ability to speak (in derision in some cases), suggested that the taxes on salt and vodka be raised and stabilized to provide more income. He hoped to be able to use the natural salt deposits at Elton lake since the traditional method of boiling salt water controlled by the Stroganovs was becoming more and more difficult. In return, so as not to harm "the people", the complicated "soul" tax was to be lowered.[16] The threat of war passed and the consideration of the plan dropped by the not-too-enthusiastic Senate.

In 1749 the issue was raised once again as the Senate and Treasury could not explain the budget differences. This coincided with the rise of Ivan Shuvalov as the chief favorite. Hence, it was possible to influence the empress directly. In addition, there was growing tension between Russia and Prussia at that point which led to the breaking of diplomatic relations in 1750. Elisabeth had agreed in 1746 to join Maria Theresa in an aggressive war against Prussia when the opportunity arose to regain Silesia for Austria. Also the peasant arrears in the "soul" tax were growing which was to necessitate the cancellation of said arrears in 1752. In 1749 the Senate passed on the suggestions of Shuvalov to the empress and she approved them early in 1750.[17]

The government already controlled the sale of vodka so Shuvalov's scheme simply introduced new elements--although important ones--of uniform higher prices. This was to become the major tax of the pre-Revolutionary governments in Russia in addition to the import-export duties. When inflation or war affected the country the government simply added to the vodka tax.

Shuvalov's scheme involved the sale of vodka at high uniform prices throughout the Empire with the exception of Siberia. The whole-sale price of vodka by the barrel (vedro) was to be 1.88 rubles or about .15 copecks for a liter. Sold in smaller quantities it was slightly higher.[18] The following table prepared by the late Soviet historian, S.M. Troitsky, gives a good example of how well the system worked.[19]

Year	Profit (in rubles)	
1744	992,150	
1747	1,141,376	
1748	1,062,024	
1749	1,263,529	
1750	1,634,798	
1751	2,273,466	(In 1751 the system was in full operation.)
1752	2,362,140	
1753	2,305,185	
1754	2,249,491	
1755	2,662,909	
1756	2,574,329	(The price was raised to .18 copecks a liter.)
1757	2,551,890	
1758	2,731,675	
1759	3,132,676	
1760	3,298,379	
1761	3,329,829	

| 1762 | 3,450,043 |
| 1763 | 5,376,000 (The price was again raised.) |

A study of these figures proves interesting. The empress was concerned that the revenue would actually drop as a result of the higher costs, but she proved wrong. The intake of the government jumped rapidly. Using the few years before the scheme went into effect (1744-1750) the yearly average profit was 1,218,775 rubles while the intake for the years 1751-1761 was 2,678,452 or an increase of 1,459,677 rubles. In other words the government was making more than twice as much from the vodka trade after the scheme of Shuvalov went into effect. The Russian muz'hk could live without paying his taxes but not without his vodka. It will be noted that with the total state income around 3.5 million rubles that the added one million was significant.

Man can live without vodka, but salt was considered necessary for the human diet in addition to being an important preservative. Thus, the salt tax would place the greatest burden upon the poorer classes. Of course, the idea for a tax on salt can be found in France where it was then one of the chief sources of revenue for the state. On the otherhand, for better or worse it distributed the tax burden better than did the "soul" tax since even the women and girls would be indirectly taxed. The information is available for the sales of salt and the income of the government from it. The table below provides the profit of the government from 1740-1761 for salt sales.[20]

Year	*Profit* (in rubles)
1740	821,346
1741	840,720
1742	804,409
1743	816,438

1744	706,102	
1745	777,747	
1746	813,344	
1747	792,654	
1748	753,484	
1749	801,255	
1750	1,223,011	(2.2 copecks per kilogram or .35 copecks per pud)
1751	1,216,156	
1752	1,296,970	
1753	1,392,200	
1754	1,318,347	
1755	1,370,517	
1756	1,404,994	(In September of 1756 the price was raised to 3 copecks a kilogram or .50 copecks per pud.)
1757	1,887,064	
1758	2,177,184	
1759	2,012,924	
1760	2,065,177	
1761	2,182,428	

Thus, not considering inflation or population growth and using the period 1740-1749 before the tax was made uniform, we find that the yearly income of the government for the period almost doubled. The average for 1740-1749 was 792,749 while for the period of the new tax from 1750-1761 the average was 1,553,081 rubles per year. In the face of this there was an actual drop in the consumption of salt, unlike vodka, as a consequence of its growing price. It is stated that towards the last months of her reign the empress felt that the tax was too heavy and asked the Senate to consider immediately lowering it.[21]

Unfortunately the salt used was from Lake Elton rather than the old boiled salt and had a high mixture of dirt and chemicals in it. Büshing claimed that the Elton salt was so poor that it would not preserve meat but apparently it did preserve fish otherwise it would have been useless.[22] So not only did the "people" find that the price of their salt had gone up but they also found it inferior in quality.

However, both reforms taken together added greatly to the state budget. It is unfortunate that there is no way to measure inflation, but the signs imply that it was not a significant factor as was indicated in the section concerning the price of serfs. Population growth would tend to push the figures up likewise but not to a major proportion. If the increase from the salt tax income yearly (831,164) are added to the vodka tax (1,459,677), the schemes of Shuvalov increased the income of the state on the average to 2,290,841 which is impressive.

But Shuvalov did not leave the needs of the lower classes out of consideration. He planned to lower the "soul" tax. This appears to have been the last effort of its type. The tax was to be lowered as the income from the salt tax started matching it. In 1751 it was lowered 3 copecks, in 1752-3.25, in 1753--5, in 1754--6, in 1755-5, 1757-8 and 1759--8. Since the basic tax was 70 copecks the average tax payer would then have been required to pay 47.75 copecks in 1758.[23] Whether the goal was the final abolition of the soul tax is not clear, but in view of the difficulty in its collection it is probable that this was the final aim. It is doubtful if the reductions really were enacted.

The success of these schemes of Shuvalov enhanced his stature with the empress and prepared the way for changes both of a positive and a negative nature.Positively the next scheme was to attack the internal tolls in Russia and abolish them. One of the chief hindrances to the internal development of Russia was the existence of numerous little tolls along the roads which made it expensive and difficult to trade any distance. These fees were used by a selected individual to maintain a bridge, bog crossings, the entrance to a city and many more. It was estimated that a serf traveling legally from Moscow to the famous Trinity Monastery sixty-four kilometers from there had to pay special fees four or five times. Even entering a city to sell some goods involved payment. Peter the Great had inherited the system and in his needs during his numerous wars had added greatly to them. When such a post was the charge of the government careful records were maintained which allow the study of the trade patterns for the pre-1753 period. Despite the fact that many of them had been quietly dropped over the years others were retained which were especially annoying to those engaged in trade. One such was the five percent tax a merchant had to pay for selling goods in another city than his own to support the local merchants.[24] A person would be put in charge of a brige, for example, and he would be expected to keep it in repair plus making some sort of payment to the government for this special right from which he also made his living. His payment to the government normally would be channeled through the local authorities.

Thus, it was difficult for merchants and serfs or even for the agents of wealthy nobles who owned factories or mines to trade. The merchants complained that local authorities nearly always held them until they paid a traditional, but illegal, bribe. The serfs of the nobles when allowed to travel to sell their wares could more easily pay their dues to the nobles. Hence, the only group benefiting from the system were the collectors themselves. All other classes had much to gain by the abolition of the internal tolls. But the question which stopped action was how they were to be replaced.

In 1752 Shuvalov made a sweeping proposal to do away with all the internal duties and replace them with an even external tariff for exports and imports of 13 percent instead of the existing 7-10 percent level. For the reason that the Senate was a social class institution of the nobles, and they had an interest in the proposal, they asked the author to work it out in more detail with some changes. Hence, Shuvalov gathered facts in order to marshall an argument convincing to the Senate.[25] His findings were of great interest. He discovered that the internal duties for the period 1742-1749 brought in yearly an average of 903,537 rubles whereas the foreign trade turnover for 1747-1751 had averaged 8,911,981 rubles.[26] The raise in the tariff to 13 percent would almost exactly off-set the loss on the internal duties. On the 18th of August, 1753, the Senate accepted the proposal and started to work out the details of its implementation.[27] Three months later the empress gave her consent and the project became reality.[28]

First it was necessary to overcome some local interests that would suffer from the change. The Senate decided to pay people for maintaining bridges and other such vital functions out of local revenues and have the local officials insure that all was maintained in order. When local fees for administrative business were abolished the local officials were allowed to retain some other revenue in compensation, as, for example, a portion of the "soul" tax. Under no circumstance were officials allowed to annoy peaceful merchants from any part of the empire in their legal transactions.

One of the most serious problems which arose concerned the Ukraine. As the empress in the past had defended the rights of the Ukrainians it was assumed by Shuvalov that she would exclude them from the new plan. Kyrill Razumovskii did, indeed, put up serious resistence to exclude the Ukraine from the new law since it enjoyed nearly free trade with its neighbors. The local officials among the Cossacks collected small sums from the merchants and naturally did not want to surrender this right. But underlying the entire situation was the above mentioned fact that the Ukraine was being forced to become more and more a part of Great Russia. Hence, the pleas went unheard. The Ukraine and the Don Cossacks were included in the system.[29]

When the law was issued, therefore, it meant the creation of a free internal market from the border of Poland to the north-west coast of America. It is curious to note how socially backward Russia was in some fields while it was ahead of such politically and economically developed countries like France and England in others. When Colbert in France tried to achieve an internal market he was forced by vested interests to settle for his famous five farms or regions with tariffs.

Traditionally, in the past, the Soviet historians have viewed this law as a class law favoring the interests of the nobility although this outlook has changed recently. The old view was that the abolition of tariffs made it easier for the serfs to market goods and thus pay their dues. It is true that the nobility did gain by this law, but so did most other social groups in the country. The fact that it was not purely a class law is indicated by the reaction to it by some of the nobles, like Shakhovskoi, who felt that Shuvalov favored abolition of internal tariffs for his own selfish needs.[30] But the serfs were given the right to travel farther to sell their goods and the interests of the merchants were also furthered. It was stated, in addition, to protect the merchants that the nobles could only trade in goods which they produced and never act as middlemen.[31] This was not the best means in which to treat the class interests of the nobles. The key here seems to have been the concepts of Shuvalov which one might call as Kahan has, a more refined type of mercantilism of the variety that proceeded free trade.[32] Shuvalov himself believed that many of his projects had as their aim the "good of the people". In addition, he had mines and factories which would suffer as a consequence of the new law because it raised the export duty on iron and copper.

There were exceptions to the new tax like the Baltic states which had acquired and retained their old rights from Peter which allowed them to import goods for local use and export from the direct hinterland at old rates. In 1757 the Senate issued a new list of tariffs which broke the principle of 13 percent. In a mercantilist spirit tariffs on the export of wax, worked-hemp products and products of Russian industry were placed in a lower export tax category and protective tariffs were placed upon their import. [33] Also certain minor exceptions were made for foreigners living or trading in Astrakhan, for merchants on the Chinese border and foreign merchants in Orenburg.

Of course, the traditional duties had to be paid such as the use of the postal service and the horses which were necessary in the transportation system by travelers which had to be maintained at the expense of those using them. Some payment was also necessary to maintain canals which had cost a great deal to construct and much to maintain.

One of the leading pre-Revolutionary historians, S.M. Soloviev, felt that this single law was the most important in the reign. Viewing it from the standpoint of the general development of Russian history from the earliest times he claimed that this action had "completed the process started by Ivan Kalita", the first strong Moscovite ruler in the 14th century.[34] This law also meant a major increase in the income from the tariff which was paid chiefly in foreign silver and gold. The following table provides information concerning the impact of this reform upon tariff income.[35]

Year	Income From Tariff (in rubles)
1742	955,302
1743	1,060,763
1744	1,001,717

156

1745	1,031,895
1746	1,055,796
1747	950,616
1748	888,637
1749	1,052,527
1750	1,227,667
1751	1,230,071
1752	1,427,640
1753	1,460,405
1754	2,134,405
1755	2,134,511
1756	2,320,941
1757	2,516,851
1758	2,559,736
1759	2,654,550
1760	2,625,036
1761	2,669,139
1762	2,881,231

Using the years 1742-1753 as a base the average tariff income was 1,111,919 rubles while under the new tariff for the period 1754-1761 it grew to 2,451,689 rubles or a yearly average increase of 1,339,977. The income from the tariff more than doubled after Shuvalov's scheme went into effect. Notable is the jump between the years 1753 and 1754 when the plan was implemented. Only sixteen more ships visited St. Petersburg in 1754 out of a total of over three hundred (see below). The internal duties were more than compensated for and the government received added revenue which it badly needed. The demand for Russian goods remained so high that foreign merchants apparently were not greatly disturbed by the change.

However, these figures must be taken with some caution. The trade was growing very rapidly in this period with foreign countries as will be indicated. For example the total turnover was 8,135,507 rubles in 1742 and 16,905,071 in 1761 or more than double.[36] But in the year of the dramatic rise in tariff income (1754) trade had risen over the previous year by only 1,026,584 rubles and had been actually 534,204 rubles higher in 1752 than in 1754.[37]

On the basis of the above material it is possible for the modern researcher to achieve something which the government at the time was unable to accomplish, namely, to determine the actual income for certain years. S.M. Troitskii estimated that the government received about 9.88 million rubles in 1749 and about 11.6 million in 1756. [38] Before discovering Troitskii's figure the present writer independently established the same income for the year 1756. It will be recalled that the estimated income for the period 1742-1747 was between 3.5 and 5 million rubles. So the income of the state had increased substantially thanks to the "successes" of the schemes of Shuvalov and the natural economic development of Russia. The expanded income of nearly two million rubles in species probably help explain the decision of the empress in 1756 to initiate war against Prussia. But despite the claim of Shuvalov that he was working for the good of the "people", it was the mass of the lower classes who were paying more although the tariff reform had little if any affect on them. It is only a conjecture, but if war had been avoided in 1756 and if the vodka tax had been increased as Catherine raised it in 1763, the "soul" tax might have been eliminated.

As the state became more affluent it was possible for it to undertake various projects impossible without a surplus. Again Shuvalov rose to the occasion by suggesting the creation of banks run by the government. The idea was not a new one. In 1733 Anna had ordered the Treasury to loan out money at the rate of 8 percent for one and later for three years.[39] As early as 1744 a merchant named Fedor Iakolev petitioned the Senate to establish a merchants' bank, but his plea went unheard then.[40] In the same year the governor of Astrakhan, Tatishchev, one of the most learned men of his time, also suggested the establishment of a similar bank-again with negative results.[41] Private lenders were charging up to 20 percent at the time which often ruined both noble and merchant if they really needed temporary funds. Anna's lending operations had been stopped after a few years.[42] Hence, there existed indigenous demand supplemented by foreign examples especially that of England and Holland. Some claim that Peter Shuvalov suggested the creation of the banks for his own advantage, but there exists no indication that he ever borrowed money from it personally since he really had no need. The empress gave him the needed money. One of the chief sources for loans in St. Petersburg was the British Consul, Wolf, who was simply a usuer. Given the backwardness of the economy and the control of the government, private banking on British lines did not develop until the 19th century. Hence, there existed a need which only the government could fill.

In 1754 Peter Shuvalov induced the empress to permit the establishment of two banks, one for the nobles and the other for the merchants. The bank for the nobles was to have offices in Moscow and St. Petersburg while the merchant bank was to operate only in St. Petersburg to stimulate trade there. The nobles bank was to have a fixed initial capital of 750,000 rubles in full bodied money which it could loan at the reasonable rate of 6 percent. [43] It was not anticipated that the bank would need additional capital since it could rely on paid debts. So the reader will not be misled, Russia then had only metalic money and since it emitted no paper money the capital amount was the limit it could loan - unlike the banks in England which could emit their own paper money and loan above their capital as a result. The banks were to be under the authority of the Senate with loans from 500 to 50,000 rubles and anyone applying for more needed personal permission of the empress.[44] Later loans for less than 500 rubles were permitted. The term for the loans was an unreasonable one year which was later extended almost indefinitely as a consequence of the war and

159

pressure from the nobles. Nobles could borrow on either moveable property or their estates. They could, for example, deposit jewelry with the bank as collateral and receive in return 75 percent of the value of the item in loan funds. If a noble wished to borrow money on his estate the valuation was made in terms of the number of "souls" he possessed with little value placed upon the land. The bank would loan ten rubles for each such "soul" of the male sex which indicates that the government valued the male serf at about 15 rubles each. Thus, the government guaranteed itself a good return if the person borrowing the money failed to repay or could not repay. At first there was no inspection of estates, and the signature of another noble was sufficient to secure a loan. In default, the item pawned or the estate would be sold to the nearest relative if possible and any extra money received above the principal and interest went to the unfortunate person having his goods sold.

The same law created a bank for the merchants, but it received only 500,000 rubles in capital which meant that the total capital of both banks was 1,250,000 rubles--a substantial sum given the period. But the terms for loans from the merchants' bank were not nearly as liberal as those for the nobles since they were required to turn over merchandise they intended to sell for collateral and could only regain it when sold and paid for. This made transactions difficult since the merchants could not display goods being held by the bank for collateral to prospective buyers and this stipulation was eventually dropped as a consequence. The merchants could borrow for only a half a year at 6 percent.

Apparently the merchants' bank worked fairly well although figures seem unavailable for the exact operations of both banks. Trade was lively in St. Petersburg and the possibility of rapid transactions good while the port was ice free. But all was not well with the nobles' bank. In

1757 two nobles were discovered to have lied about the size of their estates to obtain larger loans. They lost what little they had, were deprived of their rank of nobility and made common soldiers.[45] The empress had not sold out so quickly to the nobles as is commonly held and she or her Senate could be very severe in dealing with cases of dishonesty.

By 1761 it was possible to obtain some idea of the general, if not the particular, operations of the joint banks. By that time, under conditions of war, the banks appear to have loaned out their fixed capital and were accepting repayment and interest only in gold and silver. But a profit of 584,757 rubles was reported from all operations over the years.[46] This figure appears to be rather high but probably reflects the success of the merchants' bank. The Senate ordered that it not be reloaned, but that it be ued to pay the salaries of civil servants, who as a result of the war, were not being paid regularly if at all. But modern Russia did have its first bank despite the limitations.

One of the later schemes of Shuvalov grew directly out of his earlier activities with the abolition of tariffs internally. When this was completed a special commission concerning tariffs had been established to handle problems involving the implementation of the new law. By 1758 it had completed its task and Shuvalov suggested to the Senate that it be abolished and replaced with a much more powerful Commission Concerning Commerce. One of the aims of this was the reduction of the "soul" tax. It was proposed that this commission have extremely wide-ranging powers and that it eventually be replaced by a regular Tarriff College. The idea was accepted, but for some reason it was not passed by the Senate until 1760[47] It was to consist of members chosen by the Senate--some from among its members and others knowledgeable about matters of commerce. The Commerce College seems to have played a small role in the scheme. Merchants were to be consulted and even become members. Special bureaus were to be established in all the ports of Russia to monitor the trade patterns and more specifically to watch for the welfare of the Russian merchants themselves. An effort was to be made to get the right goods to the right place at the right time for sale to foreign merchants. In a more modern spirit an effort was to be made to attempt to remove barriers to trade and make it as free as possible. Special agents were to be sent out to keep close watch on the foreign markets to determine the demand and prevailing prices of goods so that the Russian merchants would not suffer from their own ignorance. Special emphasis was to be placed upon St. Petersburg as the chief trading center. Factories were to be checked to determine if production could be increased for goods in special demand. A large merchant fleet was to be created as Peter the Great had wished. The Commission was to work slowly and evolve a general plan along these lines. The resulting profit from increased trade would be used to reduce the "soul" tax which, in turn, would enable the serfs to fulfill their obligations more fully to their owners.[48] The Commission Concerning Commerce did start functioning, but it started so late in the reign that it produced very little. Then in January of 1762 Peter Shuvalov himself died and three months later Petter III ended the Commission.[49] Catherine the Great later revived the idea.

Certain actions of the Senate seem to reflect the activities of the Commission. In 1760 the Senate announced that it would pay the costs for sending the sons of merchants to Holland in order to study at first hand methods of trade, banking and manufacturing.[50] In 1761 the Senate announced that it was going to publish a list of current prices in Russian twice a week. Twelve hundred copies were to be printed to be sold to the Russian merchants for two copecks each.[51]

Another project which bears the imprint of the influence of Shuvalov since its aim was to help the "people" was the enforcement of standard weights and measures. This had been undertaken in previous reigns but now an attempt was made to really enforce it.[52] The Senate was bothered by the manner in which the common uneducated plain people were tricked by the use of differing weights and measures. To counter the problem the Senate issued in June of 1749 a printed manifesto which had more force than a simple Ukaz. Despite this the Senate had to repeat its order to the Treasury a few months after the manifesto.[53] According to the order, all local officials and all those in higher positions were to insure that uniform weights and measures be strictly adhered to under the threat of severe punishment. In the year 1748 the government had already issued exact examples of the various units of measures. For instance, the size of the standard barrel or vedro (12.3 liters) had been decided upon in 1737, but local authorities did not receive an official measure until 1748.[54]

The same Treasury which was criticized for not following the law at once had taken a major step itself in stablizing the system of weights in the empire by producing an exact Russian pound (.40953 kilograms) of gold in 1747 which remained the Russian pound unit until the adoption of the metric system after the Revolution. The pound was further subdivided into smaller subunits at the time.[55]

******

It appears that Shuvalov had little influence over the problem of the supply of gold and silver--these belonged to the empress. A law dating from the time of Peter the Great placed all silver and gold mines directly under the control of the ruler and until the reign of Elisabeth the only significant silver mine was that of Nerchinsk with an insignificant output of 8,297 metric tons of silver worth 234,708 rubles for the period to 1754--a small sum for 46 years of operation.[56]

For some unknown reason Soviet historians overlook one of the most important developments of the reign in this regard. Perhaps it is the fact that the empress entrusted this delicate and potentially corruption-prone operation to foreigners that explains their reticence. Be that as it may, in the period 1740-1743 Akinfii Demidov of the famous family of entrepreneurs of peasant origin from the time of Peter, discovered that, in his Altai mine named Kolyvano-Voznesensk, along with the copper there existed significant deposits of silver. In 1744 he reported this to the government and died in the next year. The Mining College upon the direct order of the empress sent an expedition to the mine headed by a Dane named Beyer (?). He reported that it was true that there was indeed much silver in the region and was given complete control over the mine which then became the personal possession of the empress.[57] The silver was used only in one brief instance for monetary purposes otherwise being retained in the privy purse of the empress until her death.

Another foreigner, I. Schlatter, at first a junior assayer in the Fiscal Chancellary which had the task of determining the actual gold and silver content of foreign coins as well as monitoring the output of Nerchinsk, was placed in charge of the output of both the Nerchinsk and the Kolyvanovo silver production with instruction to push production to the maximum. In assaying the new silver Schlatter found a large admixture of gold which he then proceeded to separate by a method he developed.[58] As production rapidly increased Schlatter was made first Chief Assayer and finally the President of the Mining College.[59]

164

It is impossible to give yearly output figures for the Kolyvano mine, but figures do exist for longer time spans. Thus, between 1748 and 1759 the Kolyvano mines produced 1.464 metric tons of gold worth 962,372 rubles and 46,266 metric tons of silver worth 2,231,087 rubles. The production increased very rapidly and most of the output took place in the last few years of the period given.[60] If all this had been struck into coinage it would have had a strong stimulating effect upon the economy and could have caused inflation if there had been no war. In the reign of Catherine the output of these mines was greatly increased, but the really serious beginning of gold and silver mining can be dated to the reign of Elisabeth. When Peter III and Catherine came to the throne it is not known how much silver and gold remained in the privy purse.

There was a side effect of this development of gold and silver which has partially misled historians. To increase production and develop farming around the mines to feed the workers, the government resorted to various measures. For example, in 1759 the empress ordered that 12,295 "souls" be attached to the mine or the region around Kolyvano to stimulate production.[61] This was not enough. During the desperate period of the war the Senate allowed any holder of serfs whether clergy, noble or merchant with a factory to ship families to Nerchinsk or Kolyvano as settlers. The government itself would pay the way for both the man, his wife and very young children. "Souls" so lost could be counted as recruits at the next call-up.[62] Usually this measure is viewed as an extension of the rights of the nobles, but in reality it was more a measure to increase the output of precious metals even though these were not being used for the war effort and were retained in storage for the satisfaction of the ruler.

Of more immediate importance to the development of Russia was the iron and copper industries which were important both for domestic industry as well as for export. The policies of the government tended to fluctuate in regard to the ownership of the mines. There always existed a private   sector alongside the large government owned one. After the downfall of the "German" party in 1742 many of the mines and mills given to foreigners for their personal exploitation were regained by the government. It will be recalled that the Blagodets iron works was one such enterprise.

In general policy towards these iron and copper works, the attitude of the ruler and her advisers changed during the reign. The concept of a mixed economy was never questioned as the basic manner in which to operate. But starting about 1752 the government returned to the dangerous policy of Anna and turned over state factories, mills and mines to private individuals. The apparent reasons for this shift were several. First, there was the eternal problem of paying the wages of high officials, and giving them economic concessions was one manner in which to subsidize their already inadequate salaries. The case of V.L. Vorontsov will be recalled in this connection. Another would be the favorites of the empress and their influence upon her. The most outstanding example of such an individual would be Peter Shuvalov, who, indeed, was one of the chief beneficiaries of the changed policy. But in considering the controversial question of the Shuvalov holdings it must be borne in mind that by 1753 Peter Shuvalov seemed to be working miracles with the economy itself. He could convince the empress that he was capable to doing the same for larger governmental works if they were given to him to operate. Whether for better or worse the empress accepted this argument.

Since the sudden increase of gold and silver was not widely known and occurred towards the end of the reign copper and iron were the chief industrial indicators for the development of the Russian industrial economy. It was held at one time by historian such as Paul Miliukov that the industrial growth of Russia actually slowed in the post-Petrine period to the level of stagnation.[63] A study of the factual data has convinced historians that this is another myth of the "dark era of the reign of women".

But for the economy as a whole despite the "reign of favorites" there were several factors which actually ac-celerated economic development. One of the most im-portant of these was the introduction of Saxon technology in the area of mining in the reign of Anna which did much to speed the output of the iron industry. Other measures which had a stimulating effect upon the economy were the stabilization of the monetary confusion by the re-evaluation of copper coins, the reforms of Peter Shuvalov, the issuance of nearly seven million rubles in copper money which stimulates an economy and has inflation potential, and last but not least, the abolition of the internal tariff.

The chief regions of importance in the development of iron and copper were in the Urals and the region to the south of them. In the reign of Anna, Tatishchev the famous historian and the Saxon engineers explored the region to the south of the Urals and made significant finds of minerals.[64] The "German party" then removed the Russians such as Tatishchev from the operation and operated these mines as they saw fit until the year 1742 when they were sent back to Germany. The economic historian, Patlaevskii, claimed that about two thirds of the trade was then controlled by the government.[65] This was to be the situation until about 1752.

The discoveries in the south caused new problems for the Russian government since it was necessary to protect the mines and mills from the plains peoples such as the Kirgiz and Bashkirs who resented the intrusion of industry upon their traditional grazing lands. Thus, a security

167

system was established with a line of forts guarded by cossacks and linked to the important new city of Orenburg. Tatishchev as governor of Astrakhan until 1745 oversaw the beginning of this new system and in 1744 Orenburg was turned into a Gubernia with the capable I.I. Nepliuev as governor.[66]

The security of the region and the need for population to settle it caused a rapid influx of persons. Many of the minor offenders were sent to the region especially if they were of the merchant class or raznochintsy. There were also many persons there "who could not remember where they were from" who were rarely bothered since the need for persons was so great. Mines and mills producing iron and copper sprang up very rapidly. To insure a labor force for these new mills the Senate set limits on the number of workers an enterprise could possess so any surplus could be moved to the new places of need.[67] Finally to stress the new orientation after 1752, the Senate ordered in 1753 that no more state mines or mills be established in the new region thus leaving it to individual initiative.[68] Of course, most of the workers were serfs and the Senate restated the law that they were fixed to their positions.[69]

The growth rate of the Ural region is clear from the number of mines or "works" established in the various reigns:[70]

Peter I	12
1725-30	10
Anna	21
Elisabeth	54
Total	97

Of these works 49 were created in the south Urals near Orenburg most of them in the reign of Elisabeth and provided a large portion of the iron and copper output of Russia. While the growth did not end with the reign of Elisabeth it slowed down in later reigns as a consequence of such factors as the rising of Pugachev and the growing influence of nobles who proved less capable of operating enterprises. In the 19th century this led to real stagnation.

The question is now posed--how much iron and copper was produced by the government and private owners and what was the price gained from these sales. Roger Portal in his book on the Urals in the XVIII century gives some information, but it is not based upon precise archival materials.[71] The flucuations in it would tend to indicate probable gaps. Thus, *Sanktpeterburgskiia Vedomosti,* the official journal again becomes a partial source for answers. Material is provided for four years (1749, 1750, 1751, and 1753). These are official sales since the source is given as the Mining College. It should be noted at this point that the state had more than twice as many possessional serfs as the private owners.[72] Hence, the figures given are merely examples. In 1749 7,169 metric tons of "Siberian" iron were offered along with 700 tons from Olents.[73] In 1750 3,253 metric tons were for sale for 36.63 rubles per ton.[74] In the next year 337 metric tons of copper from Siberia were placed on sale without a price.[75] This was interésting since in the next year several times the governmental agencies such as the mint had to offer to buy copper. Again in 1753 3,517 metric tons of iron were offered for 41.50 rubles a ton.[76] After this notices appear frequently from governmental agencies requesting "German" or "Swedish iron" (steel) for nearly three times the price of "Siberian" iron. There appear to be several explanations as to why the glut of iron and copper suddenly ended. The first is the policy of the government in turning over some of its larger producers to individuals such as Peter Shuvalov who could not manage them well (Bladodets). As cheap metals appeared on the market in the interior, small kustar or artisan producers probably increased their production for local consumption. Also, large centers such as Ekerinburg remained firmly in the hands of the government and produced copper coins and cannons in place of shipping the raw product to the market. It is unreasonable to project a downturn in general production with the large number of mines being opened at this time.

*****

As a part of the merchantilist system and for the development of Russia, companies were formed for the production of certain goods or for trade with a specified region usually carrying a monoply in either the goods produced or trade in the region. It is true that often one person constituted the sole owner of an enterprise, but for large undertakings the merchants (sometimes with the nobles) joined together to form a "tovarishchestvo" or company.[77]

In the spirit of mercantilism the empress or the Senate would desire the creaton of a special company for a single purpose. For example, in 1753 proposals were made that a a company be established to handle a monopoly of trade on the Black Sea with Turkey. At first there was little response. Pressure was brought to bare resulting in a trading company in 1757 to use Temernikov near Azov and present-day Rostov-on-the-Don. While very mercantilist in spirit, the new company also had certain "modern" features which were the precursor of the modern limited liability company in as much as it appears that the owners of shares were not responsible for its debts. The regulations for the company state that if "God forbid" it lost money it was to be taken from the capital initially invested. There is no indication as to what would happen if these debts exceeded the capital. The company was to sell 200 shares at 500 rubles each for working capital of the significant sum of 100,000 rubles. In modern fashion the shares could be sold if a merchant wanted to rid himself of them, and they could be inherited like other property.[78]

The company was named the "Russian Commercial Company for trading in Constantinople", but despite its name the Ottomans refused it permission to have its own ships on the Black Sea for the trade insisting on the use of their own. The customs post at Temernikov was founded in 1747 and witnessed a rapid growth in trade with the new company. In 1758 the turnover was 87,000 rubles and 170,000 in 1762. In 1763 the turnover dropped to 103,000 rubles.[79]

It is interesting to note the faith which the empress and the government had in this company. On May 15, 1758 it was given the concession to collect all tariff according to the new 1757 regulations (excluding Siberia and Oren-burg). The law is somewhat unclear and the profit not indicated. But it did make the president of the company a hereditary noble (Nikita Shemkian).[80] In the confusion of the Seven Years' War, it is difficult to trace the fate of this concession further without the assistance of the archives. Peter III renewed the right to collect the tax for ten more years for the company.

The apparent success of this company stimulated another group of merchants to attempt to establish a limited liability company for the trade with Persia. In 1757 Matveev, a merchant, with comrades, petitioned to be allowed to establish such a trading company with Persia capitalized,like the earlier company, at 100,000 rubles. The Senate refused because Matveev requested the capital as a loan. A year later an Armenian resident of St. Petersburg, Issakhanov, applied along with other

Armenians for the same trade right, but not for the capital. The Senate accepted with the stipulation that the company sell 4,000 shares at 150 rubles each and to permit Russians to join the company as well. Like the other company, its shares could be freely traded.[81] In consequence of the stipulation that the shares be sold widely an announcement was placed in the *Sanktpetersburgskiia Vedomosti* requesting merchants to purchase shares.[82] The success of the company is again unknown, but in 1760 the trade with Persia was 391,000 rubles.[83] With the initial capital at 600,000 this was not significant.

In a less formal manner the government handled the fur trade in the "Eastern Sea". While exploration had been in process since the opening of Siberia and the Bering Sea was reached by Russian merchants as early as 1648 the official "discovery" of Alaska is dated to the year 1741 by Bering who started his expedition in the reign of Anna and perished along with most of his crew in making his discoveries.[84] Merchants wanted the valuable furs from the region, but the government policy was to leave sufficient furs for the inhabitants to pay their tax or Iasak. In 1748 Emil'ian Iugov, a merchant, with "comrades" was given the right to hunt sea animals among certain islands in the "Eastern Sea" if they paid one-third of their income to the treasury. In view of the needs of the local population limits were set upon them. For example, they were to be allowed to use no more than four boats with 35 men on each and an official appointed by the government was to check to insure their adherence to the rules.[85] With the monopolies of the nobles coming under increasing pressure toward the end of the reign and with the spread for free trade ideas, in 1761 the Senate opened the entire "Eastern Sea" to any merchant wanting to hunt there for an established tax of 10 percent of the catch. The merchants were warned to treat the original inhabitants well.[86] The

Russian-American Company - when it was established - was a sort of reversion to the earlier concepts which were becoming outdated as the eighteenth century progressed.

Another area in which governmental policy overlaped with the private sector was in tax farming-as the French would call it. As was noted in the case of the Black Sea trading company, the customs and other collections could be farmed out to individuals or companies. Not only was this a typical practice of the ancient regimes but, specifically in the case of Russia, it was a method of attempting to avoid to as large a degree as possible the problem of corruption. Thus, if the local officials were given the charge of collecting certain revenues such as the "wine tax" covering all strong drink the temptation for corruption was greater. The local authorities already were charged with the collection of the "soul" tax, but on the basis of the censuses the central institutions knew the amount of income which should be received. With other taxes the amount was variable and it was nearly impossible for the authorities to insure honest reporting. A manner of avoiding this was using the system of "farming" or selling the right to tax a certain item to a noble or merchant in a given region.

In the official journal, for example, in March of 1750 the bids were opened for the control of the sale of strong drink for all of European Russia.[87] Such notices were frequent. And often the person whose bid for a given region was accepted was continued in subsequent years.

In line with the mercantilist spirit of the time the state also gave another type of monopoly for goods which were being imported and no native industry existed for them. A foreigner (or Russian) could apply for the right to produce such goods and receive either a monopoly, a loan or both.

To make the country independent of foreign supplies of wall hangings an Englishman named Butler was given the monopoly to produce all such wall hangings in Russia, and, to the disgust of the English, promised to stop all imports with high tariffs.[88] Five successful years later (1760) the monopoly was extended for another ten years.[89] Two other English entrepreneurs established a factory to produce printed cloth with the result that in 1757 the Senate placed a high tariff on goods of the type they produced.[90] In the same year a Belgian received from the Senate a loan of 10,000 rubles, the right to hire 500 women and 200 men to establish a lace making factory in Moscow or St. Petersburg. The loan was for ten years without interest.[91]

Perhaps the most famous "assistance" of this type was the one made to Lomonosov in 1752 after he had become the "professor" of chemistry in the Academy of Sciences. He was given a loan of 4,000 rubles for five years and the village of Opol'e with 151 "souls" to found a factory to produce small glass items and mosaics.[92] It was especially successful since the Senate banned the import of such goods and gave Lomonosov a thirty-year monopoly. Many of the art works he produced are now destroyed, but from what remains the level of artistic creation was very high.

******

The government, mainly the Senate, continued to follow a policy of encouraging the development of trade especially with foreign countries. Incentives in addition to those already mentioned above were provided. After a fire in Moscow it was ordered that a brick building be constructed for the merchants to protect their merchandize called the "Gostnyi Dvor". This was in 1755.[93] On the order

174

of the empress in 1748 the construction of a new merchant house on eastern lines was also ordered for St. Petersburg.[94] It was to be made of stone and metal and designed by the famed Rastrelli who was the official architect responsible for the Winter Palace. In 1758 it was announced that work had started and that rooms in it were already available at the cost of five rubles a year and that it was possible for a family to hold a given stall.[95] However, the entire project was not completed until 1783 by Catherine and existed as late as 1860.[96] Thus centers were created for the merchants where they could conduct business free of fear of fires which were a most serious problem in the cities of old Russia.

There were several important trade centers in the country, but in line with the policy of Peter the Great St. Petersburg was given the most important position. To attract more foreign merchants in 1750 the customs and clerical staff at Kronstadt, the port for St. Petersburg, was increased by 38 people to bring the level there to 150 persons of whom 50 were supposed to be constantly on the job.[97] Five years later the Senate issued an order to train those officials having contact with foreigners in French and German. In 1752 new docking facilities were opened at Kronstadt which had been under construction for a number of years.[98]

Other centers also enjoyed special status. These included Astrakhan and Orenburg. Astrakhan was perhaps one of the most important junctures for the goods of Persia, Indian and to a degree Central Asia. It was a point of toleration in an otherwise intolerant country. The city had a large number of foreign merchants from such places as Armenia, Persia, England and even a colony of 200 Indian merchants from Hindustan. All were allowed to follow their traditional religions without hinderance and often built special quarters for themselves. The Indian merchants smoked canabis and used the water pipe (kaljan).[99] These merchants were free to leave and enter Russia at will if they paid their 13 percent duty. When a wealthy Indian merchant died in the city he left behind a large estate of 300,000 rubles which the Senate ordered distributed according to Indian, not Russian law.[100]

Orenburg was another curious city for merchants. The situation which developed there resulted from events in Persia where the Nadir Shah was ruling the country in an arbitrary fashion and attacking his neighbors. His raid into India was one example of his policy as was his attempt to conquer Central Asia. Until his assassination in 1747 he presented a problem to the entire region including Russia which anticipated an invasion from Persia. It seems that Moslem merchants who had normally gone to markets in Central Asia to trade their goods before Nadir Shah now started coming to Orenburg. Anna had recognized the potential of this trade and allowed special rights to the merchants trading there. The tax was fixed at 5 percent before the tax reform. Also, the normal regulations were relaxed to allow merchants who were not Russian to trade among themselves.[101] Until 1751 the tax at Orenburg was only 5 percent and precious stones could be imported tax free. Until the return of the trade to the traditional cities of Khiva and Bukahara the Russian government collected only 398,902 rubles in taxes (1742-1754).[102]

The trade with China took place according to the 1727 treaty at the border post of Kaikhta which was not much influenced by the growing liberalization of trade in Europe since relations between China and Russia were not good. But both countries wanted the trade to continue since the Russians desired the luxury goods of China, and the Chinese needed furs, wax, etc. In 1751 the tax was raised to about 23 percent on the Russian side. Tax receipts for the period 1755-1761 were 1,375,928.[103]

These posts for trade were among the more interesting. In general the Russians had 16 ports of entry with St. Petersburg clearly favored by governmental policy and 27 border posts from Finland to Kaikhta. The general regulations forbid foreign merchants to trade among themselves (aimed at stopping Europeans trading with Asia merchants to the harm of the Russian merchants), forbidding the serfs to trade in the port cities, and outlawing the unnecessary export of gold and silver items. [105]

The Russian government had a long-standing most-favored-nation treaty with England. According to this treaty the English could carry raw silk from Persia through Russia paying the traditional tax for it. While England remained the chief trading partner during the reign there were signs of definite strains in the relationship. The first problem was the above mentioned Nadr Shah. The Russians had once hired an Englishman named Elton to explore the border regions in the process of which he discovered Elton Lake later the chief source of salt. After serving the Russians he was taken into the service of Nadr Shah and constructed for him a large warship on the Caspian Sea named the "Russian Emperor" which was more than the Russians could tolerate. In addition to the ship on the Caspian Sea Nadr Shah threatened to invade Russia directly and caused great concern among the officials. Hence, the Russian government started to reconsider its treaty with the English. English merchants were given increasingly difficult terms in their carrying trade. Often, coming from Persia, they were placed under unnecessary quarantine.[106] This explains the trip of Hanway to Russia and Astrakhan. His trip was a failure, but after 1747 relations improved with the assassination of Nadr Shah and finally in 1766 the trade treaty was renewed.[107] When conditions were normal again about

218,000 rubles worth of raw silk a year were passing through St. Petersburg destined for England.[108]

Another question relating directly to the policy of the government was that of the influence of the new ideas which were undermining the prevailing mercantilism. It was noted that the ideas of Josiah Tucker had been popularized through the official journals in an earlier chapter. It was noted that the trade in the "Eastern Sea" had been opened for all by the Senate with the stipulation that the local peoples not suffer. There were other indications of the change in the Senate itself. In 1756 with a war about to start and with an excellent harvest, the Ober Procurator of the Senate, Trubetskoi, suggested that grain trade be freed to improve the profit of the country and the gentry in particular.[109] Despite his extensive monopolies the vice-chancellor, M.L. Vorontsov, also favored free trade in grain.[110] Apparently the fear that English ships would take the grain to enemy Prussia to sell it killed the idea. During the short reign of Peter III this trend away from mild mercantilism accelerated when the seven monopolies of Shuvalov were abolished.[111] This change is usually attributed to Catherine II who shared the dislike of her husband for the monopolies.

******

At this point it would be appropriate to concentrate on the private sector and the results of the policies of the government. In view of the mixed nature of the economy, it is still of value to study those economic indicators which exist to see the natural growth patterns and how these might have been effected by the policies already mentioned.

Up to this point consideration has been given to the sectors in which the government dominated such as mining. There also existed the purely private sector for the production of such items as sail cloth--an important export, leather goods, waxed cloth, hats, silk cloth, etc. Often these enterprises were owned by one person or family, but it was possible to establish private partnerships without governmental interference. While the factories were scattered about the country most were centered in large cities such as Moscow where demand was great or St. Petersburg for purposes of export.

In 1755 the Commerce College prepared a list of factories operating, with the capital and the date in which they were formed. This count apparently excluded the distilleries which were becoming monopolies of the nobles. Out of the fifty-five factories in operation forty two had been founded in the reign of Elisabeth before 1754 when the report ended.[112] Despite the complaint of the factory owners that the workers were "wild, untrainable and unable to understand the business of manufacturing" most of these factories seemed to be operating fairly successfully.[113] There exist no detailed yearly reports on the exact output for each of these enterprises, some scattered indicators show a pattern of growth. Efforts to produce raw silk failed in Russia, but the processing of imported raw silk was relatively successful. Between 1754 and 1759 one silk working factory increased its finished product from 8,983 meters yearly to 18,630.[114] A St. Petersburg leather working factory raised its output between 1750 and 1762 from 4,620 rubles a year to 19,961. Since the number of units produced is also provided in addition to price there is an indication that little or no inflation existed since the price remained stable with perhaps even a slight drop in 1762 over the price in 1750.[115]

With the growth in manufacturing and mining   and   with

the development of much closer contacts with the West it is natural that this should lead in turn to a marked growth in the trade. The Russian upper classes desired the luxury goods produced in the West and the West in turn needed many of the goods which were to be found in Russia in abundance. From the standpoint of the government this development was also desirable since goods entering and leaving the country were subject to tariff. The following table gives a picture of the general growth of this trade. The general growth is especially striking in 1750 during a period of peace.[116]

Year	Import	Export	Total
1742	3.5	4.6	8.1 Million Rubles
1743	4.5	4.2	8.7
1744	3.7	5.9	9.6
1745	3.9	5.2	9.1
1746	4.2	5.3	9.5
1747	3.5	5.4	8.9
1748	4.3	4.6	8.9
1749	4.5	5.3	9.8
1750	6.0	7.2	13.2
1751	5.9	6.6	12.5
1752	7.0	5.9	12.9
1753	5.9	7.5	13.4
1754	5.2	7.2	12.4
1755	6.6	8.2	14.8
1756	6.6	8.0	14.6
1757	6.0	8.2	14.2
1758	6.4	8.7	15.1
1759	8.0	9.6	17.6
1760	7.4	9.9	17.3
1761	7.2	9.7	16.9
1762	8.2	12.8	21.0
1763	8.2	11.1	19.3
1764	9.7	11.5	21.2

Using these figures for a basis for calculations some interesting results emerge. Taking 1742-1751 as the basis and comparing them to 1752-1761 trade increased by 66 percent for the last half of the reign. The contrast for 1742--we do not possess earlier figures--with 1762 stands out even more. Imports and exports grew roughly in porportion with a slight gain of 6.3 million rubles for the exports which meant that the long term balance of payments was favorable to Russia and the trade a very important factor. In 1769 Catherine II did abolish the selective protectionist tariff of 1757 established to help finance the Seven Years' War and replaced it with a more moderate one causing the total trade to rise in that year to 26,198,000 rubles.[117] But at that point inflation was becoming not only a Russian problem, but a European one as well.

There exists another index which serves as a means of establishing the pattern of developing trade more clearly. This is the number of ships visiting the port of St. Petersburg itself which Peter the Great had given strong preference over Archangel. It was in the reign of Elisabeth that the decided shift to the new port took place. Fortunately there exist reliable figures for most years for the ships stopping in Kronstadt, the port for St. Petersburg. While there are gaps the picture is fairly accurate.[118]

Year	Ships	Year	Ships
1736	100	1750	272
1737	118	1751	298
1744	264	1752	424
1745	195	1753	305
1746	240	1754	321
1748	209	1756	356
1749	267	1758	402

Year	Ships	Year	Ships
1759	728	1763	326
1760	357	1764	360
1761	282		

With a few exceptions there is a clear relation between the number of ships stopping at St. Petersburg and the growth of trade. The year 1752 is one of the exceptions since in that year new facilities were opened at Kronstadt and many stopped merely out of curiosity.[119] In 1759 with the war against Prussia at its height the Russian government hired foreign ships to carry supplies to the army fighting in Prussia.

Again using calculations (dropping the year 1759) it is possible to find some interesting confirmation of the greatly expanding growth of Russian trade. There are seven years up to 1751 and seven years between 1752 and 1761. A count shows that the total number of ships rose from 1754 for the first period to 2447 for the second or 71 percent which is close to the count of 66 percent for the general trade increase. The higher count for St. Petersburg would probably indicate that more and more of the trade was moving through that port.

Another question of interest is the country or city of origin for the vessels visiting St. Petersburg. Fortunately there exists a partial answer to this question. Büsching provides a breakdown for the years 1744 and 1745 which correspond to the number of ships visiting the port in those years.[120]

Nation or City	1744	1745
Denmark	12	18
England	115	69
Holland	61	32
Lübeck	29	31
Sweden	15	9
Rostock	12	11
Hamburg	6	7
France	5	7
Kiel	2	2
Danzig	5	6
Stettin	2	3
Total	264	195

The importance of England is immediately evident as is the relative unimportance of France. But there are explanations for this. The English enjoyed the most-favored-nation status for most of the century and without the English trade the prospects for the Russians would have been dismal. War with England would have ruined Russia's trade and left the army without uniforms which were mainly imported. The relative unimportance of the French trade is atributable to the worsening relations between the two countries, and awar between England and France.

The trade with England gives another indication of the growth of trade and the type of goods exchanged. Iron was, of course, important.[121] But ship stores were especially important to the English. Very little grain was then exported. But hemp, flax, wax, wood, furs were all items that could be expected in the Russian trade. For example, Hanway said that in the early 1740's Russia was exporting 6,400 short tons of hemp a year,

[122] yet by 1758-1762 the yearly average had jumped to 36,281 tons of hemp and 11,335 tons of flax.[123]

The question arises--what was the nature of the goods carried to Russia for exchange? Büsching who traveled often to Russia to collect data there checked the cargo of a ship in Vyborg in 1759. The Jonge Cornelius was from Amsterdam and carried 1,261 kilos of sugar, 147 kilos of rice, 426 kilos of coffee, 393 kilos of Spanish nuts, 116 of chestnuts, 550 rolls of tobacco(?), one ton of anchovies, 1,347 liters of ordinary French wine, 210 liters of Rhine wine, 227.5 liters of French brandy, and even six coffee grinders. In exchange, the Dutch merchants purchased lumber and firewood.[124] To assist merchants the official journal listed the arriving ships and their cargos. Unfortunately the cargo lists were dropped in 1752. But up to that time imports included English New-castle coal, Bordeaux wine and cognac carried on French ships, some ships with simply "balast" and many with a mixed cargo as described by Büsching.

In addition to the battle fleet maintained by the government there were also a few vessels trading under the Russian flag. The exact number of these ships is not given by the sources, but Büsching stated that in the period 1758-1764 there were an average of fourteen such ships at St. Petersburg.[125] Peter Shuvalov owned at least one of these. In the collected laws of the Russian Empire there exists a curious law from the empress herself in reference to the Russian merchant fleet. Her special Ukaz stated that Russian merchants could go ashore in foreign ports to trade, but that the sailors of the line must remain on board their ship all the time or the skipper faced a fine of 150 rubles and a possible five years at hard labor.[126] Conditions for the sailors must have approximated those of their serf counterparts and the reaction the same--flight. But the fleet was far from the size of the fleet which Peter had dreamed of. Russia was highly dependent upon foreign carriers for the trade.

184

******

From the above materials it is evident that the long held theory that the period between the death of Peter the Great and that of Catherine II in the field of economic development was one of stagnation. Indeed, it was a period of steady and strong growth. By the end of the reign of Elisabeth Russia was not only recognized as a military power, but as an economic one as well. This is not to detract from the economic achievements of the reign of Catherine, which, in this sense, was a continuaton of the general growth of Russia.

NOTES

1 *PSZ,* XIV, No. 10,495. Senate. January 1, 1756. In this famous order the Senate told the various local and central governmental officials to send matters relating to the Commerce College to that College and not to the Senate.

2 P.A. Shtorkh, "Materialy dlia Istorii gosudarst-vennykh deneshnykh Znakov v Rossii s 1653 po 1840g", *Zhurnal Ministerstva Narodnago Prosh-cheniia,* CXXXVII, March, 1868, 776-78.

3 Bondarenko, 153-170.

4 Büsching,VI, 1771, 379.

5 *Senatskii Arkhiv,*VI, 453. June 18, 1745.

6 *PSZ,* XIV, No. 10,370. Most Highly Affirmed (by the empress). March 7, 1755.

7 Shcherbatov, 210-11.

8 Patlaevskii, 244-46. Shtorkh, *Ibid.*

9 Patlaevskii, Ibid.

10 M.M. Maksimov, *Ocherk o Serebre* (Moscow: Nedr, 1974), 132. Maksimov makes only vague reference to foreigners and their relation to the development of the gold and silver mines. The author claims that between 1751-1756 the mint was striking two million rubles a year in silver.

11 V.V. Zvarich, *Numizmaticheskii Slovar* (Lvov: "Vischa Shkola, 1957), 59.

12 M.V. Danilov, *Zapiski artillerii Maiora Mikhaila Vasilevicha Danilova, napisannyia Im v 1771 Godu* (Moscow: Selivanovskii, 1842), 105.

13 S.M. Troitskii, "Dvorianskie Proekty Ukrepleniia gosudarstvennykh Finansov v Rossii v Seredine XVIII Veka", *Voprosy Istorii,* 1958, II, 54-75.

14 Bondarenko, 368.

15 *Senatskii Arkhiv,* VII, 49. January 28, 1747.

16 S.M. Troitskii, *Finansovaia Politika russkogo Aboliutizma v XVIII Veka* (Moscow:"Nauka," 1966), 65-66.

17 *PSZ,* XIII, No. 9696. Personal. December 15, 1749. *Ibid.,* No. 9711. Personal. February 15, 1750.

18 *Ibid.,* No. 9711. Personal. February 15, 1750.

19 Troitskii, *Finansovaia,* 157-59.

20 A. Svirshchevskii, "Materialy k Istorii Oblozheniia Soli v Rossi", *Iuridicheskiia Zapiski,* I, 1908, 197.

21 Presiankov, 189.

22 *PSZ,* XIV, No. 10,262. Senate. July 21, 1754. Büsching, XIX (Halle, 1775), 128.

23 Troitskii, 142.

24 M.I. Volkov, "Tamozhennaia Reforma 1753-1757gg", *Istoricheskie Zapiski* (Moscow: Akademiia Nauk, 1962), Vol. 71, 152.

25 *Ibid.,* 137-39.

26 *Ibid.*

27 It is curious that in the printed *Senatskii Arkhiv* it records seven reports on that date but makes no mention of the Shuvalov proposal. This indicates the vast amount of materials not printed in the work.

28 *PSZ*, XIII, No. 10,164. Personal. December 20, 1753.

29 Volkov, 145-47.

30 Shakhovskoi, 141.

31 Volkov, 151.

32 Arcadius Kahan, "Continuity in Economic Activity and Policy in Russia During the Post-Petrine Period", *Journal of Economic History,* Vol. XXV (1956), 80.

33 Volkov, 154-57.

34 Solov'ev, 23, 179.

35 Patlaevskii, 169.

36 Heinrich Storch, *Supplement Band zum fünfsten, sechsten, und siebenten Theil des historisch-statishischen Gemäldes des russichen Reiches enhaltend archvalischen Nachrichten und Beweisschriften zur neuen Geschichte des russichen Handels von Heinrich Storch* (Leipzig: Johann Friedrich Hartknoch, 1803), No. 1.

37 *Ibid*.

38 Troitskii, "Finansovaia Politika russkogo Absoliutizma vo vtroi Polovina XVII i XVIIIvv", *Absoliutizma v Russii* (Moscow: Akademiia Nauk, 1963), 302.

39 *PSZ*, IX, No. 6300. Personal. February 8, 1733.

40 *Senatskii Arkhiv,* VI, 204-7. September 25, 1744.

41 S. Ia. Borovoi, *Kredit i Banki Rossii. (Seredina XVIv.-1861g.)* (Moscow: Godgonizdat, 1958), 34.

42 Bondarenko, 143.

43 *PSZ*, XIV, No. 10,235. Personal. May 13, 1754.

44 *Ibid.*, XV, No. 10,948. Personal. April 30, 1759.

45 *Ibid.*, XIV, No. 10,713. Senate. March 21, 1757.

46 *Ibid.*, XV, No. 11,226. Senate. March 27, 1761.

47 Presiankov, 167.

48 *PSZ,* XV, No. 11,117. Senate. October 9, 1760.

49 N.L. Rubinshtein, "Ulozhennaia Komissiia 1754-1766", *Istoricheskie Zapiski* (Moscow: Akademiia Nauk, 1951), Vol. 38, 217.

50 *PSZ,* XV, No. 11,171. Senate. December 17, 1760.

51 *Ibid.*, No. 11,321. Senate. September 3, 1761.

52 *Ibid.*, XII, No. 9559. Senate. December 9, 1748. This law applied to grain and bread measures.

53 *Ibid.*, XIII, No. 9681. Senate. November 7, 1749.

54 *Entsiklopedicheskii Slovar'* (St. Petersburg : Efron, 1892) V(X), 699.

55 *Despatches Received by the Department of State from United States Ministers to Russia, 1808-1906.* September 3, 1898-January 14, 1899. Enclosure in a letter to Secretary of State John Hay. St. Petersburg, December 15, 1898, No. 211 by Herbert H.D. Pierce.

56 I. Bogoliubskii, *Istoriko-statisticheskii Ocherk Proizvoditel'- nosti nerchinskago gornogo Okruga s 1703 po 1871* (St. Petersburg: Demakov, 1872), 3.

57 V. Rozhkov, "Akinfii Nikitich Demidov po svokh Kolyvano-Voskresenskikh Zavodakh. Istoricheskii Ocherk, 1744-1747", *Gornyi Zhurnal,* III, August, 1891, 331-34.

58 Shalatter. *Obstoiatel'noe Opisanie rudnago Dela.* Tom I-II. St. Petersburg, 1763-65.

59 A.M. Lornaskii, *Kratkii istoricheskii Ocherk administrativnykh Ucherzhdenii gornago Vedomstva v Rossii 1700-1900gg.* (St. Petersburg: Bernshtein, 1900), 27-29.

60 Rozhkov, 352-54.

61 *PSZ,* XV, No. 10,976. Personal to the Senate. July 22, 1759.

62 *Ibid.,* No. 11,166. Senate. December.13, 1760.

63 Kahan, 62.

64 Roger Portal. *L'Oural au XVIIIe siècle. Etud d'Historie economique et sociale* (Paris: Institut d'Etudes Slaves, 1950).

65 Patlaevskii, 157.

66 *PSZ,* XII, No. 8901. Personal. March 12, 1744. Vitevskii, I, 258-59. When the English merchant, Hanway, visited Astrakhan Tatishchev presented him with an excellent map of the new Orenburg line which Hanway included in his book about his experiences in Russia. Hanway, XV and 8-9. Hanway reprinted the map between pages 8 and 9 of his account and it was a very accurate map for the time.

67 *PSZ,* XIII, No. 10,131. Senate. August 12, 1753. The Senate provided a list of private works with too many workers and ordered them turned over to the government.

68 *Ibid.,* XIII, No.10,141. Senate. October 13,1753.

69 *Ibid.,* XIV, No. 10,494. Senate. December 30,1755.

70 Portal, 169.

71 *Ibid.,* insert between pages 156-57.

72 *Ibid.,* 264

73 *Sanktpeterburgskiia Vedomosti,* No. 38. Friday, May 12, 1749, 202.

74 *Ibid.,* No. 23. Tuesday, April 3, 1750, 214.

75 *Ibid.,* No. 92. Friday, November 15, 1751, 768.

76 *Ibid.,* No. 33. Friday, June 25, 1753.

77 The term "tovarischestvo" has a much wider meaning in Russian than simply company. It could mean a club, a gathering of friends for certain purposes, etc.

78 *PSZ,* XIV, No. 10,694. Senate. February 21, 1757.

79 Pronshtein, 102-103.

80 *PSZ,* XV, No. 10,837. Senate in consequence of a Personal Ukaz. May 15, 1758.

81 *Ibid.,* XV, No. 10,848. Senate. June 15, 1758.

82 *Sanktpeterburgskiia Vedomosti,* No. 60. Tuesday, July 28, 1758.

83 Patlaevskii, 141.

84 *The History of Kamtschatka, and the Kurilski Islands, with the Countries Adjacent with Maps and Cuts.* Published at St. Petersburg in the Russian Language, by the order of her Imperial Majesty, and translated into English by James Grieves, M.D. Glochester. Printed by R. Raikes for T. Jefferys, Geographer to his majesty, London MDCCLXIV. Reprinted by Quadrangle Books: Chicago, 1962.

85 *PSZ,* XII, No. 9480. Senate. February 12, 1748.

86 *Ibid.,* XV, No. 11,315. Senate. August 24, 1761.

87 *Sanktpeterburgskiia Vedomosti,* No. 22. Friday. March 16, 1750.

88 *PSZ,* XIV, No. 10,376. Senate. March 21, 1755.

89 *Ibid.*, XV, No. 11,080. Senate. July 12, 1760.

90 *Ibid.*,XIV, No. 10,692. Senate. February 21, 1757. Certain ports were excluded from the ban.

91 Kostomarov, III, 48.

92 *PSZ,* XIII, No. 10,057. Senate. December 14, 1752.

93 Kostomorov, III, 52.

94 *PSZ,* XII, No. 9511. Personal to the Police Chancellary. July 2, 1748.

95 *Ibid.*, XV, No. 10,840. Personal, promulgated to the Senate by P. Shuvalov. May 21, 1758.

96 *Russkoe Iskusstvo v XVIII Veka,*(Moscow: Nauk,1973) plates 50 and 51. The first plate 50 shows the original plan conceived by Rastrelli and the second 51 a picture of the stripped structure as it was in 1860 before destruction.

97 *PSZ,* XIII, No. 9702. Senate. January 29, 1750.

98 *Ibid.*, XIV, No. 10,389. Senate. April 3, 1755. As shall be indicated nearly half the ships visiting kronstadt were English which indicates that their captains and their merchants generally knew French which was then the universal language. *Pribavlenie k Sanktpetersburgskim Vedomostiam,* tuesday, October 13, 1752. As will be noted below there were an unusually large number of ships visiting St. Petersburg that year probably partly out of curiosity to see the facilities.

99 Büsching, X, 380-81.

100 *PSZ,* XV, No. 11,026. Senate. January 26, 1760.

101 Büsching, VII, 59.

102 *Ibid*.

103 Troitsky, 176.

192

104 *PSZ,* XIV, No. 10,486. Tariff Law. December 1, 1755.

105 *Ibid.,* XIV, No. 10, 503. Senate. February 1, 1755.This law is similar to the proceeding one.

106 Hanway, 221.

107 Dietrich Gerhard, *England und der Aufstieg Russlands. Zur Frage des Zusammenhanges des europäischen Staaten und ihres Ausgreifens des 18. Jahrhunderts* (München & Berlin: Oldenbourg, 1933), 42-43.

108 Patlaevskii, 140.

109 *Senatskii Arkhiv,* IX, 704. December 12, 1756.

110 Troitskii, *Russkii Absoliutizm,* 354.

111 *PSZ,* XV, No. 11,489. Personal of Peter III. March 28, 1762. Peter did extend the right of the leaders of the company to continue to collect taxes for the next ten years.

112 A. Lappo-Danilevskii, *Russkie promyshlennei i torgovie Kompanii v pervoi Polovine XVIII Stoletiia. Istoricheskii Ocherk* (St. Petersburg: Balashev, 1899), 124-26.

113 *Ibid.,* 35.

114 *Ibid.,* 96.

115 *Ibid.*

116 Patlaevskii, 164. N.L. Rubinshtein, "Vneshniaia Torgovlia Rossii i Russkoe Kupechestvo vo vtoroi Polovine XVIIIv.", *Istoricheskie Zapiski,* Vol. 54, 1955, 345-346. Troitsky used the same figures. The figures are rounded off to make it easier to understand. It will also be noted that when the war ended in 1762 and the principle of free trade

gradually accepted there was another jump in the trade similar to that of 1750.

117 Troitsky, *Finansovia Politika,* 185.

118 Büsching, (Hamburg: Buchenröder, 1767), III, 342. The official journal *Sanktpeterburgskiia Vedomosti* also provided figures for the number of ships visiting St. Petersburg for the period before the war (1757). When compared with those provided by Büsching they proved exact. The years compared were 1746, 1748, 1749, 1750, 1751, 1752, 1753, 1754, 1760. The figure for the year 1756 came from the journal alone and was not provided by Büsching.

119 *Pribavlenie k Sanktpetersburgskim Vedomostiam,* Tuesday, October 13, 1752.

120 Büsching, (Halle: Curt, 1776), X, 314.

121 David S. Macmillan, "The Scottish-Russian Trade: Its Development, Fluctuations, and Difficulties, 1750-1796 ", *Canadian Slavic Studies,* IV, 3 (Fall 1970), 426-442.

122 Hanway, 370-71.

123 Kahan, 47.

124 Büsching, (Halle: Curt, 1775), IX, 314.

125 *Ibid.,* (Hamburg: Buchenröden, 1767), III, 344.

126 *PSZ,* XIV, No. 10,474. Personal. October 11, 1755.

CHAPTER SEVEN

TO IMPROVE THE INTERNAL ORDER

The reign of Elisabeth witnessed several initiatives which were to be of special importance for the future, but which as a consequence of circumstances, did not come to full fruition in her reign. Three initiatives are of special importance, mainly, the start of a modern general survey of the country, the attempt to create a new law code and the efforts to bring settlers into the country to occupy the unused lands along the Volga. In each case the need had been recognized in previous reigns but as a consequence of circumstances, such as wars, were set aside. But often the fact that these efforts were major concerns of the Russian government of Elisabeth is underrated by those who attribute more initiative to subsequent reigns.

The problem of land survey in European Russian was not a new one. The Ulozhenie of 1649 (Law Code) carried instructions for primitive surveys based upon traditional methods such as the use of outstanding landmarks for separating the lands. In 1684 such a survey was undertaken by Alexis, father of Peter the Great. But the inaccuracy of such a survey soon sparked problems and the succeeding reigns of Peter the Great and especially Anna Ioannovna witnessed much governmental concern over the developing problems. it will be recalled that Peter the Great had himself been interested in mathematics mainly for purposes of navigation for which he had established a school for exactly this purpose. Hence, there now existed Russians trained for the modern task, but too few at first.

Then there were the subsequent efforts of the Academy of Sciences after the death of the Great Reformer to carry out his wishes to study Russia and produce modern maps of the country. By hiring and importing leading mathematicians such as Euler and d'Ilse a group of Russians was trained in the art of cartogrophy, cestial measurements and land survey. The result of the application of these new methods to the Russian Empire culminated in a series of maps as well as atlases of which the one published in 1745 is perhaps the most famous since it contained regional maps as well as a complete map of the Russian Empire as it was known at that time. The use of scientific instruments in fixing the exact locations of cities, rivers, etc., prepared for a more exact survey.

Some modern survey work had been undertaken. Peter had ordered a general survey of the region around St. Petersburg (called Ingermanland) so that exact information could be obtained similar to that existing in the newly acquired Baltic states where the Swedish government had already undertaken a survey. For the remainder of Russia it appears that he was content with the results of the materials from 1684. Only if a petition was received requesting a survey as a consequence of a dispute did the Estates College (Votchina) despatch a few trained geodeitic experts of the government to fulfill the request.[1]

But with time condition started to change. The movement of peoples into new lands, the fading of memories concerning exact boundaries, the taking of state lands and including them in an estate and most important the growth of population made it imperative for the government to undertake a new modern scientific survey. The famines, which were localized and general, also caused small rights to be called into question. For example, the serfs on neighboring estates might fish in the same river in good years without dispute, but if a famine affected the region the fish in that same river could represent the only source of food and thus become a matter of life or death for many of the serfs on both estates. This problem and the population growth led to outright clashes in which the landowners or his prikazchik would arm the serfs on one estate to fight those on another. The central region of the empire, especially the regions around Moscow, were especially curtial in regard to this problem.[2]

By 1731 these little "wars" had become so serious that Anna issued a manifesto calling for an end to them and promising a general survey to settle these problems.[3] During her reign (1730-1740) a general set of rules for the survey were prepared and sent to the Senate where they were shelfed since the state was at war and lacked people capable of the undertaking. Hence, these rules of 1735 were the last effort in her reign to work out a general survey. Local surveys were still possible upon request and the survey of St. Petersburg continued its slow and inaccurate course.[4]

Early in the reign of Elisabeth there were a few minor surveys to determine the boundaries of the Guerniias or even the national borders as will be recalled in the case of Poland. In 1750 the Don Cossacks encountered problems with their neighbors over fishing rights, and in 1751 the order was issued that a survey be made of their boundaries especially along the rivers.[5] But a full survey was a completely different matter. It would require a large staff of persons trained in geodetics, careful orders and a special court to adjudicate conflicting claims. Even after such a survey the nobles often would consider land assigned to their neighbor as truly theirs as witnessed in Chekhov's play *The Marriage Proposal*.

The wars between various estates continued into the reign of Elisabeth with many of them not reported by the local officials. But these tended to become larger battles which could not be concealed. Finally in 1750 the prikazchiks of two neighboring estates armed their respective serfs to fight over disputed land in the Kashirskii region near

197

Moscow. The result was 26 persons killed and many more wounded. The local authorities tried unsuccessfully to cover the incident but apparently the losing side pushed the claims relating to the incident to the highest level in the land--the empress. In 1752 the empress herself following the example of Anna ordered these little wars ended and threatened severe punishment to the prikazchiks responsible for them. This was issued again as a manifesto and read in all the Orthodox churches in the same manner in which the whole society was informed of the drafts of men and horses.[6] The initiative for this move came when Peter Shuvalov reported before the Senate on January 22, 1752 that the empress wanted a general survey to end the trouble. It will be noted that this was the period when his influence with the empress was at its height. He suggested that the Senate prepare the necessary measures for the survey which he thought should start first in the Moscow Guberniia.[7] The whole country was to be prepared for an eventual survey except Siberia and Orenburg where there existed sufficient land and no trouble. In a second manifesto a month after the first, it was ordered that all documents needed for the survey and information from elders be collected first in Moscow Guberniia which should prepare itself at once for a survey.[8] The elders of the communities seem to have been trusted more than the landlords since in the absence of documents they were to be relied upon to truthfully state what lands and rights pertained to a given estate.

Since an undertaking of such magnitude was very complex it took two more years to work out the exact details of the survey. The next immediate warning came to Moscow in April of 1754 and in May of that same year the rules for the survey were publshed. These rules occupy fully 57 pages of the collected laws of the Russian empire and seem to have covered most cases of conflict.[9] The persons commissioned with the survey were given strict rules to follow. First, they were required to take a most solemn religious oath that they would be perfectly honest, not take bribes or be influenced by outside factors like threat of force, friendship for a given landowner or hatred for another. In preparing these rules Shuvalov and those helping him (about whom we know little) used the 1735 rules plus information from the 1684 survey and probably assistance from the Academy of Sciences which had extensive experience in geographical and mathematical matters. The people preparing the survey missed little, if anything. For example, fishing rights and how to determine them are spelled out in detail. To determine the exact boundary several methods were provided. First the surveyors were to use any legal documents relating to the land such as those from the 1684 survey. Such documents were probably rare since in 1684 the average Russian noble could not read and therefore discarded them. The Estates College did have some of the records left to it when it replaced the Pomestie Prikaz in 1721. It also was responsible for knowing the location of the various estates and the males on them with a duty to serve the state. Often the Estates College had the duty of selling estates when a family line became extinct and it was able to provide information concerning the size and number of souls for each.[10]

It is curious that in the absence of written records the first people to be trusted were the elders of the villages who, of course, in most cases were serfs with no rights. They were preferred over the landlords or prikazchiks since it was feared that the owners and their hirelings would be more likely to lie. Heavy fines were threatened against those providing false information knowingly. Landlords and prikazchiks were warned not to undertake anything before the survey which would tend to hinder access to correct information. Then if a section of land was in dispute and there was no clear owner such land was to be given to the estate with the most serfs and least land for them. This humane measure would reduce the effect of famines on poor estates and permit the serfs to carry through more easily their obligations. In general, the plan involved typical Russian situations and therefore does not seem to be a direct copy of regulations of other countries. It was original and comprehensive.

The law had certain other features which were certain to annoy the nobles. Land which had formerly belonged to the state, but was being used by the landowner, either reverted to the state or the landowner had to purchase it. Certain people such as the Onehouseholders whose lands and rights were being gradually usurped by the nobles were protected and given land. Much time had passed since the 1684 survey, but not enough for all the older people to have forgotten it. But most of the nobles had occupied governmental lands which had then been passed down in the family losing memory of the factual situation in the process. Hence, according to the 1684 survey they owed the government for that land. But the power of the nobility had increased greatly since the death of Peter the Great to the point that they--the nobles--actually controlled possessions of the crown. By 1754 the nobles had also forgotten the source of their wealth and attributed it to their being "well born". Peter had abolished the distinction between the hereditary (Votchina) and the pomestie tenure which was originally temporary. Hence, estate ownership was considered a "right" which could only be forefeited for a crime against the state. Another problem was the widespread dishonesty of the landowners. Many, especially those with influence and friends in high positions, saw this as an occasion to make gains at the expense of their neighbors. Hence, claims were put forth for lands belonging in reality to other estates. This produced constant squables.[11] One of the aims of the 1754 survey was to give the nobles fixed tenure in their ownership of the land (sobstvennost) often attributed to the reign of Catherine.[12]

200

In early 1755 the Chief Land Survey Chancellary was opened and General Fermor, who was responsible for the slow survey of Ingermandland, was named its first commander upon the suggestion of Peter Shuvalov himself. [13] The Senate continued to busy itself with preparations for the big survey which it anticipated would rapidly include all of Russia except Siberia and Orenburg. The form of the maps to be used was published in 1755.[14] A special law was issued concerning the type of marker to be used to separate land.[15] Then the official announcement appeared in the state journal in January of 1756 on the eve of the Seven Year's War. The announcement consisted of a general order to survey all of Russia (with the noted exceptions) and named the staff selected to complete it. For the survey the students from the Cadet Corp, then the best educational institution in Russia, were selected partly because of their noble background and partly because they understood mathematics and would be capable of using the necessary scientific instruments. The names of eighty-three were provided out of a proposed total force of ninety-three men which was insufficient for the task.[16] With the opening of Moscow University Catherine had a larger number of qualified persons to assist her in her survey.

Despite the outbreak of the war the Senate attached great importance to the survey. Once the announcement was made publicly the Senate ordered that the survey was of great importance and the surveyors must be obeyed in fulfilling their assigned functions.[17] When the war broke out in Europe the Senate ordered all officers to their duty posts except those chasing bootleggers and the land survey people, all of whom were officers.[18] Some writers assume that the war ended the survey since so little was accomplished. However, the survey team continued to struggle on in a limited region near Moscow. In December of 1756 the Senate named itself as a court of appeal for the survey Commission.[19] The fine for moving a marker was set at 100 rubles.[20] By 1760 the financial crisis of the war bore down upon the resources of the government, but the Senate ordered that the surveyors be given salaries plus provisions while other governmental officials were receiving only part of their normal pay.[21] It is difficult to trace the survey from this point since the war all but drained the country of its financial resources and the empress was ill. But in the final accounting the survey in the Moscow region 62,500 hectars of land and 359 villages (dachas) had been covered.[22] There it ended until Catherine II started it again this time with much more success.

The question then posses itself as to the relative lack of success of the survey after such a heavy commitment of administrative time and men. The answer appears to be related to the manner in which the nobility viewed their land. Many years had passed since the 1684 survey and during that period the nobles had taken much state land and land from Onehouseholders which, if the materials from 1684 were used, they would be forced to relinquish. The nobles would have been forced to pay for land illegally in their possession, but held in their family so long that they considered it to be theirs. Catherine simply allowed them to retain this land. Also, she abandoned the principle that in cases of disputed lands the estate with the most needy serfs should have the first right. This allowed the powerful to gain at the expense of the poorer nobles. It was under these circumstances that the nobles would support a real survey which, despite this, still proceeded slowly.[23]

******

Another important initiative was put forth by Peter Shuvalov before the Senate in the presence of the empress on March 11, 1754. His sweeping proposal called for abandoning the fruitless effort to re-establish the "pure" Petrine system of laws in favor of a completely new law code which would be "clear and understandable". [24] This was one of the rare meetings which the empress attended and part of the reason for her being there was to support Shuvalov, although it appears that he wanted a completely new code, while she thought that the code would be based upon the ideas of her father, Peter the Great.

The idea of creating a new law code was not new. Russia was operating under the Ulozhenie (Law Code) of 1649 which was clearly out of date by then. The Ulozhenie was supplemented by the Ukzes or direct orders of the ruler or the Senate. But even these were inadequate in consequence of the westernization of the country and the growth of the power of the nobility. The volume of the output of laws for specific cases was very great. When the most important laws of the past were collected and printed in 1830 there were fifteen volumes for the twenty year reign of Elisabeth alone. And this was only half the actual number of laws issued since many were petty and related to specific cases.

There had been a long history of attempts to create a new law code since the rulers after Alexis, the father of Peter the Great, knew that it was necessary to update the old code. Peter himself had made several attempts. In the year 1700-1703 he established a commission to write a new code, and it did produce such a new statute, but apparently Peter did not like it so he disregarded it. [25] In 1714 Peter returned to the problem and instructed the newly created Senate to follow the 1649 code in all matters except those that had been changed by subsequent laws issued by the rulers. He then established a commission to study the laws enacted after the code of 1649.[26] Capriciously in 1718 he ordered that the Russian laws be compared with those of Sweden to see where they differed. This proved impossible given the resources and time. Then shifting again Peter ordered the Senate in late 1719 to have a new code prepared by October of 1720 which was simply impossible. It was then decided to call in select nobles and officers to create and approve a new code.[27] In short the changes in policy in the lifetime of Peter prevented him from achieving his goal. But Peter had raised the question of a new code and some sort of input from the "free classes". Peter's wife Catherine I, Peter II and Anna all tried to create a law code and accepted the principle that it, like the Ulozhenie of 1649, should have some sort of "popular" approval, but again nothing came of these efforts.[28] The constant wars during the reign of Anna probably account for her failure to achieve anything in updating the laws.

Hence, the efforts of Elisabeth and later of Catherine II were not really innovations. Each ruler or the advisors were aware of the need for a code, but none ever reached the goal. Shuvalov thus had a strong argument to present to the empress and Senate for a new code. Especially strong for the empress were the efforts of her father and her own attempt to achieve what had eluded him.

The first step in the process was to order all governors and courts to make special reports of cases which they had judged which might be of assistance to those composing the code.[29] This law of the Senate included a brief history of the past efforts to create a new code and the failures. But as was usual the local authorities were slow in answering the order of the Senate and work on the code proceeded without much helpful materials. Reports from this request and the one mentioned earlier concerning the nature of the local bureaucracy were still being submitted in the reign of Catherine II. One of Catherine's justified complaints about the Russian system was that it took three orders to obtain an answer or to have a law obeyed.

For the actual composition of the proposed law a special commission was created under the jurisdiction of the Senate.[30] These persons were to be selected on the basis of their knowledge of the law. It was to work as rapidly as possible and report to the Senate as it completed its work. The code was to be divided into four sections: (1) all judicial matters, (2) the "rights" which the subjects of the state have according to their status and personal possessions, (3) moveable and immoveable property, how it is to be divided (inheritance and divorce) and to whom it is fixed, and (4) a criminal code concerning such matters as when to apply torture, fines and other punishments. The project enumerated the individual headings for the chapters which indicates that Shuvalov had probably studied previous efforts before submitting his proposal to the Senate.[31]

The members of the initial commission appear to have been selected with care. Among the members were Justice College Active Civil Advisor, Iushkov, Vice President of the Justice College, Emme, State Advisor Bezobrazov, College Assessor, Liapunov, former Professor of the Academy of Sciences, Struve de Pirmont, and the burgomeister of the Chief Magistrate of St. Petersburg, Bikhliaev. [32] Of the persons identifiable all seem to have had some experience with the law and several were subsequently promoted in the reign of Catherine II. Alexander Vorontsov, known for the excellence of the education he received, had Struve de Pirmont as a tutor and considered him to be excellent.[33] However, two also had "experience" in the shameful trials of Ostermann and Münnich. Glebov, an original member of the commission and later Ober-Procurator of the Senate during the reign of Catherine, was later discovered to have been taking bribes. So one had on-the-job training for his position.

The commission was given powers to obtain the necessary materials wherever such existed. Its agents were widely distributed throughout the higher governmental system to obtain information. The commission was in full operation one week after the law creating it was issued, and it went to work at once with a speed rarely seen in old regime Russia. It held its first sittings in August of 1754 and was already writing the first parts of the proposed code by the 23rd of September of that year. When matters concerning religion were considered two persons selected by the Synode were consulted by those composing the code. On the 10th of April, 1755 two parts of the code were sent to the Senate for approval--one on judicial matters and the other on criminal. After the Senate and the Synode had approved the codes they were forwarded to the empress for her approval on July 25th which was almost exactly one year after the start of the project.[34]

At that point the empress could simply have signed the codes and they would have become law and she the great lawgiver. But one of the puzzels of her reign arises at this point. She left them unsigned for the rest of her reign. This cannot be explained by laziness since the matter was so urgent. The assertion of Shcherbatov that the cruel punishments included in the code touched the soft-hearted empress so much that she could not bring herself to sign is questionable since she could easily have ordered those punishments changed.[35] Another theory states that she wanted an assembly to approve them is also weak, since when an assembly was called to consider all the laws, it was through the action of the Senate.[36] Perhaps I.I. Shuvalov who as was noted was deeply influenced by the Enlightenment found the first two sections distasteful and induced her not to sign. The Soviet scholar N.L. Rubinshtein claims that it was the result of the conflict of two parties at court. Such parties did exist.[37] In any case even with the use of the archieves neither the pre-Revolutionary historian, Latkin, nor the Soviet historian, Rubinshtein, could provide a conclusive answer.

The commission continued to work on the other two parts of the code despite the war which almost stopped its meetings. According to Latkin it convened only once in 1757 and five times in 1758.[38] Shuvalov, whose brainchild the code was, by then devoted much of his time to the problem of obtaining money to conduct the war. That there was no intention to drop the program is evidenced by the addition of two members in 1760 one of whom was the honest State Advisor, Shakhovskoi,and the other, R.L. Vorontsov, brother of the Chancellor M.L. Vorontsov and one of the richest landowners in Russia. Both of the new members were enemies of the Shuvalovs as was Catherine. According to Rubinshtein's study of the archives there were several drafts of the next portions especially the one dealing with social groupings. It appears that the Shuvalov group wanted to maintain as much of the Petrine system as possible while the opposing group was more favorable to the interests of the nobles. Shuvalov, for example, wanted the merchants to retain the right to factories with serfs while his opposition wanted more freedom for the nobles and a monoply in owning serfs.[39] Apparently the addition of new figures to the commission in 1760 speeded up work on the last portions, and a changed code was presented to the Senate in September of 1761. However, on the 27th of March Alsuf'ev, the private secretary to the empress, conveyed the order of the empress to the commission that the entire code should be rewritten with the death penalty removed.[40] There is no evidence that any such effort was undertaken and the death of the empress several months later completely removed this concern.

Thus, there were two periods of extreme activity in the writing of the code the first 1754-55 and the second starting in 1760. While the laws passed during the reign of Peter the Great appear to have played a strong role in the codes, there were also some new items which had developed as a consequence of the judicial problems facing the Senate and the courts. Also, apparently complete drafts of two sections were completed by the commission since these were published under the old regime in Russia. [41] The commission was probably reworking the whole code as the composition and orientation of the code commission slowly changed with the dropping and adding of members.

One change does stand out--mainly the treatment of the nobles. In the 1755 code they were not given the special treatment they felt that they deserved, but were often treated the same way as other classes whereas in the 1766 version after the "freeing" of the nobility from state service the nobles and merchants of the first guild were never to be executed, but for serious crimes they were to lose their rank and sent to free Siberian villages "eternally". For lesser crimes these groups were subject to a year in prison, a half a year in a monastery to do penance and regained their titles after that.[42] As was typical under the old regime, before the ideas of the Enlightenment prevailed in law, the punishments were very severe for even minor crimes. But the proposed code was mild compared to the 1649 law code. It will be recalled that a woman who murdered her husband (justly or unjustly) was buried alive. The new code merely had them beheaded.

The most serious crime a person could commit was lesè majesté for which in Russian practice a person was to be "fifthed" instead of the usual quartering in common practice.[43] The next worst crime seems to have been that of misleading Orthodox people from their religion especially in the case of self-immolators, who, were themselves burned for their "crime". Other serious crimes could lead to breaking on the wheel, but this was becoming a rare punishment. Most common punishment for severe crimes was beheading, the use of the knutor which could result in death, whipping, burning a V in the forehead and sending to a Siberian mine to work eternally. The use of torture was allowed only in the cases of proven criminals between the ages of 15 and 70 to obtain information.[44] There still existed a belief in witches in Russia and their punishment was not burning at the stake but beheading.[45]

It is difficult to imagine that such a criminal code could have been written in a country without the death penalty. A whole generation grew up without witnessing an execution! There is no evidence to indicate if it had any influence, but it is doubtful if the lower classes knew of the practice--it was never written into a law, all death sentences were simply commuted to "eternal" exile in some place after appropriate punishment. As early as 1744 foreigners, such as Hanway, were aware that the death penalty was not being applied in Russia.[46] On the other-hand in a book published by a Frenchman in 1802 we find the following quotation about the "terrible" reign of Elisabeth: " ... the executioner's axe was occupied without stop at sacrificing of persons of all classes, even women of the most distinguished rank...."[47]

The third part of the code published by Latkin was entitled: "About the Situation of the Subjects Generally". Published on the press of the St. Petersburg Solitary Confinement Prison (?), it was apparently completed as a draft in 1762 whereas the second part had been submitted to the empress in 1755. This would mean that it was last reworked after the death of the empress and about the time Peter III released the nobility from obligatory service. Like the first code it was a class code in that all were not to be equal before the law. The "well born" nobles and merchants of the first guild were given special treatment. The key quote is the following:

> The nobility alone has complete power over its owned people and serfs both male and female without limit, except for the taking

of life, punishment with the knout or and
making them undergo torture.[48]

Non-noble factory owners (merchants) with serfs attached
to their factories who were not of the first guild had
restriction placed upon them. The serfs held by lower
guild merchants had a degree of freedom, could not be
sold, could not be forced to marry against their will and
were to be insured sufficient time to raise food for their
support.[49]

Yet even though it was completed later than the second
part many of the prejudices of the empress were reflected
in it. People of Hebrew faith and Jesuits were forbidden
to enter the country. There were anti-Moslem and anti-
Armenian articles. In addition, under the proposed code
the Old Believers were to be subjected to even worse
restrictions than existed. The Ukrainians were to be left
alone. This proved to be one of the last references to
their freedom which was soon to be violated.

Many of the old laws were simply repeated. For example,
laws about the return of runaway serfs was in the code
along with the fine of 50 rubles for keeping them one
month and 100 for each year. Yet there were original portions of the code as well arising from the problems which
faced the Senate and courts. The most original in this
respect was the part dealing with orphans or persons incapable of handling their own affairs. While obviously for
the nobles and wealthy merchants it established special
regulations for the persons selected to oversee their affairs. Guardians were to be honest and be able to provide
an orphan with a full accounting of the running of an
estate (or business) when the orphan came of age. Mentally ill persons and compulsive gamblers were treated in a
similar manner to preserve their estates for their families.
In passing gambling was also made illegal.[50] The law on
gambling was promulgated in 1761.[51]

These codes were, of course, suggestions for regularizing the legal system in the country. While the empress herself could have accepted them and given them the force of law there existed the tradition of calling on the social classes to provide input, but in retrospect it would have been wiser for the empress to simply have ignored "public" opinion, made what changes she deemed necessary, and signed them. Such an action would have done much to simplify the legal system in the country. The codification was reasonable for the time even if it is harsh by modern standards. Much confusion would have been removed from the administration of the country. Many of the problems which came before the Senate repeatedly in differing forms wold have been solved and the Senate could have become a court of last appeal. The local administration would have been forced to have been more honest since a printed code was harder to evade than the dozens of orders issued by the empress, the Synode and the Senate. But without a code the machine continued to operate as before. As the old Russian peasant saying goes: "The law is like a wagon's tongue, whichever way it is turned, there it goes".

With the commission still writing the last portions of the code, and the empress dying, the commission itself returning to the old idea of representatives of the "public" for ratifying their work, called upon the Senate to determine the people to judge the code as in 1649, and had been tried several times subsequently. Hence, in September of 1761 the Senate issued an order to the nobles of each province except Kiev, Astrakhan, Vyborg, Latvia, Estonia and Siberia to select two persons to come to St. Petersburg to consider the code. In addition, the Senate decided to include representatives of the other free class--the merchants--who were ordered to select one person instead of two from the same regions to consider the economic sections of the code affecting them.[52] The nobles were to gather in the chief city of the provinces or Guberniia and elect their delegates. The Magistrates (roughly mayors) and the Rathusha (roughly city council) had this function for the merchants. The Synode was charged with selecting delegates from among the clergy, but it apparently did nothing. The noble delegates were to be in St. Petersburg on the first of January 1762 to discuss the codes--which, as fate would have it, was to be seven days after the death of the empress.

In December of 1761 in a new order, the Senate called for the election of two merchants from Irkutsk, Tobol'sk, Kiev, Orenburg, Kiev and Nyzhin as well as two nobles from Latvia and Estonia.[53] This belated action would have helped redress the unbalance between nobles and merchants while it also brought into the considerations regions which had been excluded before, often because as in the case of Siberia, serfdom and nobles did not exist.

The elections took place as scheduled and the Senate was generally pleased with the choices. But the delegates arrived very slowly. Only five arrived on the date of the scheduled opening of the conference and twenty-two more in January probably in time for the funeral of the empress. But even in June work could not even begin in view of the heavy absences.[54] The merchants were a little more successful probably because many of the wealthy ones traded in St. Petersburg. Often, in contrast, the nobles seleted were poor and found it difficult to attend. Also, the manditory state service meant that few of the nobles were then in the countryside to take part in the elections. This was in the middle of a serious war.

The revolution of Catherine the Great came in June 1762 and changed the entire picture. After obtaining the throne Catherine took the delegates on hand to Moscow for her coronation and eventually released them. Despite this the commission continued to work on the codes until 1766 and Latkin claims that some of the proposed laws in the instructions of the nobles to

Catherine's conference were taken directly from the proposed codes of Elisabeth.[55] It has been established that
at least thirty-nine and probably many more of the
approximately ninety delegates elected to the law conference of Elisabeth were in Catherine's assembly.[56] Rubinshtein has established that two of the instructions of
the merchants that remain from Elisabeth's conference
were nearly identical to those put forth in much greater
quantity by the merchants to Catherine's commission.[57]

Catherine then merely picked up where Elisabeth left off,
but she apparently wanted a fresh start. While her effort
drew more attention chiefly because she used the ideas of
the Enlightenment in preparing for her conference and
also included representatives of the state serfs her failure
was also more manifest. In reality, Elisabeth came closer
to creating a new system than Catherine since the proposed laws were almost completely prepared. But if Elisabeth
had lived and if she had convened her conference she
would have encountered the same class conflicts which
undermined the efforts of Catherine.

******

Another development of the reign of Elisabeth which
bore fruit during the reign of Catherine was the inviting
of foreigners into the country with skills, such as farming,
to assist the growth of the economy. It had long been the
policy of the Russian government to accept into its
service people with skills lacking among the Russians. Ivan
the III had built much of the Kremlin with such foreign
(Italian) assistance. This tradition Peter had inherited. But
since the close of the "gathering of the Russian lands"
which might conveniently be dated to the treaty of
Andrusovo in 1667 in which Smolensk was finally and eter-

nally added to the Russian state, matters had changed. It was true that there were still pockets of orthodox Russians and Ukrainians in Poland. But the new expansion of the state had the goal of obtaining strategic areas such as the Baltic States and access to the Black Sea in which non-Orthodox peoples were gained as subjects.

As is well known Peter the Great admired the West and its technology to such an extent that he hired large numbers of people to come to Russia to modernize his country. He stated that foreigners were welcome as long as they had something to contribute to the state and that their religious convictions were of no importance as long as they were Christians. But admitting individuals and admitting groups were different matters. In addition, the Russian government was showing increasing interest in the Orthodox peoples in the Balkans then under the rule of the Ottoman Port. Hence, Orthodox peoples were especially welcome in the empire. In 1703 Peter accepted into his service a Serb named Savva Vladislavich Raguzhinskii whose contribution to the development of the Russian state was considerable. He was provided with large estates in the Ukraine where he established a flourishing broadcloth industry.[58] He was also used by the Russian government as a financial advisor and diplomat.[59] He was especially important at the time of the disaster on the Pruth when he acted as an agent for the Russian government in attempting to arouse the Orthodox peoples of the Balkans, but he had little success since only 148 Serbs were in the Russian camp.[60]

Although the campaign of 1711 on the Pruth was a disaster for Peter personally, it did have some beneficial results for the state. The Gospodar of Moldavia, Dmitrii Konstantinovich Kantemir (1673-1723) joined the Russian army with a following of about a thousand personal retainers.[61] Kantemir was an extremely intelligent person who had advanced through the civil service of the Port to the point that he was appointed Gospodar of Moldavia. His interests were wide-ranging and his knowledge of languages beyond belief--Turkish, Persian, Arabic, Greek, Latin, Italian, Russian, Rumanian and French. Kantemir was given extensive estates in the Kharkov region and living quarters in Moscow. In 1718 he was appointed a Senator.[62] His followers were given various posts, and, as in Muscovite times, merged with the Russian nobility. His son became a famous poet and diplomat dying in 1744. Hence, Peter had established a precedence for his daughter to follow. Thus, it was no surprise, that when the ambassador in Vienna, Bestuzhev-Riumin brother of the Grand Chancellor, announced in December of 1751 that a large group of Serbs then living on the border of the Austrian Empire desired to settle in Orthodox Russia and take service there,[63] that after a long session the Senate eagerly agreed to accept two hussar regiments consisting of 4,000 men and 1,000 foot-soldiers.[64]

Considerable time was devoted by the Senate to the coming of the Serbs with the aim of making conditions as ideal as possible to induce others to emulate them. Unlike the follower of Kantemir, the Serbs requested and were permitted to have special settlements of their own which would allow them to maintain their ethnic identity. Their commander, Khorvat, was to be given the salary of a major-general and the subordinate officers rank comparable to their Russian counterparts.[65] They were provided with good land in the Ukraine in the proximity of the Turkish border with the stipulation that they serve Russia in war and watch the Turkish border.[66] Their principle fortress was to be named Saint Elisabeth after the patron of the empress. Money was despatched to Kiev at once to assist them and on March 23rd, 1752 it was reported that they had accepted the offer.[67] Smaller groups followed and received lands to the east of Saint Elisabeth, but the Serbs in these settlements were apparently so few in number compared to the first group that they soon lost their identity whereas the St. Elisabeth Serbs were a recognized group well into the 19th century.

Maria Theresa of Austria started reconsidering the advisability of losing good potential border guards who might be induced to change from the Orthodox to the Catholic faith. Simultaneously the Ottoman Port protested the existence of these people, and the construction of a fort so close to their border, which they claimed violated the treaty of 1739.[68] Hence, there were no more large-scale movements of peoples to join the Russian service. After Khorvat in New Serbia, and Shevich and Preadovich in the region now called the Donbass which they named "Slaveno-Serbia".[69]

In the reign of Elisabeth the colony of "New Serbia" once again came to the attention of the authorities. In 1760 Khorvat reported that there were 283 people, mainly fleeing from Poland, working as day laborers for "New Serbia" for 2,838 rubles a year. He petitioned the Senate to allow him to turn these unfortunate people into serfs to save money. The Senate responded in a positive manner but stating that if they were Ukrainians they would have to submit of their own free will. The number of households was to be divided among the Serbs according to their rank.[70]

This incident was to prove to be the prologue to an even more fruitful one in the future. During the reign of Elisabeth it was decided to allow colonies of people of other Christian faiths settle in Russia. This started initially when individuals in the government such as the Chancellor, Bestuzhev-Riumin, noted the great contributions which the French Huguenots had made to the various countries in which they had settled after Louis XIV had revolked the Edict of Nantes in 1692 depriving them of their religious freedom. Some Huguenots did enter Russian service and suggested various schemes such as the creation of the silk industry in Russia (which failed) and the growing of grapes

216

in the south for the production of wine. Little came of these efforts since there were so few Huguenots in Russia and the government did not always provide the means to support their enterprises. By the end of the century Russia still depended upon imported raw silk for its own factories. But as late as 1748 Denmark had issued a manifesto inviting the Huguenots to settle in that country and had had a moderate success. On the 8th of June 1752 a French Huguenot, de Lafon (?), in Russian service, suggested to the Chancellor Bestuzhev-Riumin that the Russian government attempt to induce the immigration of Huguenots to stimulate the silk industry. He noted that the Protestant Huguenots in the regions of Nîmes and Carcassone in France were being persecuted and could be induced to move to Russia bringing their special skills with them. He suggested the notices be placed in appropriate foreign journals inviting them and that they, like the Serbs, be offered land in the rich Ukraine near Kiev. Bestuzhev-Riumin was attracted by the concept also, but he preferred to have settlers along the relatively unpopulated Volga where pirates were a problem. A report was sent to the empress who was likewise impressed and ordered that a committee be established to consider the matter. The commitee started to consider lands along the Volga suitable for such colonies.[71] Lafon reported that the Prussian appoach had been most successful in which complete religious freedom was guaranteed, freedom from taxes for a fixed period set, and the proximity of river transportation stressed.[72]

But as was the case with much in this reign the project was lost in the administrative process (probably with the empress herself) and was still there when the Seven Year's War broke out in 1756. This created a new situation since the war encompassed several large regions of Europe. Much of the fighting took place in Germany and many families were left destitute. Prussia was heavily affected by the war and the Huguenots there probably had second thoughts about the country in which they had settled. An impressive report was received from a Frenchman in Russian service, de Larivier, who had been sent into Germany to purchase horses for the Russian government. Here he found thousands of families suffering from the war that actually wanted "to settle in Russia by colonies".[73] His report was considered by the special Imperial Conference established to conduct the war on the 2nd of May, 1759. Larivier was instructed that when approached by such people to inform them that:

> ... as is known here all foreigners in whatever their own religion have complete freedom and are favored in everyway; then, of course, as in the past all will be accepted with all favor who have the zeal to come here, settle and to live, upon which the artisans will accept them in the guilds and the farmers will receive rich and abundant lands with the freedom for several years from all imposts and taxes, and this in order to be able to transfer and provide for all special assistance, but that for *the present distressing war* it is not possible to transfer them here from their fatherland since there is no sort of dependable means. [74]

Thus, the real origins of the Volga Germans predates Catherine.

******

Numerous measures were taken in the period of Elisabeth to improve the country or the general morals and welfare of the masses many of which were simply restatements of former laws which were being ignored. Peter the Great

218

had, for example, established a system of regular police for the cities and the localities. In the cities he used the Hamburg police system as his model. These police were subjected to the Magistrate in the cities where such existed or the local authorities in the countryside.[75] The ruler often gave these police direct orders for improvements, but in the reign of Elisabeth few of the police were of the younger age group and hence were becoming less effective.

There are a number of such orders given by the empress to the police for the beautification of the city of St. Petersburg. For example it was ordered that all refreshment shops be removed from the main streets of the city to the side streets to maintain the appearance of the important avenues.[76] Other types of shops with unpleasant appearance were likewise ordered to shift their entrances to side streets. The police were slow in enforcing this order so it had to be repeated in 1752 and 1758.[77] It is doubtful if these orders were ever carried through. In 1750 the empress ordered that a series of substandard buildings along the Fontanka River be torn down and nothing built there in the future.[78] In the same year orders were issued that trees not be thrown into the canals, for which St. Petersburg was called The Venice of the North.[79]

The government had made it policy to attempt to keep the lower classes out of the center of the cities. Anna had forced many of the fuel-using factories out of the center of St. Petersburg and Moscow. In connection with this policy there existed one of attempting to preserve the woods and wildlife in the immediate vicinity of these cities. Hence, factories were often required to move a distance of 200 kilometers (200 versts) from the city, to use wood only from a greater distance and under no circumstance destroy the good forest lands nearby.[80] In a partial effort to control the construction of factories in undesirable locations it was ordered that the Manufacturing College give prior approval.[81]

The cities had the eternal problem of beggars. The police were ordered to round up the men and put them to a use for which they were suited such as the army, returned to their owners or to serve as Court serfs. In addition, certain "free" retired lower servants or those incapable of work were sent away to the provinces. In May of 1750 all "base" people were ordered out of the "better" sections of St. Petersburg.[82] The police did maintain a sort of poor house, but it was so limited that it had no means of coping with the large numbers of poor drawn to the city.

The empress herself was given to bursts of charity which had both a religious and personal basis. Once she saw a poor woman with open sores begging on the streets and was greatly moved by it. As one English writer later noted:

> Indeed I have heard another reason alleged for the few lame and deformed people that appear in Petersburg. The Empress Elisabeth, it is said had so delicacy, that she could not bear to behold such persons; and therefore prohibited their appearing in the places where she chose to reside. This cause, however, now ceases to operate; nor have I heard that her present majesty [Catherine II] was ever afflicted with such aversions.[83]

One of the chief reasons that so few deformed persons were seen begging was that the empress Elisabeth, after seeing the ill woman, ordered the opening of an almshouse for these people in 1758.[84] Of course, this was only for St. Petersburg.

Public morals were another concern for the government and empress. For example the mixed bathing of the sexes in public bathes was outlawed twice during the reign.[85] This was an indication of the probable existence of prostitution. Another indication that this was a problem is to be found in the proposed law codes. In these codes the penalties were not severe. Women caught twice in prostitution were to be retained in curcumstances which appear to have been mild for the period and the time was not long.[86] When a house of prostitution was discovered it was to be closed at once. The person responsible for the operation of the house was to be punished by light whipping which was mild for the day. While a problem, this appears to have been one with which the government was not preoccupied.

As mentioned above gambling was at first outlawed everywhere except at court, but this was later modified to allow gambling for moderate stakes. If high stakes were involved the losing party had no obligation to pay.[87]

A series of measures were also directed to improving the order in the cities. During the winter especially around holiday seasons the nobles liked to race their triokas about the city very rapidly. They were ordered to travel at moderate speeds and to stay on the right side of the road.[88] Public cursing and moving about the cities in a state of intoxication were forbidden. Taverns were required to close at respectable hours.[89] It was not legal to keep bears in either Moscow or St. Petersburg since there was always the possibility of escape which could cause the authorities a great deal of trouble and endanger life.[90] The firing of weapons in the city and fisticuffs were also illegal.[91]

******

Secret police in one form or another seem to have been a part of the Russian heritage from at least the time of

Ivan the Terrible. The Law Code of 1649 (Ulozhenie) had established plots against the royal power or royal persons and inciting to riot as capital crimes. When Peter the Great carried through his famous reforms he encountered resistance, as his problems with the Streltsi and his own son indicate. To handle such problems Peter created a special chancellary named the Preobrazhenskii Prikaz to investigate such cases with the use of torture which was typical of the period. At the head of this dreaded body he placed the vicious figure of Andrei Ivanovich Ushakov (1672-1747) for whom terrible tortures to obtain evidence were routine. In 1731 Anna created her own secret police named the Kantseliariia Tainykh Rozyskhykh Del or in English The Secret Chancellary for Investigative Purposes headed again by the cruel Ushakov. It was directly responsible to the ruler alone and in the reign of Anna gained a terrible reputation. Its goal was to discover plots "about any evil plans against 'our person' " or "treason" and about disturbances and riots.[92] "Our person" included Biron and any of the persons, Russian or German, in favor with the court. Hence, with the high level of discontent the Chancellary had much work to keep it occupied. Misspelling by a clerk of the name of the empress or one of her titles could place a person under the jurisdiction of the Chancellary. But the general punishments in the reign of Anna were known for their severity. A woman who killed her husband was buried alive with her head above ground and lived for a full month as noted above. Two persons convicted of trying to start a revolt against her were placed on pikes--then one of the most painful methods of punishment.[93]

In the time of Peter the Great laws concerning crimes against the state were tightened and a new system intro- duced. Not only was a person guilty of treason or lesè majesté to be punished, but any party knowing about the attitude of the "criminal" was also subject to punishment. The accessory charge came to be known in Russian as

"Slovo i Delo", or word and deed. This placed innocent parties who heard a remark against the "ruling power" subject to punishment if they did not report it at once. This system, with the torture built in, became one of the true terrors of the period. It divided families and friends. In addition, the reign had started with the show trial of the "German party".

Elisabeth who inherited this unenlightened policy made some immediate changes. It was no longer a crime to misspell the name of the ruler or forget one of the titles. "Word and Deed" cases continued as before under the supervision of Ushakov, but few real plots were uncovered. A fourteen year old boy said "word and deed" (so it appears in the Russian original) while being lightly lashed by officials and immediately activated the hated Secret Chancellary. The inquiry which followed indicated that he had learned them from his mother who was then appropriately punished. Another typical case was that of a monk turned in by someone for complaining about the rule of "babi" or women in Russia. The investigation proved that he made the remark while under the influence of strong drink. He was ordered whipped and returned to his monastery while another monk who had overheard the remark but had not reported it was whipped and sent to Orenburg.[94] When Ushakov died in 1747 the Chancellary was placed in the hands of Alexander Shuvalov (1710-1771) the brother of Peter Shuvalov. This seems to have marked a turing point in the use of torture in Russia. The use of torture to discover where a person obtained a small quantity of vodka illegally was dropped in 1751.[95] It is generally agreed that in this period the tools of torture were used less and less often or not at all. This was a long step in the direction of the complete abolition of torture which took place in the reign of Catherine II and provides an example of another bridge between the two reigns.[96] Ikonnikov, who wrote the standard work on the abolition of torture, noted at the beginning of his work on its abolition in the reign of Catherine that it gradually was being abolished in practice and spirit during the reign of Elisabeth. Peter the third abolished the Secret Chancellary and the crime of "word and deed", but not lesè majesté or treason.[97]

In 1753 the penalties for political crimes were lightened. The wives of male convicts, who were branded, whipped and had their nostrels ripped before being sent into exile, were allowed to retain the estates of their husbands. Also, women criminals were freed from the ripping of the nostrels which marked a person for life as a criminal, but not from other forms of bodily punishment.[98]

******

One of the constant concerns in Russia from the development of populated communities was that of fires. Once out of control whole cities could be destroyed by just one careless act with fire. This was especially important in a colder country where heating fires were required during certain times of the year. Moscow and St. Petersburg had their periodic fires. The government was attempting to induce builders to utilize more bricks and stones to hinder these fires. This had been traditional policy for a number of years. As early as 1743 the empress ordered the construction of a brick yard near St. Petersburg in contradiction to the policy of keeping such works over 200 kilometers from the cities.[99] In 1752 Moscow suffered a severe fire which caused extensive damage. The Treasury together with the Magistrate and the Moscow Governor's Chancellary upon an Ukaz of the Senate ordered that prices were to be kept low--nobody was to make over 10 percent profit--for all essential materials. The price of grain and flour was fixed. Construction iron prices were set and the purchaser could obtain a thousand bricks for 2.50 rubles or less.[100] It is probable that Peter Shuvalov had much to do with this since this was the period in which his power was the greatest, and it was in just such matters that he interested himself. Several days later the empress ordered the police chief to insure that the city be rebuilt according to a uniform plan with wide streets to serve as fire gaps in the future. It was likewise ordered that anyone unable to afford the new plan be reimbursed by the government.[101] Further steps were taken to forbid the use of tar on roofs, removing shops such as forges which were fire hazards from the city and completely rebuilding the Kitai Gorod section of the city. The Senate and the empress repeatedly ordered governmental offices to keep water barrels filled on their roofs with tubes to stop fires before they could become dangerous.

Elisabeth had been given a good education by her father which inculcated in her a great respect for Russia's past. Hence, when fire destroyed the Troitsky Sobor church in St. Petersburg, she ordered it rebuilt exactly as it had been before the fire.[102] Later in 1759 during the war she also ordered that the walls of the Kremlin in Moscow be restored along with the towers and the Ivan clock exactly as they had been originally.[103] Catherine II, being German by origin, is said not to have had the same respect for Russia's past and at one time even considered destroying the walls of the Kremlin to build other structures, but was only prevented from doing so by the lack of funds.

While there were initiated a number of important projects and trends in Russia in the reign of Elisabeth few came to completion. Critics would attribute this to the laziness of the empress or her servants. But the true cause was the undying hatred of the empress for the king of Prussia which culminated in the Seven

Years' War. The war turned the attention of the empress and her progressive servants from the problems of improving Russia to winning the war.

NOTES

1 I.E. German, *Istoriia russkago Mezhevaniia*   (2nd ed.; Moscow: Rikhter, 1910), 155-57.

2 A.A. Golubev, 29-32.

3 German, 164-65.

4 *Ibid.*, 165-67.

5 *PSZ*, XIII, No. 9891. Senate. October 23, 1751. In this case the Don Cossacks were in conflict with the Volga Cossacks over fishing rights. In the forties they had had a similar conflict with the Zaporozhian Cossacks. Pronshtein, 27-31.

6 *PSZ*, XIII, No. 9932. Personal Manifesto. January 24, 1752. A reprint of this manifesto dating to 1776 is available in the Biblicthequé nationale in Paris.

7 Solov'ev, 23, 107-08.

8 *PSZ*, XIII, No. 9948. Personal Manifesto. February 28, 1752.

9 *Ibid.*, XIV, No. 10,237. Survey Instructions.   May 13, 1754.

10 *Sanktpeterburgskiia Vedomosti*,No. 91. Tuesday, November 15, 1754, 728. Here the Vochina or Estates College offered for sale two pieces of property of Isiia Shafirov.

11 German, 181-82.

12 *Ibid.*, 174.

13 *PSZ*, XIV, No. 10,360. Senate. February 16, 1755.

14 *Ibid.*, XIV, No. 10,402. Senate. May 5, 1755.

15 *Ibid.,* XIV, No. 10,429. Senate, on a signed order of the empress. July 6, 1755.

16 *Sanktpeterburgskiia Vedomosti,* No. 3. Tuesday, January 9, 1756.

17 *PSZ,* XIV, No. 10,518. Senate. March 7, 1756.

18 *Ibid.,* XIV, No. 10,549. Senate. May 4, 1756.

19 *Ibid.,* XIV, No. 10,669. Senate. December 11, 1756.

20 *Ibid.,* XV, No. 10,878. Senate. September 10, 1758.

21 *Ibid.,* XV, No. 11,065. Senate. June 6, 1760.

22 German, 183.

23 *Ibid.,* 181-222. For other views expressed about the surveys see: Paul Dukes, *Catherine the Great and the Russian Nobility. A Study Based on the Materials of the Legislative Commission of 1767* (Cambridge: Cambridge University Press, 1967), 126-28. Robert E. Jones, *The Emancipation of the Russian Nobility* (Princeton: Princeton University Press, 1973), 78. Some see the survey as the beginning of a new age in Russian administration. Yaney, 113.

24 V.N. Latkin. *Zakonodatel'nyia Kommissii v Rossii v XVIIIst.* (St. Petersburg: Panteleve, 1887) 1, 81-82.

25 *Ibid.,* 14-15.

26 *Ibid.,* 18.

27 *Ibid.,* 20-27.

28 *Ibid.,* 42-79.

29 *PSZ,* XIV, No. 10,274. Senate. August 12, 1754.

30 For a brief treatment of this code and its relation to that of Catherine see: Kerry R. Morrison, "Catherine II's Legislative Commission: An Administrative Interpretation",*Canadian Slavic Studies,* Vol. IV, 3 (Fall, 1970), 467-73.

31 *PSZ,* XIV, No. 10,283. Senate. August 24, 1754.

32 N.L. Rubinshtein, "Ulozhennaia Kommissiia 1754-1766gg.", *Istoricheskie Zapiski,* Vol. 38, 1951, 220.

33 *Arkhiv Kniazia Vorontsova,* V, 15. "Ce professeur étoit un homme de grand mérite".

34 Latkin, 85-89.

35 Shcherbatov, 68.

36 Latkin, 89-90.

37 Rubinshtein, 208-51.

38 Latkin, 90.

39 Rubinshtein, 208-51.

40 A.A. Vostokov (editor), *Proekty ugolovnago Ulozheniie 1754-1766 Godov. Novouloznennoi Knigi Chast' Vtoraia; O pozyshnykh Delakh i kakiia za raznyiia Zlodeistva i Prestupleniia Kazni, Nakazaniia i Shtrafy Polozheny.*With a forward by N.D. Sergeevskii (St. Petersburg, Stasiulevich, 1882), XIV. This information is provided in the introduction by the legal historian Sergeevskii.

41 V.N. Latkin (editor), *Proekt novago Ulozheniia Sostavlennyi Zakonodatel'noi ·Kommissei 1754-1766gg. (Chast' III, "O sostoiniiak Poddannykh Voobshche').* St. Petersburg: Tipografiia Odinochnoi Tiur'my, 1893. For some reason Rubinshtein did not use the Vostokov work when he wrote his article on the commission.

42 Vostokov, 18.

43 *Ibid.,* 76.

44 *Ibid.,* 27-29.

45 *Ibid.,* 148.

46 Hanway, I, 373.

47 M. de Saldern, Ambassadeur de Russie dans plusieurs cours de l'Europe, *Histoire de la vie de Pierre III, Empereur de toutes les Russies, Presantent, sous un aspect important, les causes de la révolution arriveé en 1762* (Francfort-sur-le-Main: Chez Frédéric Esslinger, An X, 1802), 13. This is a defense of Peter III but containing many factual errors like the one given in the text.

48 Latkin, *Proekt,* 119.

49 *Ibid.,* 120-21. The rights of the religious over their serfs were to be likewise limited.

50 *Ibid.,* 33-84.

51 *Sanktpeterburgskiia Vedomosti,* No. 51. Tuesday 26th of June, 1761.

52 *PSZ,* XV, No. 11,335. Senate. September 29, 1761. Rubinshtein, 228.

53 PSZ, XV, No. 11,378. Senate. December 8, 1761.

54 Latkin, *Zakonodatel'nyia,* 102,27.

55 *Ibid.,* 169-70.

56 Rubinshtein, 230.

57 *Ibid.,* 248-49.

58 Romanovich-Slavatinskii, 163.

59 *Ocherki Istorii SSSR. Period Feodalizma. Rossiia v pervoi Chetverti XVII v. Preobrazovaniia Petra*

(Moscow: Akademiia Nauk, 1954), 622, 674.

60 *Ibid.,* 529-30.

61 *Sovetskaia Istoricheskaia Entsiklopediia* (Moscow: Sovetskaia Entsiklopediia, 1965), Vol. 6, 965-66. *Entsiklopedicheskii Slovar* (St. Petersburg: Brokgauz-Efron, 1895), Vol. LIV (27), 317. G. Kogol'nichan, "Petr Veliki na beregakh Pruta," *Zhurnal Ministerstva Narodnago Proshcheviia,* LIII (January 1847) Otdel II, 111-23.

62 Solov'ev, 16, 453. *PSZ,* IV, No. 2413. Most Highly Affirmed Answer to the Petition of Prince Kantemir. July 31, 1711. In this law the term "raznochintsy" is to be found for the first time.

63 *Senatskii Arkhiv,* VIII,402. December 26-27, 1751.

64 *Ibid.,* 402-15.

65 *Ibid.*

66 *Ibid.,* 415-16. January 4, 1752.

67 *Ibid.*

68 *Ibid.,* 681-92. September 22, 1752.

69 N.A. Popov, "Voenyia Poseleniia Serbov V Avstrii I Rossii ",*Vestnik Evropy,*6 (June, 1870), 604-11. "Izvestie o Pokhozhdenii Simeona Stepanovicha Syna Pischevicha", *Chteniia v Obshchestve Istorii i Drevnostei Rossiiskikh,* Vol. II, 1883, 483-561.

70 *PSZ,* XV, No. 11, 058. Senate. May 10, 1760. This order was not written with clarity.

71 Grigorii Pisarevskii, "Iz Istorii inostrannoi Kolonizatsii v Rossii v XVIIIv. (Po neizdannym arkhinym Dokumentam)",*Zapiski Moskovskago Arkheologecheskago Instituta,* Vol. V, 1909, 30-32.

72 *Ibid.,* 34-36.

73 *Ibid.,* 43.

74 *Ibid.,* 44. Underlining author's.

75 Gote, 197-222. Kostomarov, III, 6.

76 *PSZ,* IX, No. 8674. Personal. December 2, 1742.

77 *Ibid.,* XIII, No. 10,032. Personal. October 14, 1752. *Ibid.,* XV, No. 10,904. Senate, in consequence of a personal order. December 11, 1758.

78 *Ibid.,* XIII, No. 9788. Personal to the Police Chief Tatishchev. July 27, 1750.

79 *Ibid.,* XIII, No. 9792. Senate. August 27, 1750.

80 *Ibid.,* XII, No. 9438. Senate. September 3, 1747. *Ibid.,* XV, No. 10,914. Senate. January 12, 1759.

81 *Ibid.,* XIII, No. 9889. Senate. October 15, 1751.

82 L.N. Semenova, "Pravitel'stvo i rabochii Liud Peterburga v pervoi Polovine XVIII Veka", *Vnutrenniaia Politika Tsarizma (Seredina XVI-Nachalo XXv)* (Leningrad: "Nauka," 1967), 134-36.

83 William Richardson, *Anecdotes of the Russian Empire in a Series of Letters Written a Few Years Ago, from St. Petersburg* (London: Frank Cass & Co. Ltd., 1783), 201-02.

84 *PSZ,* XV, No. 10,824. Senate in consequence of a Personal Order. April 13, 1758.

85 *Ibid.,* XI, No. 8842. Senate. December 21, 1743. *Ibid.,* XV, No. 11,094. Senate. August 31, 1760.

86 Vostokov, *Proekty,* 169-70.

87 *PSZ,* XII, No. 9380. Senate. March 11, 1747.   The Senators opposed this law but were forced to

approve it. Later the "compromise" appeared in a lead editorial to *Sanktpeterburgskiia Vedomosti,* No. 51. Tuesday the 26th of June, 1761.

88 *PSZ,* XIV, No. 10,679. Personal. December 31, 1756. Since this law was repeated nearly each subsequent year it was apparently little obeyed. Kostomorov, III, 19.

89 *PSZ,* XV, No. 11,017. Personal. December 20, 1759.

90 *Ibid.,* XIII, No. 9959. Personal to the Police Chief. March 13, 1752.

91 Kostomorov, III, 19.

92 V.I. Veretenikov, *Iz Istorii Tainoi Kant-seliarii. 1731-1762gg. Ocherk.* (Kharkov, 1911), 3-22.

93 S.A. Gol'tsev, *Zakonodatel'stvo i Nravy v Rossii XVIII Veka.* (2nd ed.; St. Petersburg: Iakobson, 1896), 50. Got'e, 412.

94 A.V. Arsen'ev, "Nepristoinyia Rechi. (Iz Del Preobrazhenskogo Prikaza i Tainoi Kantseliarii XVIII Veka)", *Istoricheskii Vestnik,*Vol. 69,July, 1897, 68-70.

95 *PSZ,* XIII, No. 9912. Senate. November 28, 1751.

96 N.B. Goikova, "Organy politicheskogo Syska i ikh Razvitie v XVII-XVIII vv.", *Absoliutizm v Rossii (XVII-XVIIIvv)* (Moscow: Akademiia Nauk, 1963), 269. V.S. Ikonnikov, *Stranitsa iz Istorii eka-terininskogo Nakaza. (Ob Otmene Pytki v Rossii)* (Kiev: Zavadskii, 1890), 1-3.

98 Got'e, 197-200. Kostomorov, III, 6.

99 *PSZ,* XI, No. 8746. Personal. June 11, 1743.

100 *Ibid.*, XIII, No. 10,000. June 17, 1752.

101 *Ibid.*, XIII, No. 10,003. Personal to the Police Chief. June 30, 1752.

102 "K   Istorii   Postoroiki   St.   Petersburgskago Troitskogo Sobora", *Russkaia Starina,* Vol. 148, November, 1911, 426.

103 *PSZ,* XV, No. 10,958. Personal. May 24, 1759.

CHAPTER EIGHT

WAR AND THE STATE

Several times references have been made to the Seven Years' War in regard to its effects on some aspect of the development of Russia. It is sad to note the number of times Russia went to war for just or unjust reasons, but it seems to be a part of human nature to solve problems by resorting to military force. Of the Romanovs only Peter II and Alexander III managed to avoid war.

The causes of the Seven Years' War have been debated at length and there has been no final decision as to the "guilty" party in initiating it.[1] Actually the Russian negative attitude towards Frederick the Great played a large role in its outbreak, but it is really not correct to blame it soley on this factor since Austria, France, England and Prussia all shared the blame as well. As indicated previously Russia was one of the few powers maintaining the Pragmatic Sanction which guaranteed the Hapsburg holdings to Maria Theresa. This had been the policy of Ostermann and it was also the policy of the Grand Chancellor, A. Bestuzhev-Riumin. Having spent several years in the service of the British, Bestuzhev understood well the intricacies of international relations and the problem of the Balance of Power. This fact is often missed by person writing on the origins of the war. The English had likewise supported the Pragmatic Sanction. The French had induced the Swedish government to initiate a war with Russia to keep that country occupied so that it could not intervene as the French and their numerous German allies, including Frederick, tried unsuccessfully to divide the Hapsburg holdings. Frederick, like the French, thought that the victory of Elisabeth in 1741 was favorable news, but both were soon disabused of their anticipation. As early as 1742 Elisabeth ordered the movement of troops into the Baltic States in preparation for a possible campaign against Frederick.[2] As soon as the Swedish War ended and Frederick made a temporary truce with Maria Theresa relations seemed normal and the tradition gifts were traded between the Russian and Purssia courts.

But relations between the two courts then took a marked turn for the worse for reasons still under debate. Perhaps, as some say, it was the influence of Bestuzhev-Riumin, but this alone seems unconvincing. There were several other factors which might explain the deterioration of relations between the two courts. Frederick broke his truce with Maria Theresa when she seemed to be doing too well against her other enemies. The fact that Elisabeth and Maria Theresa were both women and the only women rulers at the time, must have played some role in the attitude of sympathy between the courts--even this the French tried unsuccessfully to destroy.

There was the problem created by the "giant soldiers" given by Peter and Anna to Frederick's father. By 1742 they were aging and the Russian ambassador in Potsdam was flooded with requests that they be allowed to return to die in Russia and be buried in Orthodox soil.[3] Frederick could easily have acquisced without any real loss, but for some unknown reason he refused claiming that they had been given to his father outright without conditions and he would not return them. In view of the religious attitudes of the new empress this was a gross error. Then the empress was informed, perhaps by Bestuzhev-Riumin, that Frederick did not go to church and held skeptical attitudes towards established religions.

Matters became very strained in 1746 when Frederick absolutely refused to return the old giant soldiers.[4] In addition in that year the sister of Frederick married the future king of Sweden who had been selected by Elisabeth herself, but now the possibility of an alliance between Sweden and Prussia became an obsession with the Russian court. In late 1745 the Russian diplomatic corp abroad was instructed to report their perception of Prussian power and the Balance of Power. On May 22, 1746 a famous treaty was concluded between St. Petersburg and Vienna in which there were two parts. The first called for non-aggression whereas the second which was secret stated that when the time became proper the two courts, hopefully with the support of England, would attack Frederick to regain Silesia and Glats taken by him from Maria Theresa. This secret clause meant an aggressive war started by both when conditions were deemed proper.[5]

Before signing the treaty the empress resorted to a meeting of her top advisors which she did when especially difficult situations arose. On the 11th of August, 1746, at Peterhoff Bestuzhev-Riumin, Prince Kurakin, Graf Rumiantsev, General-Procurator of the Senate Prince Trubetskoi, General Buturlin, General-Prince Repnin, General Apraksin, Lieutenant-General Peter Shuvalov and Secret Advisor Baron Cherkasov gathered to consider the treaty and the problem of Prussia. From the composition of the meeting it is doubtful that one person such as Bestuzhev-Riumin could have controlled the outcome. The reports from the embassies were read, other related documents including some in German were considered. All the reports were anti-Prussian and a long discussion took place which lasted until the next day. As might be expected all the decisions regarding Prussia were negative.[6] Hence, the collision course was set which was to culminate in the Seven Years' War.

In 1750 a sort of cold war started between Russia and Prussia when the empress recalled her ambassador from Potsdam without the customary leave-taking. Frederick could only respond by recalling his ambassador after which diplomatic relations between the two countries ceased.[7] To complicate matters Sweden and Russia came close to open warfare over actions by the Swedish crown which the Russians considered threatening. But the Swedes backed off and the situation normalized. Thus, Russia had broken diplomatic relations with both France and Prussia, but not with the other courts.

At this point the internal situation in Russia came to play a leading role. It will be recalled that the empress had asked for an accounting and had not been able to ascertain income and expenditure for the period 1742-1747. She was concerned about expenses in wartime. In 1750 the reforms of Peter Shuvalov started and soon the government appeared to be in the black for a change. This was why it was possible to open the state bank and capitalize it with silver and gold. The situation was especially good by 1756 and there had been a series of years of good harvests after the mini-famines of 1749-1750. Hence, from the standpoint of the empress this was a "good" time to start a war.

There were a number of warnings earlier that had gone largely unheeded. The English ambassador to St. Petersburg writing as early as 1750 noted that there was a high likelihood of a war between Russia and Prussia:

> When I consider, how greatly the Empress is provoked against this court [Prussia], I am much more afraid of trouble beginning on that side than with Sweden; for, from the chicaneries and rude proceedings towards each other, we may see them come to blows, when it will be least thought or expected. [8]

In July of 1753 the English ambassador quoted others as having heard the empress state with pleasure in her eyes

238

"that there was nothing she desired more, than to be at war with that prince [Frederick]"[9] In June of 1755 an article appeared in the official monthly journal based upon English reports about the outbreak of fighting in the New World which was taken by the writer as a signal that a general European war was about to start.[10] Apparently in late 1755 or early 1756 the empress decided that the time was ripe to "attack the king of Prussia". The first mentioned written reference to this decision is dated March 30, 1756 o.s.[11] A special executive council named the Conference was established for the purposes of conducting the war. In theory the empress was to preside over it, but it is doubtful if she attended many of its later meetings as her illness grew worse. The Senate became an executive for it. Shakhovskoi, the head of the Synode and later the Senate, was appointed to handle the provisioning of the military since the empress trusted his honesty.

It will be recalled that the income for the Russian government in 1756 was approximately 11.6 million rubles which was very favorable. The anticipated initial costs of the war based upon the calculations of the Senate appear to have been 6,683,96[0] rubles which meant that slightly less than five million was to be allocated for the other aspects of the expenses of the government.[12] The Conference and the Senate were occupied with problems of forage, food for the troops and crossing Poland to reach East Purssia to pursue the war. The Austrians were at once informed and replied as rapidly as they could, which took sometime in that period, that their army would not be ready for action until the next year. The Conference then had to put all operations except maintainance on hold. But before this action was taken Frederick could hardly have missed the build-up of a massive Russian army in the Baltic States and its preparations for major action. Thus, he panicked and signed an alliance with the British, which, in passing, annulled a similar alliance Russia had with England. Then the Austrian Foreign Minister, the astute

Kaunitz, engineered the famous diplomatic revolution which made Austria, France and later Russia allies against Frederick. But Russia did not and would not war with England. War broke out when Frederick siezed Saxony in the fall of 1756 because he suspected it was an ally of Austria. Thus, started he Seven Years' War which was to damage the Russian economy and cause unbelievable chaos within the country.

******

The question poses itself at this point concerning the status of the Russian military forces on the eve of the war. There was one significant change in this reign which proved to be lasting: that is, the shift from foreign commanders to Russians. After the defeat on the Narva in 1700 when foreign officers deserted leaving the soldiers leaderless, Peter determined that he would train Russians to fill the commanding posts. At the battle of Poltava Peter himself was in command with his favorite Menshikov second. Foreigners were utilized for secondary roles. This was one of the motivating forces behind his requirement that all the male nobles had to serve the state as long as they were able to do so. In addition, he created schools to train them in such matters as mathematics and naval affairs In the reign of Anna foreigners held nearly all the important positions in the Russian military. The case of Münnich has already been mentioned. In the Swedish war at the beginning of the reign Lacy (1678-1751) replaced the disgraced Münnich and his second in command was the Jacobite, Keith. But with the advent of Elisabeth and her attack upon the "German party" many of the foreigners started to leave Russian service. While Lacy remained in Russian service until his death, his son took service with Austria where he rose to the rank of Marshal and was one of the few friends of the tragic emperor, Joseph II. With the death of Lacy senior in 1751 the command definitely shifted to the Russians. There were, indeed, still many foreigners in lower positions. Frederick realized that the departure of many officers with experience in Russia presented him with a real opportunity to obtain expertice in case of a war with Russia. He did hire a number of Germans and Jacobites leaving Russia into his service. In 1744 Manstein took service with Frederick and the Prussian king desired to obtain his views on the Russian military capabilities. He suggested to Manstein that one Prussian soldier could easily take on four or five Russians alone. Manstein replied that one Prussian would have difficulty with one Russian soldier.[13] Frederick replied by losing his composure and stating that their officers were poor. When the Jacobite Keith took service with Frederick and was asked the same question he was surprised when Keith praised the Russian army. Frederick replied: "The Russian army is a wild hord; they are not capable of fighting ordered troops". Keith politely replied: "It is obvious, your highness, you will shortly learn their wildness". [14] Keith, a friend of Lacy senior, was killed during the Seven Years' War and his body was spotted on the battle field by Lacy junior who ordered that he be given a decent burial according to his religion.

In 1732 the government of Anna upon the advise of Münnich opened a special school for the nobles from about 11-17 to train them in military matters. About two hundred students were taught a curriculum which mixed the liberal arts with a military training. They were the same Cadet Corp which helped found the Russian theater in St. Petersburg. It produced several generations of good officers before obligatory state service was ended in 1762. The highly critical Locatelli considered it poor as he did all things Russian.[15] The best witness as to its value was the English ambassador to St. Petersburg, Colonel Guy Dickens, who as the name implies, knew a good deal about military matters. Once fantastic rumors so frequent in this period started curculating that the fun-loving empress planned to enter a convent and that singers, dancers and domestic servants were receiving commissions in the army. The normally pragmatic British government believed these incredible stories and asked Dickens for his view on the subject. He was blunt:

> I am much surprised at another intelligence your grace received, viz-t: that singers, dancers and domestic servants have commissions in the army. Since I came here, there has not been any one instance of such persons being employed in a military capacity. They have, here, a foundation which does not yield to any in Europe for the education of youth and what is called the *cadets corps*. The number which is constantly kept there is between three and four hundred; the greater part of whom are, chiefly, of the best families in the Empire. They have there, not only a complete military-education from the age of ten to seventeen or eighteen, but learn foreign languages, as, french and german. It is from this corps of cadets, that the vacancys are filled up, and I can truely (sic) say, I never saw anywhere a prettier corps of subalterns, capitans and field officers than they have here; it were to be wished they had in proportion as many good generals to command the fine and numerous army they have.[16]

Subsequent events proved how correct he was in his analysis. It was the initiative of the junior officers and the courage of the soldiers of the line that enabled the Russian army to repeatedly maul the Prussian army. As he indicated with few exceptions the senior officers proved

242

to be substandard. It was not until the younger generation moved up and replaced the older generals that figures like Suvorov emerged.

Some of the officers were trained at home by tutors. Usually such future officers came from wealthy and influential families and received rank at an early age although they did not report for duty until about eighteen. There was a preference for the military over the civil service since Peter the Great had decreed that the military ranks receive double the pay of the civil. However, often persons in the civil service held military rank which raised their pay. But in general, except during actual combat, the life of the officer was not difficult. The nobles were allowed to take wagons and servants with them on campaign. Bolotov is a good example. On the first Prussian campaign he was extremely disappointed that the junior officers could have only one wagon with their goods.[17] Of course, this did not apply to the commander, the incompetent Apraksin, whose baggage train looked like a city of wheels.[18] Bolotov was allowed to use two serfs as servants one of whom he sent back to his estate periodically to collect money and goods to support his lifestyle.[19]

The army used against Frederick was very large about the level of the armies Peter the Great used against Charles XII. In the Swedish war of 1741-43 the Russians had 17,500 men facing 17,000 Swedish troops. In 1757 when the Russian army crossed the border of Poland in the direction of East Prussia it consisted of 134,000 troops of whom 99,000 were infantry, 19,000 mounted and 16,000 irregulars.[20]

In contrast the fleet was in terrible condition. It had been allowed to decay over the years by rulers lacking the committment of Peter the Great. In 1748 the Admiralty College asked the Grand Chancellor to inform the empress of the situation.   Four years later when Shuvalov was at

243

the height of his power the naval school underwent a major reorganization and followed the lines of the Cadet Corp.[21] There existed a great need for officers in the Russian navy but the nobles much preferred the land service. This, in part, reflected the condition of the fleet.

According to Büsching in 1745 Russia had one ship with 114 guns (but he provided no crew size), one with 90 guns and 800 sailors with 3 decks, a 76 gunner with 550 sailors, 12 ships of 66 guns and crews of 407 each, one of 60 guns and eight with 50 guns and 350 sailors. Most of these ships were in poor condition having been built between 1731 and 1744. There were only 80 rowing galleys in contrast to the 160 which Peter used in his campaigns.[22] thus, the fleet needed more care as well as more qualified officers. In 1749 the Admilarty College requested funds to construct 112 ships in the years 1749-1750 but could obtain only money and men for twenty-nine.[23] In May of 1750 the Senate ordered that the galley fleet be built up to the level of 130 ships in the face of the threat of a war with Sweden.[24] This was followed by an order to send all prisoners who would normally have been executed to Rogevik which apparently was the main ship-building center.[25] It seems that the situation was improved somewhat in that many of the old rotting ships had been decommissioned and a few new ones constructed, but actually the overall naval situation had not improved greatly by 1757.[26] This was in marked contrast to the army. But it must be recalled that Russia and England had been on excellent terms and the Russian planners probably expected British help in case of a war. Instead they got neutrality at best.

******

In 1757 the Russian field army under the command of Apraksin moved across Poland into East Prussia where it easily defeated the army despatched by Frederick to stop

244

it. The Russians then really had East Prussia in their control when for some reason not clear, Apraksin ordered a withdrawal. From a reading of the Senate archives it is evident that he had an irrational obsession with a shortage of forage and especially feared that other shortages a long distance from the supplies in the Baltic States might be disasterous to the Russian army. Another story is provided by Büsching, upon which much doubt has been thrown as a consequence of the time framework, that the Grand Chancellor, Bestuzhev-Riumin warned him to withdraw since the empress had what appeared to be a very serious stroke and a change in the government favorable to Frederick was imminent.[27] The rapid recovery of the empress led to a serious change in leadership. Apraksin was immediately fired and placed under investigation where he died from fright. The Austrians protested the retreat as well. This was a factor in the downfall of the Grand Chancellor in the next year. But the empress ordered the army to take East Prussia which it proceeded to obey and where it was to remain until 1762. According to some sources the Russian soldiers, especially the irregulars, treated the inhabitants without mercy.[28] They were ordered to treat the local people in the same horrible manner in which Frederick had treated the Saxons in the previous year.

Peter Shuvalov, whose name appears frequently the latter part of the reign, made a contribution in a completely unexpected field. People working under his direction developed a new artillery weapon which caused great controversy. this was the "Shuvalov howitzer" which was conically shaped and was capable of firing small missiles of many types. Its range was about twice that of existing cannons and it could be used to cover attacking troops since it was the first weapon that could fire directly over the heads of the advancing troops upon the enemy-probably a consequence of its range. Not a large number of them were ever made and the soldiers trained to use them had to take a strict oath of secrecy concerning them.[29] It is difficult to judge just how advanced this new weapon was. Western military historians unacquainted with Russian ignore it while Russian military historians, even of the pre-revolutionary school, have a high regard for the weapon. Their consensus is that it was premature and thus not suited to its time.[30] After the death of the empress they were dropped from the army. Despite the small number of these weapons some of the victories of the Russian army were attributed to this weapon.[31] In 1758 Frederick captured several of these weapons and put them on display in Berlin to the chagrin of Shuvalov.[32] The plans were thereupon forwarded to the Austrian government by Shuvalov himself in a letter in excellent French signed by "Piere comte de Schouwalow" addressed to "Madam" or Maria Theresa.[33]

Shuvalov wanted an extensive reform of the higher military schools and put forth several suggestions which could not be put into practice as a consequence of the outbreak of the Seven Years' War.[34] Like Peter the Great he considered the artillery to be one of the most important components in the military. In 1757 he reformed the artillery school by bringing in better instructors and in 1759 even obtained a typograph for the reorganized school.[35] Still even in 1762 it had only 132 students in it.[36]

******

The far most important problem which faced the court was finding the monetary means to carry on the war. The Russian state, as was the case with most of the states with the possible exception of England, underwent serious financial strain during a war. Louis XIV had stated that the country winning a war was the one having the last silver piece in its possession. The record of the Russian state was rather poor in this regard. Peter the Great had forced the recources out of the state by strong means. Anna's feeble attempts at reform as will be recalled were twarted by her two wars and the lack of money to carry them through. The Seven Years' War was no exception.

As was the tradition the taxes were raised very rapidly. Vodka and salt were the earliest to be affected. The State serfs had an additional one ruble added to their dues so they were paying 1.7 rubles a year.[37] Later even the raznochintsy were required to pay a tax of one ruble a year.[38] Notices were sent to all local officials receiving money for the government that they sent it at once to the treasury or report it at least.

Once again Peter Shuvalov enters the picture. Noting the worsening finances he suggested that the copper coins be reduced from the heavier weight (five rubles to the pud) to .92 copecks to the kilogram (16 rubles to the pud). Later he suggested that the amount of copper in the coins be dropped even further to 1.95 rubles to the kilogram (32 rubles to the pud), but fortunately this was ignored until the reign of Peter III who used this unfortunate rate briefly.[39] One of the reasons that the government emitted so much copper money was not only to raise its own income for the war, but also to try to attract the silver and gold money out of circulation to be used for purchases of needed goods abroad. Hence, much encouragement was given to people to trade in the valuable metals for the copper pieces coming from the mints.

Shuvalov made another suggestion at the very outset of war. He proposed to establish a special bank capitalized upon the new copper money loaning at an unknown interest for the purpose of establishing a special "Observation Corps" of 30,000 special reserves. It was created and the Corps as well, but the Observation Corps played no useful role in the war. The government then had to take control over the copper supplies to insure that the value of that metal would remain high to support its

247

policies.[40] Shuvalov and other nobles were the chief beneficiaries of the loans of this bank.

As the situation became more desperate Shuvalov again made a suggestion to assist the artillery section. He noted the large number of outdated cannons made of copper and otherwise useless, and suggested they be used to fund a second bank in 1760.[41] The first bank, the Copper Bank, was in operation since 1758 and must have been a moderate success if Shuvalov thought that a second bank could be established. This was also justified on the grounds of stimulating commerce which had been little affected by the war. In the reign of Elisabeth the cannon bank was not a great success, but Catherine continued using the old cannons for money well into her reign.[42] It clearly took a long time to process the old cannons.

The mine at Kolyvano-Vosnenskii which was producing silver and gold in significant quantities by this time was not producing that for purposes of producing money or revenue for the state, rather it went into the privy purse of the empress. As the situation became more and more desperate the empress finally opened the privy purse and released 16.380 metric tons (1000 puds) of silver.[43] Most of this silver went to Königsburg to be issued as high probe silver coins with the picture of the empress on one side and the Prussian coat of arms on the other.[44] By this means the Russians hoped to take out of curculation the lower silver probe coins of Frederick.

As the financial situation became more critical the Conference considered the issuance of paper money as was being successfully done in England. At first it appears that Peter Shuvalov opposed this recalling John Law's scheme and claiming that the Russian people would not accept it.

But he was convinced otherwise and became one of its advocates.[45] thus, in 1760 the government issued about one million rubles in the form of "printed ukazes" or paper money. They were intended to be term notes good for a year and bearing 6 percent interest.[46] Soon thereafter it was ordered that these be circulated like regular money and that they must be accepted by all in payment of debt except the state bank which would only accept silver and gold.[47] Peter III ordered five million more issued, but this was not achieved before his "death" in 1762 and Catherine II cancelled the plan.[48] Thus, the first paper money in Russia was issued during the reign of Elisabeth and not Catherine. It is clear where Catherine obtained her financial ideas. Combining the copper and cannon banks of Shuvalov with the paper money of Elisabeh she had the basis for her assignat bank.

******

While he economy continued to deteriorate the war itself followed a course favorable to Russia. Austria was fighting very hard with mixed results. The French were for all practical purposes put out of the land war by their defeat at Rossbach in 1757. But while the Russians and the Prussians fought several very bloody battles Frederick was unable to achieve his chief goal of running them off the battlefield. Once he was nearly totally defeated.

One factor annoyed all the parties in the war except, of course, Russia and that was the Russian occupation of East Prussia. The treaty of 1746 had made no mention of what compensation Russia was to receive in case of the defeat of Frederick. But the Russians acted in East Prussia as if they had every intention of staying, - which they did. They issued special money for the region. The people there, including the philosopher Kant, were forced to take an oath of allegiance to the Russian empress. In addition, in 1760 in a sudden lunge the Russian army took the city of Berlin which was an extreme humiliation for Frederick even though the troops stayed only briefly and did not loot the city upon the payment of 1.5 million thalers. Needless to say this caused a real sensation in Europe.[49]

It was clear that the retention of East Prussia became one of the major aims of the Russians for, as was indicated, such retention was a way of insuring that the ambitions of the Prussian king would be restrained and his power greatly reduced. This argument was very cleverly developed and presented to the Austrians and French in 1760 with the personal approval of the empress.[50] The other powers realized that this would cause an imbalance in the Balance of Power in favor of the Russian which was as undesirable as a powerful Prussia. But as after World War II there was really not much choice but to permit it or to fight another war against Russia in the name of the Balance of Power. It was noted that Frederick had stated that he would prefer to die behind the last standing wall in his country before he would give up East Prussia. Such a fate for her enemy would have given the Russian empress the greatest of pleasure. This was one of the chief reasons that it became difficult to end the war when the resources of all the powers were seriously depleted. But in 1760 in an interview with the Austrian ambassador, Joseph Esterhazy, the empress told him:

> I do not make up my mind quickly on any-
> thing, but once I decide there is no
> changing my decision. I will continue the
> war with the allies even if it is necessary
> for me to sell half of the dresses and dia-
> monds.[51]

While the attitude of the empress was unchanging that of

other persons in high positions was. In particular a major turning point was the replacement of Bestuzhev-Riumin in 1758 by the more flexible, if less experienced, M.L. Vorontsov. The new Chancellor did not share the same hatred towards Prussia as the empress and to a lesser extent his predecessor. Vorontsov recognized the extent to which the war was ruining the state. In addition, it was clear after the stroke of 1757 that the empress was dying and had little interest in small routine matters. She simply wanted to win the war.

The state was also being deprived of manpower. This author estimates that from official figures between 1754 and 1759 about 231,664 "souls" in their prime were drafted for the war.[52] In 1759 Peter Shuvalov worked out a system of regular drafts, but it is doubtful if any people were drafted under his system. The last draft of the reign appears to have been in 1759 since in 1761 the authorities were trying to obtain the recruits called up in 1759.[53]

Since the field army was out of the country it was very difficult to maintain order inside. Catherine later claimed that 100,000 church serfs were about to take up arms. The factories were the scenes of growing disorders, and robbery was increasing in the countryside. Generally there was much discontent among the lower classes and one could almost feel that a general rising was in the not-too-distant future. Conditions within the country can only be described as chaotic.

The government was running a much greater deficit than normal. In 1760 civil servants getting half of their assigned salaries were considered lucky. The soldiers in the field were owed some 300,000 rubles.[54] It was clear that this situation could not continue. But with Russia holding tightly to East Prussia and Maria Theresa desiring to have at least part of her beloved Silesia returned, it was exceedingly difficult to initiate peace negotiations.

Despite the fact that some considered the Chancellor, M.L. Vorontsov, to be limited in his abilities, he seemed to have realized better than the other members of the government how critical the situation really was. By the end of 1760 he was willing to face the situation directly. He therefore composed a report for his government and the allied governments which he presented to the Conference on November 10, 1760.[55] He then passed it on to the Austrians where it appears in their archives in the handwriting of the secretary of Vorontsov entitled: "Reflections sur l'Etat actuel des Affairs politiques, et militaries, et sur quel fondement il est possible de farie presentement la paix sans une plus longue continuation de la Guerre.".[56] In his report Vorontsov simply stated that there was no money left for the war and that the war had already cost the Russian government forty million rubles in silver and gold much of which had gone out of the country thus adding to the internal chaos. He noted that the financial condition of Austria was similar and that peace was essential.

The Russians could not even take care of the veterans from the war who were no longer able to serve as a consequence of injuries suffered during the war. The monasteries did not want them. Therefore the Senate had to order that special houses be established in some Gubernia supported by local funds and supposedly benefitting from the lower price of grain.[57] Efforts were made to establish a lottery to obtain money for these people which appears to have been a moderate success.[58] Yet nearly a million rubles went into the construction of the winter palace and it is estimated that the costs of the court were about 2.65 million rubles in 1762.[59] Thus, palaces and diamonds seem to have had priority over the suffering people who had served their country, which itself, was near the point that it could no longer take the burdens of war without some type of internal explosion.

Thus, the determination of the Russian empress was the

chief block to peace. Only her death allowed the policy to be changed. One curious dilemma arises out of this situation. The empress must have known that her chosen successor, Peter, was actually pro-Prussian and would reverse her policy upon her death. She must certainly have been aware that her own death was impending, although it was a practice of the time to try to ignore death. Funeral processions were not allowed to pass the palace, for example. But given the level of hatred of the empress for Frederick and the known inclination of Peter in his favor, the empress certainly could have taken some measure to insure a continuation of her policy. She had the sole right to select her successor and had selected Peter. But she also had the power to replace him with a regency of some sort for his supposed son, Paul. The answer seems to reside in the very strong attachment which she had for her family and the memory of her dead sister Anna whose only son, Peter, had a stronger claim to the throne than that of the empress herself since the will of her mother, Catherine I, placed Anna and her offspring before Elisabeth.

On the other hand to attribute the change in Russian policy completely to the whims of Peter III would also be folly. The state was in such terrible condition that he had little choice but to end the long and costly war.[60] Not to have done so could have led to an immediate palace revolution in favor of Paul or his mother, Catherine. Thus, when the empress died on December 25 o.s. the "miracle of the house of Hohenzollern" took place partly out of the change of rulers and partly out of necessity.

NOTES

1 Herbert Kaplan, *Russia and the Outbreak of the Seven Years' War.* Berkeley: University of California Press, 1968.

2 "Winch to the right honourable lord Carteret. No. 126. Moscow, June 21, 1742. Doneseniia i Drugi Bumagi angliiskikh Poslov, Poslannikov i Rezidentov pri russkom Dvore s 7 marta 1741 g. po iiulia 1742g.", *SIRIO,* Vol. 91, 503-04.

3 "Russkie Soldaty v Prussii. Iz Donoseniia Graf P.G. Chernysheva, nashego Posla pri prusskom Dvory, ot 28 sent 1742.", *Russkii Arkhiv,* No. 7, 1866, 1539-1541.

4 Sovo'ev, Vol. 22, 406. *Sbornik moskovskago glavnago arkhiva Ministerstva Inostrannykh Del.*Vypusk I (Moscow, 1880), 172-73.

5 Louis-Olivier de Maconnay, *Lettre d'un voyageur actuellement à Dantzig a un ami de Stralsand sur la guerre qui viet de s'Allumer dans l'Empire,* Traduction libre de l'Allemand (n.p.: MDCCLVII), VIII. The author defends Frederick and blamed the entire war on Maria Theresa apparently totally unaware of Russian actions. The secret clause in the treaty was known by the author which means that it was known by 1757.

6 *Arkhiv Kniazia Vorontsova,* Vol. 7, 112-209. The length of the citation provides the reader with an idea of the magnitude of the materials considered.

7 *Privalenia k Sanktpeterskim Vedomostiam,* Friday, January 25, 1751. In this unusual special addition to the regular bi-weekly journal nearly all

the blame for the problems between Russia and Prussia are placed upon the refusal of Frederick to return the old giant soldiers.

8   "Colonel Guy Dickens to the duke of Newcastle. No. 36. 24 of April o.s. (5 May) 1750 ", *SIRIO,* Vol. 148, 59-60.

9   *Ibid.,* "Colonel Guy Dickens to the duke of New-castle. No. 193. Moscow 7th (18th), July, 1753", 437.

10 "Izvestie o Ssorakh Anglichan i Frantsuzov v Amerike", *Ezhmesiachniia* ...June, 1755,538-48.

11 "Protokoly Konferentsy pri vysochaishem Dvore. Tom I. 14 Marta 1756--13 Marta 1757 g.", *SIRIO,* Vol. 136, 50. No. 7. March 30, 1756.

12 *PSZ,* XIV, No. 10,547. Senate. May 1, 1756.

13 Solov'ev, 22, 432.

14 A. Veidemeir, *Tsarstvovanie Elisavety Petrovny.* Tom II. (St. Petersburg: Department Vneshnei Torgovlei, 1835), 9. This is probably the earliest work on the reign before the archives were opened.

15 Locatelli, 227.

16 "Colonel Guy Dickens to the duke of Newcastle". No. 213. January 28, 1752, *SIRIO,* Vol. 148, 322.

17 Bolotov, 400-12.

18 *Ibid.,* 453-54.

19 *Ibid.,* 630.

20 *Ibid.,* 481. Bolotov writing when aged claimed that he had strong nationalist feelings when leaving Russia in 1757, 428.

21 *PSZ,* No. 10,062. December 15, 1752. Veselago, *Kratkaia Istoriia Russkago Flota* .Vypusk I (St. Petersburg, 1893), 106. Two formerly existing schools were united into one which was to have 120 midshipmen and 240 noble cadets of whom 30 were to be trained for the artillery.

22 Büsching, IX, 259-74.

23 Solov'ev, 23, 10-11.There was also a shortage of labor.

24 *PSZ,* XIII, No. 9742. Senate. May 10, 1750.

25 *Ibid.,* XIII, No. 9871. Senate. July 31, 1751.

26 Büsching, IX, 259-74.

27 *Ibid.,* II (Hamburg: Ritter, 1768), 420-21.

28 Pastor Pege, "K Istorii Semiletnei Voiny", *Russkii Arkhiv,* XI-XII, 1101-63. Bolotov, 491-92.

29 Bolotov, 420.

30 A. Nilus (editor), *Istoriia material'noi Chasti Artilleri* Tom I. *Istoriia material'noi Chasti Artillerii ot pervobytnykh Vremen do XIX Veka* (St. Petersburg: Soikin, 1904), 261-71. The author has a very high opinion of Shuvalov and his weapon, but he does conceed that it was before its time.

31 *Anhang zu den St. Peterburgischen Zeitungen.* Freitag den 10 julii 1759. Ausführliche Relation an IHRO JAISERL MAJEST ... so von dem herrn General Grafen von Soltykow, den 18 Jul. aus Grossen ... worin von den Gänzlichen Verreibung der Preussischen Arme aus Pohlen. ... Austrian Archives; Russland II Berichte 1758 X-1759 VII No. 41. The victory reported here is attributed to the Shuvalov howitzer.

32 Danilov, 110-11.

33 "Piere comte de Schouwalow, Madam.... 19 December 1758. Austrian Archives: Russland II Berichte. 1759 IX-1760 VI.

34 S.O. Shmidt, "Proekt P.I. Shuvalova o Sozdanii v Rossii Vysshe Voennoi Shkoly. (1755)", *Voprosy Voennoi Istorii Rossii. XVIII i pervaia Polvina XIX Vekov* (Moscow: Nauka, 1969), 390-404.

35 *PSZ,* XV, No. 10,961. Senate at the request of Shuvalov. June 17, 1759.

36 Nilus, 271.

37 *PSZ,* XV, No. 10,617. Senate in consequence of a Personal. October 3, 1756.

38 *Ibid.,* No. 11,219. Senate. March 19, 1761.

39 Troitsky, *Finansovaia,* 209-10.

40 *PSZ,* XIV, No. 10,617. Senate in consequence of a Personal. October 3, 1756. *Ibid.,* No. 10,624. Senate in consequence of a Personal. October 9, 1756.

41 P. fon-Winkler, *Iz Istorii monetnago Dela v Rossii. 8. Peredel mednykh Pushek v Moneta (1756-1767)* (St. Petersburg: Soikin, 1899), 8.

42 *PSZ,* XV, No. 11,037. Senate. March 10, 1760.

43 fon-Vinkler, 6.

44 I.G. Spasskii, *Russkaia monentnaia Sistema. Istoriko-Numismaticheskii Ocherk* (Leningrad: Avrora, 1970, 4th ed.) 219-20. *PSZ,* XV, No. 11,170 Senate, given to the President of the Berg College, Shlatter, December 15, 1760.

45 Troitskii, 248.

46 *PSZ,* XV, No. 11,016. Senate. December 18, 1759.

47 *Ibid.,* No. 11,027. Senate. January 28, 1760.

48 Troitskii, 249.

49 *Anhang zu dem St. Peterburgischen Zeitungen.*
Dienstag den 24sten octobr, 1760. Unständliche
Beschreiburn dessen, was bei der Einnahme der
Stadt Berlin durch IHRO KAISERL. MAJESTAT trup-
pen vorgefallen. Austrian State Archives: Russland II Berichte.1760 VII-1761 III. No. 43. Enclosure in a letter. The Russians lost 45 men in
the capture and Berlin had to pay 1.5 million
thalers. There was even a Russian army song
which the soldiers composed and sang about the
event: P.B. Sheina (ED), "Istoricheskiia Pesni
XVIII Veka", *Russkaia Starina,* Vol. VIII, November, 1873, 814.

50 "Prisoedinenie Prussii k Rossii, Proekt ", *Russkaia Starina,* Vol. VII, May, 1873, 705-13.

51 Solov'ev, 24, 545.

52 *Senatskii Arkhiv,* XI (St. Petersburg: Senatskaia
Tipografiia, 1904), 359.

53 *PSZ,* XV, No. 11,387. Personal. December 21,
1761. This was the last personal Ukaz of the
reign since the empress died four days later.
While it is general in calling for those who
have deserted to return, special mention is
made of those who failed to respond to the draft
of November, 1759.

54 Solov'ev, 24, 595. Troitskii, 247.

55 Troitskii, 247.

56 Austrian State Archives: Unsigned enclosure.
Esterhazy to Kaunitz. St. Petersburg. February
15, 1761. Russland II Berichte 1760 VII-1761 III
No. 43. A Russian copy dated November 10, 1760
in the handwriting of the Chancellor Vorontsov

258

in *Arkhiv Kniazia Vorontsova,* 4, 174.

57 *PSZ,* XV, No. 11,139. Senate. November 5, 1760. This law applied only to the Gubernia of Kazan, Nizhnyi-Novgorod, Voronezh and Belgorod.

58 *Ibid.,* XV, No. 11,083. Senate with Most High Approval. July 5, 1760.

59 Troitskii, *Absoliutizm,* 309.

60 Troitskii, *Finansovaia,* 247.

CHAPTER NINE

CONCLUSIONS

Although Catherine the Great would have preferred that historians and her contemporaries view the change of power in 1762 as a major turning point for Russia such was not true. The economic growth of the country continued as it had in the reign of Elisabeth with perhaps some slowing of the development of the metallurgy industry. Many of the projects for which Catherine was so famous such as her Nakaz found their roots in the previous reign. French culture captured the court and upper classes which it continued to hold.

under Elisabeth

There were some areas of definite improvement. Peter III abolished the Secret Chancellary and Catherine continued this policy. Peter ended many of the monopolies which was easy to accomplish since the chief holder of such was Peter Shuvalov who outlived the empress only by two weeks. The policy towards the religious dissenters was also improved as was the policy towards the Moslems. However, other national groups such as the Baltic peoples were not subject to oppression as well as the Laminist Buddhists Kalmyks the majority of whom attempted to escape Russia in the reign of Catherine.

The otherside of the coin relates to the court. The conditions of the court have been covered adequately in the memoirs of Catherine as well as by the older works on the English historian, Nisbet Bain, and the Pole, Kazimierz Waliszewski.[1] There is no need to dwell upon the many lovers of the empress, her large wardrobe of 18,000 dresses, court intrigue, etc. Really little changed with her departure. There seems to be little if any criticism of her construction of the Winter Palace which was built during the Seven Years' War and just ready for occupation upon her death.

Then there was the problem of the so-called "sycophants and young favorites" of the reign of Elisabeth. Panin, one of the leading advisors to Catherine II, was very critical of them and attempted to induce her to divide the functions of the over-worked Senate and create a sort of cabinet to avoid such persons in the future.[2] But the chief "sycophant" of the reign was, of course, Peter Shuvalov who, for all his harmful monopolies, did much actual good for the Russian state with his many projects. Why were Panin and other historians so critical of these people that they could not see the positive side of their activity? As has been noted Peter Shuvalov was responsible for the general stabilization of the economy, the creation of a funded state bank for nobles and merchants, the start of the land survey, the effort to write "clear and understandable laws", his military projects, his Commission About Commerce and even his efforts to create a Russia merchant fleet all aimed at the welfare of the state. His monopolies are palled into insignificance by his major achievements. A few monopolies, a feeling of self importance and a love of luxury have little meaning when compared to one single action such as the abolition of the internal tariffs in Russia.

The chief "young favorite" of the reign was without doubt Ivan Shuvalov who Voltaire considered to be one of the best educated persons he had ever met and for whom Catherine herself later developed the highest esteem. He was responsible for most of the cultural and educational initiatives of the government. While he did not have a direct connection with the development of the opera or the theaters these were about the only fields his influence did not touch. He was the protector of Lomonosov which in itself made him one of the key figures of his day. Deeply emersed in French culture and the enlightenment, Ivan did much to further the development of Moscow University which, until the 19th century, was to be the only real university in Russia. Lomonosov on his own could have done little, but with support in the court he could produce needed reforms. The attempt to found primary and secondary schools in the provinces also bears the imprint of the ideas of Ivan, but bore fruit only in the establishment of the gymnaziia in Kazan. These were typical goals of the men of the enlightenment.

In a secondary, but nearly as important a field, mainly in art, Ivan played an important role. The Academy of Fine Arts was most clearly Ivan's idea given his later interest in art in his years in exile.

While the standard interpretation attributes most of the negative and positive aspects of the reign to "sycophants and young favorites" noting the love of luxury and the laziness of the empress, a closer look indicates that she did have a strong impact upon Russia. First it can be noted that she was the first modern ruler or state which abolished the death penalty. While this was never carved in stone in the form of a law, it was a well known fact. The slow change of the methods of handling criminal cases of the past by the ending of torture can be attributed to her as Solzhenitsyn does. In fact, for the Slavophile Solzhenitsyn, Elisabeth is his favorite ruler primarily on these accounts.

A further study of the important laws issued in the reign tends to prove a more active role for the empress. The footnotes referring to the collected laws of the Russian Empire indicate that a large number of those of special significance are listed as "personal" or those issuing directly from the empress. She would also attend the meetings of the Senate when Peter Shuvalov took an especially important initiative. Her influence upon foreign policy was also decisive despite the persons responsible for guiding her views. Her determination to remain in the Seven Years' War is a clear example of this factor in action.

Elisabeth was the last ruler to maintain the Universal Service State as established by her father. Although there is no doubt about the growing power of the nobles in the state, Elisabeth tended to resist this development. Such facts are adduced as the right of the nobles to send select serf families to Siberia and later to count them as recruits for the army. But as it has been noted the reason for this law was really more related to the desire to have farmers in the vicinity of the silver and gold mines to produce food to feed the miners and thus increase production of these metals. Others say it was easier to retire from the army during her reign.[3] Yet she issued a law during the Seven Years' War repeating one of her father's that if a noble in the military service in good health attempted to resign he was to be turned "eternally" into a soldier of the line and by implications lose his title of nobility.[4] Indeed, the government under the proding of the empress continued to pressure the nobles into service and they could lose their estates if they failed to report as had been ordered in her father's time. It is little wonder that the nobles should desire to build a golden statue to Peter III for his "edict of emancipation" of the nobles in 1762.

In respect to the serfs themselves some effort was directed at maintaining the old Petrine system under which, in theory, but not practice, the serfs were supposedly attached to the land they worked and not the nobles. This was being universally ignored and serfs sold like cattle. Apparently to maintain the facade that the serfs were fixed to the soil the official *Sanktpeter-burgskiia Vedomosti* published no announcements that serfs were being sold apart from the soil. Perhaps the low price of the serfs explains this. Authors often

264

state as true fact that during the reign of Elisabeth such announcements for the sales of serfs were constant. None such appeared in 1743, 1746, 1748, 1749-1754, 1756-1761. Even the laws restricting the economic activities of the serfs were repeated from previous reigns and sought to protect both the serfs and merchants. These did not represent a clear increase in the servitude of the serfs.[5]

Hence, the pattern emerges. The reign represented a sort of transition from the Petrine Universal Service State maintained by the empress in large part as a measure of respect for her father, and of new reforms which represented the future needs of the state and the nobility. True, the power of the nobility was too great for subsequent rulers to reduce it as the experience of Paul I was to prove and the fact that Catherine herself owed the throne to this same nobility.

******

Within six months after the death of Elisabeth, Catherine who had long been plotting to overthrow her husband, Peter III, became ruler in a coup d'Etat in which the support of the nobles was essential. With her husband quickly removed from the scene she took full power against the advice of Panin who suggested that she be regent for her son, Paul.[6] Being in no direct manner related to the Romanovs she had no pretext except her son for holding power. Catherine retained the services of the best of the officials of Elisabeth especially the ones known for their honesty such as M.L. Vorontsov who remained Chancellor until that post was abolished, Bestuzhev-Riumin, Ia. Shakhovskoi, I.I. Nepliuev and Alexander Shuvalov, head of the former Secret Chancellary and brother of Peter Shuvalov. The governor of Novgorod, Sievers, became one of her most helpful advisors.

An additional factor which clouds the reign of Elisabeth was the attitude of Catherine towards existing conditions. She vented her rage upon such figures as Ivan Shuvalov and the Princess Dashkova-Vorontsova. In addition, Catherine was highly critical to the existing situation as she found it in Russia. Of course, the economic situation was chaotic as a consequence of the long war just ended. Peter III had increased the problems by issuing debased copper coinage as Peter Shuvalov had suggested so that three different weights of copper coins were in circulation. Peter III had also ordered the continued issuance of paper money, but this Catherine stopped at once.

But there is one curious aspect to the situation which developed. There are few who would question the intelligence and drive of Catherine, but it appears that during the period of neglect when she had provided the Russian throne with the desired heir, Paul, she had emersed herself in the French classics of the Enlightenment. She appears to have displayed a remarkable degree of ignorance of the real conditions inside Russia itself. For instance she appears not to have read the literature which was being issued by the Academy of Sciences. She claimed that the Senate did not know where the towns were located to which it appoined officials such as governors or voevodas.[7] Thus, she seems to have failed to read the monthly journal of the Academy which had a series of articles on just this subject. She purchased a map for the Senate but chose an older version over the much improved 1745 atlas which was considered excellent.

Catherine's account of the condition in Russia when she came to power has its amusing side when compared with the situation faced by Catherine herself a few years after she had written her account. She claimed that the credit of the state had been ruined when Elisabeth borrowed two million rubles abroad to finance the war. She also claimed that Elisabeth had discarded the "good" reforms of Münnich without any reference to the Cadet Corp. She claimed that the silver content of the coins had been dropped for the first time which was correct. She was also annoyed by the internal disorder which appeared to be on the verg of open revolt.[8] In the year in which she wrote that account she drew Russia into the Turkish war (1767) and started to finance the war with paper assignats which provided two-thirds of the needs of the state. She steadily raised the other taxes except the salt tax. She borrowed nearly seven million abroad.[9] By 1774 she faced a much more serious situation than Elisabeth. It is interesting to speculate what a person replacing her in 1774 would have written concerning the state of Russia. Heavy debts undreamed of before existed in the form of paper money and foreign loans. There was a real uprising which nearly overthrew the government under Pugachev. The field army in the region of the campaign was in need of food and supplies. The inflation was becoming a serious problem and was accompanied by shortages of grain. Hence, many could look back to the reign of Elisabeth with a degree of sympathy.

267

NOTES

1   Robert Nisbet, Bain, *The Daughter of Peter the Great*. Westminister: Archibald Constable & Co., 1899. To date still the best account of the reign of Elisabeth in English. Kazimiers, Waliszewski, *La dernière des Romanov, Elizabeth 1-ière, 1741-1762*. Paris, 1902. The best account of the reign in Russian and French, but the scholarship of the author is sloppy and the stories often little more than fantacies without concrete factual support.

2   "Bumagi, Kasaiushchiiasia Predlozheniia ob Uchrezhdenii imperatorskogo Soveta i o Pazhdelenii Senata na Departmenty v pervyi God Tsarstvovaniia Ekateriny II", *SIRIO,* VII, 200-09. Ransel, Davil L. *The Politics of Catherinian Russia. The Panin Party.* New Haven: Yale University Press, 1975. David Ransel, "Nikita Panin's Imperial Council Project and the Struggle of Hierarchy Groups at the Court of Catherine II", *Canadian Slavic Studies,* IV, 3 (Fall, 1970), 443-63.

3   Marc Raeff, *Origins of the Russian Intelligentsia: The Eighteenth-Century Nobility* (New York, 1966), 69.

4   *PSZ,* XV, No. 11,063. Personal to the War College. May 26, 1760.

5   Michael Confino, *Domaines et Seigneurs en Russie vers la Fin du XVIIIe siècle* (Paris: Institut d'Etudes slaves, 1963), 23.

6   Ransel, *Nikita Panin,* 443-63.

7   "Razskaz imperatritsy Ekateriny II-oi o pervykh Piati Godakh Eia Tsarsvovaniia", *Russkii Arkhiv,*

1865, 3, 480.

8   *Ibid.*, 485.

9   John T. Alexander, *Autocratic Politics in a Na-
    tional Crisis: The Imperial Russian Government
    .and Pugachev's Revolt, 1773-1775* (Bloomington: In-
    diana University Press, 1969), 15-16.

SELECT BIBLIOGRAPHY

PRIMARY SOURCES

Akty i Dokumenty, otnosiashchiesia k Istorii kievs-koi Akademii Otdelenie II (1721-1751gg), III (1751-1762gg). Kiev, 1906.

Arkhiv Kniazia Vorontsova. 40 Volumes. Moscow, 1870-1895.

Andrei Timofeevich Bolotov. *Zapiski Andreia Timofee-vicha Bolotova.* St. Petersburg: Semevskii, 1871-1875. IV Volumes.

Catherine II. *The Memoirs of Catherine the Great.* Edited by Dominique Maroger. New York: Collier Books, 1961.

------. "Razskaz imperatritsy Ekateriny II-oi o per-vykh piati Godakh Eia Tsarstvovaniia", *Russkii Arkhiv,* volume 3, 1865, 481-494.

M.V. Danilov. *Zapiski artillerii Maiora Mikhaila Vasilevicha Danilova, napisannyia Im v 1771 Godu.* Moscow: Selivanovskii, 1842.

Despatches Received by the Department of State from United States Ministers to Russia, 1808-1906.

Dokumenty i Materialy po Istorii moskovskogo Univer-siteta vtroi Poloviny XVIII Veka. Moscow: Mos-kovskii Universitet, 1960, Volume I.

Ezhemesiachnyia Sochineniia k Pol'ze i Uveseleniiu Sluzhashcchiia. Monthly journal of the Academy of Sciences in St. Petersburg where it was iniated as a journal for public information in 1755. In 1758 it was renamed *Sochineniia i Pe-*

271

revody k Pol'ze i Uveseleniiu Sluzhashchiia and
continued to appear until the reign of Catherine the Great.

*Polnoe Sobranie Postanolenii i Rasporiazhnii po
Vedomostu pravoslavnago Ispovedaniia
rossiiskago Imperii.* Volumes 1-3. St. Petersburg: Synode, 1912.

Polnoe Sobranie Zakonov rossiskoi Imperii. 46 Volumes. St. Petersburg, 1830-1839. Volumes 11-16
were especially valuable for this work.

"Protokoly Konferentsy privysochaishem Dvore. Tom I.
14 Marta 1756-13 Marta 1757g.", *SIRIO,* Volume
136, St. Petersburg, 1912.

Sbornik imperatorskago russkago Obshchestva. Volumes
1-148. St. Petersburg, 1867-1916. Referred to
as *SIRIO* as is standard among historians.

Sanktpeterburgskiia Vedomosti. 1743, 1746, 1749-54,
1756-61. St. Petersburg: Akademiia Nauk. This
was the official journal of the government
which appeared twice a week on Tuesdays and
Friday carrying foreign and domestic news in
addition to official notices and paid ad-
vertizements.

Iakov Petrovich Shakhovskoi. *Zapiski kniazia Iakova
Petrovicha Shakovskogo pisannykh Im Samin.* Moscow: Vsevolozhskii, 1810.

M.M. Shcherbatov. *On the Corruption of Morals in
Russia by* M.M. Shcherbatov. Translated and
edited by Professor Lentin. Cambridge:
Cambridge University Press, 1969.

*Senatskii Arkhiv.*12 Volumes. St. Petersburg: Senatskaia Tipografiia, 1892-1904. A most useful
source for the ruling of the country, but much
material appears to have been deleted.

272

ARCHIVES

Oesterreichs Staats- und Hof-Archiv. Referred to as
    Austrian State Archives. *Berichte aus Russland.*
    1740-1762. Especially valuable were the fre-
    quent letters from the ambassadors themselves
    in French.

SECONDARY SOURCES

Absoliutizm v Rossii. (XVII-XVIIIvv.) Moscow: Akademiia Nauk, 1964.

P.K. Alefirenko. *Krest'ianskoe Dvizhenie i krest'
ianskii Vopros v Rossii v 30-60-Godakh XVIII
veka.* Moscow: Akademiia Nauk, 1958.

-----. "Russkaia obshestvennaia Mysl' pervoi poloviny XVIII, vek o Znachenii sel'skogo Khoziast-
va", *Akademiku Borisu Dmitrievichu Grekovu ko
Dniu Semidesiatiletiia. Sbornik Statei,* (Moscow:
Akademiia Nauk, 1952), 261-265.

John T. Alexander. *Autocratic Politics in a National
Crisis: the Imperial Russian Government and
Pugachev's Revolt, 1773-1775.* Bloomington: In-
diana University Press, 1969.

-----. "Communicable Disease, Anti-epidemic Policies, and the Role of the Medical Professions
in Russia, 1725-62", *Canadian American Slavic
Studies,* volume 12, No. 1 (1978), 154-169.

V.K. Andreevich. *Istoricheskii Ocherk Sibira. Tom
III. Period ot 1742 do 1762 Goda.* Tomsk, 1887.

A. Andrievskii. *Iz Zhizni Kieva v XVIII Veka (Ark-
hivnyia Zametki).* Kievskaia Starina: Kiev,
1899.

N.G. Apollova, "K Voprosu o Politike Absoliutizma v
national'nykh Raionakh Rossii v XVIII V.", *Absoliutizm v Russii* (Moscow: Nauka, 1963), 355-
388.

A.V. Arsen'ev. "Nepristoinyia Rechi. (Iz Del Preobrazhenskogo Prikaza i Tanoi Kantseliarii
XVIII Veka)", *Istoricheskii Vestnik,* Volume 69
(1897) June, 59-80; July, 375-398.

Wilson R. Augustine, "Notes toward a Portrait of the Eighteenth-Century Russian Nobility", *Canadian American Slavic Studies,* Volume 4, No. 3 (1970), 373-425.

I.S.B., "Oponuditel'nom Obuchenii dvorianskikh Detei v 1743 Godu", Russkaia Starina, Volume 148 (1911) November, 343-344.

Robert Nisbet Bain. *The Daughter of Peter the Great.* Westminister: Archibald Constable & Co., 1899.

Petr Bartenev. *Biografiia I.I. Shuvalov.* Moscow: Semen, 1857.

D. Bantysh-Kamenskii. *Istoriia Maloi Rossii. Chast' Tret'ia. Ot Izbrannia Mazepa do Unichtozheniia Getmanstva.* Moscow: Stepanov, 1841.

P. Bezobrazov, "Neurozhai proshlago Veka", *Russkoe Obozrenie,* Volume I, (1892) February, 693-749.

B.L. Bil' basov. *Istoriia Ekateriny Vtoroi.* Volumes I-II. Berlin, 1900.

I. Bogoliubskii. *Istoriko-statisticheskii Ocherk Proizvoditel'nosti nerchinskago gornogo Okruga s 1703 po 1871 God.* St. Petersburg: Demakov, 1872.

M.M. Bogoslovskii, "Smolenskoe Shliakhetstvo v XVIII Veke", *Zhurnal Ministerstvo Narodnogo Prosveshchenia,* CCCXXII, (1899) March, 25-61.

V.N. Bondarenko, "Ocherk finansovoi Politiki Kabenta Ministrov Anny Ioanovny", *Zapiski imperatorskago arkheologicheskago moskovoskago Instituta imen Imperator Nikolaia II,* Volume 29 (1913), 1-390.

A.M. Borisov, "Krizis tserkovnogo i monastyrskogo Zemlevladeniia i Khoziaistva v 40-60 Godakh XVIIIv", *Istoriia SSSR,* No. 2 (1968) May-July, 142-151.

M. Borodkin. *Istoriia Finliandii. Vremia Elizavety Petrovny.* St. Petersburg, 1910.

S.IA. Borovoi. *Kredit i Banki Rossii. (Seredina XVIv.-1861g.).* Moscow: Godgonizdat, 1958.

F.A. Brockhaus i I.A. Efron.*Entsiklopedicheskii Slovar.* 86 Volumes. Leipzig, 1890-1987.

Anton-Friedrich Büsching.*Magazin für neuer Historie und Geographie.* 1767-1793. The author lived in Russia from 1761-1767 and obtained his facts on the scene from primary sources and persons still alive.

N. Chupin, "Otdacha kazennyk Zavodov v chastnykh Ruki v proshlom Stoletii", *Gornyi Zhurnal,* Volume 2 (1861), 551-591.

Michael Confino. *Domaines et Seigneurs en Russie vers la Fin du XVIIIe Siècle.* Paris: Institut d'Etudes slaves, 1963.

A.G. Cross. *By the Banks of the Thames.* Newtonville, Maine: Oriental Research Partners, 1979.

Deistviia nizhegorodskoi Gubernskoi Uchenoi arkhivnoi Kommissii. Volume XXV. Nizhnyi-Novgorod, 1913.

"Delo o Volnenii Krest'ian statskogo Sovetnika Demidova i Assessor Goncharova fabrichnykh Liudei v kaluzhskoi Gubernia 1752 Goda", *Chteniia v imperatorskom Obshchestve Istorii i Drevnosti Rossiikikh pri moskovskom Universitet,* Volume II (1863), 17-44.

N.F. Demidova, "Biurokratizatsii gosudarstvennogo Apparata Absoliutizma v XVII-XVIIIvv.", *Absoliutizm v Rossii...* 206-242.

A.A. Dmitriev. *Istoricheskii Ocherk permskago Kraia.* Perm, 1896.

N.V. Drizen, "Liubitel'skii Teatr pri Elisavete Petrovne", *Istoricheskii Vestnik,* Volume 61 (1895), 701-721.

I.I. Dubasov. *Ocherki iz Istorii tambovskago Kraia.* Volume I. Moscow, 1883. Volume III. Moscow, 1884.

Paul Dukes. *Catherine the Great and the Russian Nobility. A Study Based on Materials of the Legislative Commission of 1767.* Cambridge: Cambridge University Press, 1967.

.... "Some Aberdonian Influences on the Early Russian Enlightenment", *Canadian American Slavic Studies,* Volume 13, No. 4 (1979), 436-451.

James A. Duran, Jr., "The Reform of Financial Administration in Russia during the Reign of Catherine II", *Canadian American Slavic Studies,* Volume 4, No. 3 (1970), 485-496.

S. Efremenko, "Dvizhenia Tsen na krest'ianskii Dushi i na Khleb s 1689. Po arkhivym Dokumentam ",*Izvestiia Kurskogo Obshchestva Kraevedeniia,* 3(9) (1928), 1-29.

S.V. Eshevskii, "Ocherk Tsarstvovanyia Elizavety Petrovny ", *Otechesvenyia Zapiski,* 178,5 (1868) May, 17-58; June, 337-419; 179,7, (1869) June, 4-62.

G. Esipov, "Samosozhigateli", *Otechestvennyia Zapiski,* 156 (1863), 605-627.

------. *Liudi starago Veka. Razskazy iz Preobrashenskago Prikaza i Tainoi Kantseliarii.* St. Petersburg: Suvorin, 1880.

L.V. Grashdanskii. *Chinoproizvodstvo v Rossii. Istoricheskoe Ocherk.* St. Petersburg: Surovin, 1888.

277

E. Feoktistov. *Otnosheniia Rossii k Prussii v Tsarstvonie Elisavety Petrovny.* Moscow: Katkov, 1882.

A. Filippov, "Doklad Imperatritse Elizavete Petrovne o Vostanovlenii Vlasti Pravitel'stvuiushchogo Senata", *Zhurnal Ministerstva Narodnago Prosveshchenia,* (1897), February, 274-291.

N.N. Firsov. *Vstuplenia na Prestol Imperatritsy Elizavety Petrovny.* Kazan: Kazanskii Universitet, 1887.

P. Fon-Vinkler. *Iz Istorii monetnago Dela v Rossii. 8. Peredel mednykh Pushek v Moneta (1756-1767).* St. Petersburg: Soikin, 1899.

Gregory L. Freeze, "Social Mobility and the Russian Parish Clergy in the Eighteenth Century", *Slavic Review,* Volume 30, No. 4 (1974), 641-662.

E.I. Gavrilov, "Lomonosov i Osnovania Akademii Khudozhest", *Russkoe Ikusstvo XVIII Veka.* Moscow: Nauka, 1973.

Dietrich Gerhard. *England und der Aufstieg Russlands. Zur Frage des Zusammenhanges der europäischen Staaten und ihres Ausgreifens des 18. Jahrhunderts.* Munich & Berlin: Oldenbourg, 1933.

E.I. German. *Istoriia Russkago Mezhevaniia.* 2nd.ed.: Moscow: Rikhter, 1910.

A.P. Glagoleva, "K Istorii pripisnykh Krest'ian v XVIIIv. ", *Akademiku B.D. Grekovu,* 273-283.

N.B. Goikova, "Organy politicheskogo Syska i ikh Razvitie v XVIIIvv. ", *Absoliutizm v Rossii,* 243 -280.

P. Golovachev. *Irkustskoe Likholet'e. 1758 - 1760gg.* Moscow: Kas'ianov, 4-19.

S.A. Gol'tsev. *Zakonodatel'stvo i Nravy v Rossii XVIII Veka*. 2nd Ed., St. Petersburg: Iakobson, 1896.

A.A. Golubev. *Opisanie Dokumentov i Bumag', Khraniashchikhsia v moskovskom Arkhiv Ministerstva Iutitsii*. Volume 4. Moscow: Snegirev, 1894.

Iu. Gote [Greuthier]. *Istoriia oblastnogo Upravleniia v Rossii ot Petra I do Ekateriny II*. Volume I. Moscow: Moskovskii Universitet, 1913. Volume II. Moscow: Akademiia Nauk, 1941.

-----. "Proekt o Popravlenii gosudarstvennykh Del Artemiis Petrovich Volynskogo", *Dela i Dni,* Volume 3. (1922), 1-31.

Gosudarstvennyi Arkhiv. Razriad II. *Delo sobstvenno do imperatorskoi Famili otnochiashiesia*. St.Petersburg: Alesandrov, 1913.

Ia. K. Grot, "Pis'ma Lomonosova i Sumarokova k I.I. Shuvalovu. Materialy dlia Istorii Russkogo Obrazovanie", *Prilozhenie k pervmu Tomu Zapisok Akademii Nauk,* No. 1, St. Petersburg, 1862.

Jonas Hanway. *An Historical Account of the British Trade over the Caspian Sea with the Author's journal of the Travels from England into Persia, and back through Russia, Germany and Holland ... The Second Revised and Corrected Edition*. Two Volumes. London: J. Sewell, 1754.

Emile Haumant. *La Culture française en Russie.(1700-1900)*. Paris: Hachette, 1910.

Peter von Haven. *Reise in Russland aus dem Däischen in Deutsch übersetst von H.A.R*. Copenhagen: Gabriel Christian Rothe, 1744.

Adolf Wilhelm von Helbig. *Rüssiche Günstlinge*.Tübingen, 1802.

279

Christian-Friedrick Hempel. *Leben, Thaten und Betrübten Fall des Weltberufenen Russishen Grafen Burchard Christoph von Münnich.*Bremen:Sauvmann, 1743.

-----. *Merkwürdiges Leben des unter dem namen eines Grafen von Biron Weltbekanten Ernst Johann, gewesenen Regentens des Russisches Reichs.* Bremen: Sauvmann, 1742.

-----. *Merkwürdigs Leben und trauriger Fall des Weltberufene russischen, Staats-Ministers, Andrei Grafen von Osterman.* Bremen: Sauvmann, 1742.

The History of Kamtschatka, and the Kurilski Islands, With the Countries Adjacent With Maps and Cuts. Published at St. Petersburg in the Russian Language, by the order of her Imperial Majesty, and translated into English by James Grieves, M.D. Glochester. Printed by R. Raikes for T. Jefferys, Geographer to his majesty, London MDCCLXIV. Reprinted by Quadrangle Books: Chicago, 1962.

E.I. Idova, "Rol' dvortsovoi Drevni v Formirovanii Kupechestva ", *Istoricheskie Zapiski* (Moscow : Akademiia Nauk, 1961), Volume 68, 181-210.

V.S. Ikonnikov. *Stranitsa iz Istorii ekaterinskago Nakaza. (Ob Otmene Pytki v Rossii).* Kiev:Zavadskii, 1890.

Irkutskaia Letopis'. No. 5. Trudy vostochno-sibskago Odela imperatorskago Russkogo geograficheskogo Obshchestvo. Irkutsk, 1911.

"Izvestie o Pokhozhdenii Simeona Stepanovich Syna Pischevicha ", *Chteniia v Obshchestve Istorii i Drevnostei Rossiiskikh,* Volume II (1883), 482-561.

"K Istorii Postoroiki St. Peterburgskago Troitskago
    Sobora", *Russkaia Starina,* Volume 148 (November, 1911), 426.

V.M. Kabuzan. *Narodonaselenie Rossii v XVIII-pervoi
    Polovine XIXv. (Po Materialom Revizii).* Moscow:
    Akademiia Nauk, 1963).

Arcadius Kahan, "Continuity in Economic Activity
    and Policy in Russia During the Post-Petrine
    Period", *Journal of Economic History,*Volume 25,
    (1956), 61-85.

-----. "The Costs of 'Westernization' in Russia:
    The Gentry and the Economy in the Eighteenth
    Century", *Slavic Review,* Volume 35, No. 1
    (1966) 40-66.

Herbert Kaplan. *Russia and the Outbreak of the
    Seven Year's War.* Berkeley: University of
    California, 1968.

B. Kel'siev. *Sbornik pravitel'vstvennykh Svedenii
    ob Raskol'nikakh. Vypusk tretyi. O Skoptsakh.*
    London: Trübner & Co., 1862.

M.D. Khmyrov, Avraam Petrovich Gannibal. (Bio-
    graficheskii Ocherk po Dokumentam), *Istoriches-
    kiia Statl M.D. Khmyrova* (St. Petersburg:
    Pechatkin, 1873), 1-66.

-----. "Graf Lestok", *Istoricheskiia* ...67-240.

Walther Kirchner. *Commercial Relations between Rus-
    sia and Europe, 1400-1800.* Bloomington: In-
    diana University, 1966.

V.O. Kliuchevskii. *Kurs Russkoi Istorii.* Volume 4.
    Moscow: Sotsial'no-ekonomicheskaia Literatury,
    1958.

P.I. Khrushchov. *Ocherk iamshikh i pochtovykh
    Uchrezhdenii ot drevnikh Vremen do Tsarst-*

    vovaniia Ekateriny II. St. Petersburg: Suvorin, 1884.

A.A. Kizevetter. *Posadskaia Obshchina v Rossii XVIIIst*. Moscow: Moskovskii Universitet, 1903.

Iu.R. Kloman, "Gorod v Zakonodatel'stve Russkogo Absoliutizma vo vtoroi Polovine XVII-XVIIIvv.", *Absoliutizm v Russii* ... 320-354.

------. *Ocherki sotsial'no-ekonomicheskoi Istorii Gorodov severo-zapada Rossii v Seredine XVIIIv*. Moscow: Akademiia Nauk, 1960.

G. Kogol'nichan, "Petr Veliki na beregakh Pruta", *Zhurnal Ministerstva Narodnago Prosveshchenia,* Volume 53 (1847), January, II, 111-123.

D.A. Korsakov, "Artemii Petrovich Volynskii i ego 'Konfidenty' ",.*Russkaia Starina,* Volume 68, (1885), October, 17-54.

------. *Votsarenie imperatritsy Anny Ioannovny.*Kazan: Kazanskii Universitet, 1880.

N.I. Kostomarov, "Imperatritsa Elisaveta Petrovna. Istoricheskii Ocherk", *Vestnik Evropy,* Volume 44, No. I (1887), 61-104; No. II, 522-561; Volume 45, No. III (1888), 5-57.

V.D. Kuz'mina.*Russkii demokraticheskii Teatr XVIII Veka*. Moscow: Akademiia Nauk, 1958.

A. Krupenin, "Krotskii istoricheskii Ocherk Zaselenii i Tsivilizatsii permskago Kraia", *Permskii Sbornik,* No. 1, (Moscow, 1859), 1-32.

Lafermier, "Russkii Dvor v 1761 Godu, perevod s frantsuzskoi Rukopsei Lafermiera, krania shcheisia v Biblioteke Ego Imperatorskago Vysochestva Gosudaria Velikago Kniazia Konstantina Nikolaevicha v Gorode Pavlovske",*Russkaia Starina,* 13, (1878), 187-206.

282

K.L. "Voeno-Uchenyia Zavedeniia v Rossii", *Istori-cheskii Vestnik,* II, (1880), 100-118.

A. Lappo-Danilevskii. *Russkie promyshlennye i tor-govye Kompanii v pervoi Polovine XVIII Stole-tiie.* St. Petersburg: Balashev, 1899.

V.N. Latkin (Editor). *Proekt novagc Ulozheniia Sostavlennyi zakonodatel'noi Kommissei 1754-1766gg. (Chast' III O Sostoianiiakh Pod-dannyk Voobshche).* St. Petersburg: Tipografiia SPB Odinochoi Tiur'my, 1893.

------. *Zakonodatel'nyia Kommissii v Rossii v XVIIIst.* St. Petersburg: Pantelev, 1887.

V.S. Lechnovich, "K Istorii Kul'tury Kartofelia v Rossii", *Materialy po Istorii Zemledeliia SSSR,* II (1956), 285-400.

John P. Le Donne, "The Evolution of the Governor's Office, 1727-64", *Canadian American Slavic Studies,* Volume 12, No. 1 (1978), 86-115.

V. Leshkov, "Cherty Upravleniia v Rossii po Ukazam XVIII Veka. 1725-1762", *Russkii Vestnik,* Volume 46 (1863), July, 168-190.

Francis Ley. *Le Maréchal de Münnich et la Russie aux XVIII-e siècle.* Paris: Plon, 1959.

A Lipskii, "A reexamination of the 'Dark Era' of Anna Ioannovna", *American and East European Review,* Volume 15, No. 4 (1956), 477-488.

------. "Some Aspects of Russia's Westernization during the Reign of Anna Ioannovna, 1730-1740 ", *American Slavic and East European Review,* 18, No. 1 (1959) 1-44.

Graf Francisk Locatelli. *Lettres moscovites.* Paris: La Compagnie, 1736. Born in Italy in 1691 he entered the service of France and had to flee

France for personal reasons about 1734. Arriving in Russia he claimed to be an Italian merchant and was admitted into the country. When visiting Kazan he admitted his real occupation and was seized as a French spy. He wrote his book apparently to try to regain his position with the French government.

"Natal'ia Fedorovna Lopukhina, Stats'-dama Dvore Imperatritsy Elisavety Petrovny. Biograficheskii Ocherk ..." *Russkaia Starina*,Volume 9 (1874), 1-43; 191-235.

A.M. Loranskii. *Kratkii istoricheskii Ocherk administrativnykh Ucherzhdenii gornago Vedomstva v Rossii, 1700-1900gg.* St. Petersburg: Bernshtein, 1900.

David S. Maᴗmillan, "The Scottish-Russian Trade: Its Development, Flucuations, and Difficulties, 1750-1796)", *Canadian American Slavic Studies,* Volume 4, No. 3 (1970), 426-442.

Louis-Olivier Maconnay. *Lettre d'un voyageur actuellement à Dantizig a un ami de Stralsund sur la guerre qui vient de s'Allumer Dans l'Empire.* Np, MDCCLVII.

M.M. Maksimov. *Ocherk o Serebre.* Moscow: Nedr, 1974.

Evfim Malov. *O novokreshchenskom Kontore.* Kazak: Kanazskii Universitet, 1878.

Christopher Marsden. *Palmyra of the North. The First Days of St. Petersburg.* London: Faber & Faber Limited, 1943.

Walter Mediger. *Moskaus Weg nach Europa. Der Aufstieg Russland zum europäischen Machstadt im*

Zeitalter Friedrichs des Grossen. Braunschweig: Georg Westermann Verlag, 1952.

B.N. Menshutin. *Russia's Lomonosov. Chemist, Courtier, Physcists, Poet,* Princeton: Princeton University Press, 1952.

Vladimir   Osipovich   Mikhnevich,   "Semeistvo Skrovronskikh", *Istoricheskii Vestnik,* Volume 26 (1885) March, 536-572.

Miliukov, Seignobos, and Eisenmann. *History of Russia.* Translated by Charles Lam Markmann. New York: Funk & Wagnalls, 1968.

[V.A. Miliutin], "Ocherki russkoi Zhuralistike. Preimushchestvenno   Staroi.   Ezhemesiachyia Sochineniia. Zhurnal, 1755-1764 Godov", *Sovremennik,* Chast' II (1851), 1-52.

Kerry R. Morrison, "Catherine II's Legislative Commission: An Administratie Interpretation", *Canadian American Slavic Studies,* Volume 4, No.3 (1970), 464-484.

Johan Ernst Münnich. *Die Memoires des Grafen Ernst von Münnich, nach des deutschen Originalhandschrift herausgegeben* ...Stuttgart: J.C. Cotta, 1896.

A. Nilus (Editor). *Istoriia material'noi Chasti Artillerii. Tom I. Istoriia material'noi Chasti Artillerii ot pervobytnykh Vremen do XIX Veka.* St. Petersburg: Soikin, 1904.

Ocherki Istorii SSSR. Period Feodalizma. Rossiia v pervoi chetverti XVIIIv. Preobrazovaniia Petra. Moscow: Akademiia Nauk, 1954.

Ocherik Istorii SSSR. Period Feodalizma. Rossiia v vtroi Chetverti XVIIIv. Moscow: Akademiia Nauk, 1957.

Ocherki Istorii voronezhskogo Kraia s drevneishikh Vremen do velikoi sotsialisticheskoi Revoliutsii. Voronezhskii Universitet, 1961.

Jay L. Oliva. *Misalliance: A Study of French Policy in Russia During the Seven Years' War.*New York: New York University Press, 1964.

*Opisanie Dokumentov i Bumag', Khraniashchikhsia v moskovskom Arkhive Ministerstva Iustitsii.*No.4. Moscow: Snegirev, 1884.

K.V. Ostrovitianov (Editor).*Istoriia Akademii Nauk SSSR. Tom I. (1724-1803).*Moscow:Akademiia Nauk, 1958.

I Patlaevskii. *Denezhiy Rynok v Rossii ot 1700 do 1762 Goda.* Odessa, 1868.

"Pechatnoe Delo ", *Entsiklopedicheskii Slovar* (Leipzig: Brokhauz & Efron, 1898), Volume 46, 522-530.

Pastor Pege, "K Istorii Semiletnei Voiny ", *Russkii Arkhiv,* Volumes 11-12 (1864), 1101-1163.

P.P. Pelarskii, "Redaktor, Sotrudniki i Tsenzura v russkom Zhurnale, 1755-1766 Godov ",*Zapiski imperatorskoi Akademii Nauk,*XII, Volume 5 (1867), 1-88.

F.H. Strube de Piermont. *Ebauche des Loix naturelles et du Droit Primitif.* Nouvelle Edition; Amsterdam: Ryckoff, 1744.

Grigorii Pisarevskii, "Iz Istorii inostrannoi Kolonizatsii v Rossii v XVIIIv. (Po neizdannym arkhinym Dokumentam). ", *Zapiski Moskovskago Arkheologecheskago Instituta,* Volume 5 (1909), 30-32.

D. Planer, "Istoriko-statistcheskoe Opisanie permskikh kazennykh mediplavilennykh Zavod", *Permskaia Starina,* No. 1, III (Moscow, 1859), 1-34.

Polnaia Istoriia nizhegorodskoi Iarmarka, prezhde byvshei makar'evskoi. Moscow: Stepanov, 1833.

Kseniia Polovtsova, "Nakazanie Freilin za 'neporia-doshkoe Provedenie'," *Russkaia Starina,* Volume 124 (1905) November-December, 726-729.

Stanislav Avgust Poniatovskii, "Iz Zapisk Korolia Stanislava Augusta Poniatovskago," *Russkaia Starina,* Volume 165 (1915), December, 271-285.

N.A. Popov, "Voennyia Poseleniia Serbov v Avstrii i Rossii," *Vestnik Evropy,* No. 6 (1870), June, 604-611.

Roger Portal, "Les Bachkirs et la gouvernement Russe aux XVIIIe Siècle," *Revue d'Etudes slaves,* No. 1 (1946), 82-104.

------. *L'Oural au XVIIIe siècle.* Paris: Institut d'Etudes slaves, 1950.

[A.E. Presniakov]. *Istoriia Pravitelstvuiushchego Senata za dvesti Let', 1711-1911. Pravitel-stvuiushchii Senat v Tsarstvovaniia Elisavety Petrovny i Petra Feodorovich.* St. Petersburg: Senatskaia Tipografiia, 1911. Volume II of four volumes.

"Prisodinenie Prussiiu k Rossii, Proekt'," *Russkaia Starina,* Volume 7 (1873), 705-713.

Ieremila Poz'e, "Zapiski Brillianshchika Iremelia Poz'e. 1729-1764gg.", *Russkaia Starina,* Vol.I, 1879, 42-127.

"Prodazha Liudei, 1760g.," *Russkaia Starina,* Volume 2 (1875), 399.

A.P. Pronshtein. *Zemlia donskaia v XVIII Veke.* Ros-tov-on-the-Don: Rostovskii Universitet, 1961.

Marc Raeff. Origins of the Russian Intelligentsia: The Eighteenth-Century Nobility. New York, 1966.

David Ransel, "Nikita Panin's Imperial Council Pro-ject and the Struggle for Hierarchy Groups at the Court of Catherine II," *Canadian American*

Slavic Studies, Volume   4,   No.   3   (1970), 443-463.

------. *The   Politics   of   Catherinian   Russia.   The Panin Party.* New Haven: Yale University Press, 1975.

Georg von Rauch, "Political Preconditions for East-West Cultural Relations in the Eighteenth Century", *Canadian American Slavic Studies,* Volume 13, No. 4 (1979), 391-411.

William Richardson. *Anecdotes of the Russian Empire in a Series of Letters Written a Few Years Ago, from St. Petersburg,* London: Frank Cass & Co. Ltd., 1783.

Hans Rogger. *National Consciousness in Eighteenth-Century Russia.* Cambridge: Harvard University Press, 1960.

A. Romonovich-Slavatinskii. *Dvorianstvo v Rossii ot Nachala XVIII Veka do Otmmeny Krepostnogo Prava.* 2nd ed.: Kiev: Iakoleva, 1912.

V. Rozhkov, "Akinfii Nikitich Demidov po svokh kolyvano-voskresenskikh Zavodakh. Istoricheskii Ocherk, 1744-1747", *Gornyi Zhurnal,* Volume III (1891) August, 327-355.

------. "Materialy k Istorii gornogo Promysla v Tsarstvovanie Imperatritsy Elisavety Petrovny", *Gornyi Zhurnal,* Volume   IV   (1890), 328-353; Volume I (1891), 133-153.

N.L. Rubinshtein. *Sel'skoe Khoziaistvo Rossii vo vtoroi Polovine XVIIIv. (Istoriko-ekonomicheskii Ocherk).* Moscow: Gozpolitidat, 1957.

------. "Ulozhennaia Komissiia 1754-1766",*Istoricheskie Zapiski,* Volume   38   (Moscow: Akademiia Nauk, 1951), 208-251.

288

-----. "Vneshniaia Torgovlia Rossii i Russkoe Kupechestvo vo vtoroi Polovine XVIIIV.", *Istoricheskie Zapiski,* Vol. 54 (1955), 343-361.

Claude-Carloman de Rulhiere. *Historie, ou anecdote sur la Revolution de Russie en l'Annee 1762.*Paris: Chez Desenne. Jardin Egalité. An V de la Rep. 1797.

Russkii Biograficheskii Slovar. 25 Volumes. St. Petersburg, 1896-1918.

M. de Saldern. Ambassadeur de Russie dans plusieurs cours de l'Europe. *Histoire de la vie de Pierre III, Empereur de toutes les Russies, Presantent, sous un aspect important, les causes de la revolution arrivée an 1762.*Francfort-sur-le-Main: Esslinger, An X, 1802.

D.I. Sapozhnikov. *Samosozhenie v russkom Raskole.* Moscow: Moskovskii Universitet, 1891.

Sbornik moskovskago glavnago Arkhiva Ministerstva Inostrannykh Del. Vypusk' I. Moscow, 1880.

A.I. Shakhmatov. *Istoricheskie Ocherki Goroda Saratova i ego Okrugi.* Vypusk' I. Saratov, 1891.

M.M. Shcherbatov. *On the Corruption of Morals in Russia.* Edited and translated by A. Lentin. Cambridge: Cambridge University Press, 1969.

K.N. Shchepetov. *Iz Zhinzni krepostnykh Krest'ian Rossii XVII-XIX Vekov. Po Materialam sheremetistikh Votchin.* Moscow: Uchpedgiz, 1963.

-----. *Krespostnoe Pravo Votchinakh sheremetevykh. 1708-1885.* Moscow, 1947.

Iohann Wilhem Schlatter. *Obstoiatel'noe Opisania rudnago Dela.* Tom I-II. St. Petersburg, 1763-1765.

August Ludwig Schlözer. *Newverändertes Russland oder Leben Catharinä der Zweiten Kaiserin von Russland. Aus authentiscchen Nachrich beschrieben.* 3rd ed.; Riga: Hartknoch, 1771.

Christoph von Schmidt-Phiseldek. *Materialien zu der russichen Geschichte seit dem Tode Kaiser Peter des Grossens, mit Tafeln. Dritter Theil 1741-1762. Erste Abtheilung 1741-1756.*Frankfurt und Leipzig: Hartknoch, 1788.

Christian-Friedrich Schwan. *Anecdotes Russes ou Lettres d'un officier Allemand à un gentilhomme livonien, écrite de Peterbourg en 1762.*2nd.ed.; London: De-la-March, 1769.

L.N. Semenova, "Pravitel'stvo i rabochii Liud v pervoi Polovina XVIII Veka", *Vnutrenniaia Politika Tsarizma (Seredina XVI-Nachalo XXv).* (Leningrad: "Nauka", 1967), 127-167.

Mikhail Semevskii, "Elisaveta Petrovna do Vosshestviia svoego na Prestol, 1709-1741. Istoricheskii Ocherk", *Russkoe Slovo,* (1859), February, 178-209.

------. "Pervii God Tsarstvovaniia Elizavety Petrovny, 1741-1742.Istoricheskii Ocherk", *Russkoe Slovo* (1859), June, 221-326; August, 277-352.

------. "Tsarstvovanie Elizavety Petrovny, 1743. Istoricheskii Ocherk", *Russkoe Slovo* (1860), February, 88-118.

V.I. Semevskii.*Krest'iane v Tsarstvovanie Imperatritsy Ekateriny II.* St. Petersburg: Stasiulevich, 1903. Volumes I & II.

P.V. Shein, "Istoricheskiia Pesni XVIII Veka", *Russkaia Starina,* Volume 8 (1873), 813-822.

S.O. Shmidt, "La politique interieure du Tzarisme au Milieu de XVIIIe siècle", *Annales,* (1966), janvier-fevrier, 95-110.

-----. "Proekt P.I. Shuvalova o Sozdanii v Rossii vyshei voennoi Shkoly (1755)", *Voposy Voennoi Istorii Rossii. XVIII i pervaia Polovina XIX Vekov* (Moscow: "Nauka," 1969), 390-404.

-----. "Proekt P.I. Shuvalov 1754 g. 'O raznykh gosudarstvennoi Pol'zy Sposobakh'", *Istoricheskii Arkhiv,* Volume 6 (1962), 100-117.

P.A. Shtorkh, Materialy dlia Istorii gosudarstvennykh deneshnykh Znakov v Rossii s 1653 po 1840g.", *Zhurnal Ministerstva Narodnago Proshcheniia,* Volume 137 (1868), March, 133-153.

S.N. Shubinskii, "Aresty i Ssylka Regenta Rossiiskoi Imperii, gertsogo kurlianskago Birona 1740g. Stat'ia po neizdannym Dokumentom", *Russkaia Starina,* Volume 3 (1871), 537-561.

E.S. Shumigorskii, "Osnovanie smolnago Monastyrié", *Russkaia Starina,* Volume 159 (1914), 306-351.

I.G. Spasskii. *Russkaia monetnaia Sistema.*Leningrad: Avrora, 1970. 4th.ed.

Baron von Strahlenbery. *Description historique de l'Empire russien.* Amsterdam, 1757.

I.M. Snegirev, "Ivan Ivanovich Shuvalov", *Zhurnal Ministerstva Narodnago Prosvescheniia,* Volume 15 (1837), 396-405.

Ia Solov'ev, "Ob Odnodvortsakh", *Otchestvennyiia Zapiski,* Volume 64, Otdel II, 81-100.

S.M. Solov'ev. *Istoriia Rossii s drevneishkh Vremen.* Moscow: "Mysl' ", 1962-1966. 15 volumes.

Sovetskaia Istoricheskaia Entsiklopediia. Moscow: Sovetskaia Entsiklopediia, 1961-1976. 16 volumes.

Heinrich Storch. *Supplement Band zum fünsten, sechsten, und siebenten Theil des historisch-statischen Gemäldes des russichen Reiches enhaltend archvalischen Nachrichten und Beweisschriften zur neuen Geschichte des russichen Handels von Heinrich Storch.* Leipzig: Johann Friedrich Hartnoch, 1803.

V.T. Stroev. *Bironovshchina i Kabinet Ministrov. Ocherk vnutrenei Politiki Imperatritsy Anny.* Moscow: Mokovskii Universitet, 1909.

G.I. Studenkin, "Saltychikha, 1730-1801gg. Istoricheskii Ocherk", *Russkaia Starina,* Volume 4, (1874), June, 497-546.

A. Svirshchevskii, "Materialy k Istorii Oblozheniia Soli v Rossii", *Iuridicheskie Zapiski,* Volume 1 (1908), 171-196.

"Tainaia Kantseliariia v 1741-1761gg.", *Russkaia Starina,* Volume 12 (1875), 523-539.

S.M. Troitsky, "Dvorianskie Proekty Sozdaniia 'tret'ego China' ", *Obshchestvo i Gosudarstvo feodal'noi Rossii. Sbornik Statei, proviashchennyi 70-letiiu Akademika L'va Vladimorovicha Cherepnina* (Moscow: Nauka, 1975), 226-236.

-----. "Dvorianskie Proekty Ukrepleniia gosudarstvennykh Finansov v Seredine XVIII Veka", *Voprosy Istorii,* Volume 2 (1958), 54-75.

-----. "Finansovaia Politika russkogo Absoliutizma vo vtroi Polovina XVII i XVIIIvv.", *Absoliutizma v Rossii,* 281-319.

-----. *Finansovaia Politika russkogo Absoliutizma v XVIII Veke.* Moscow: "Nauka", 1966.

-----. *Russkii Absoliutizm i Dvorianstvo v XVIII Veke. Formirovania Biurokratii.*Moscow: "Nauka", 1974.

-----. "Soltsial'nyi Sostav i Chislennost' Biurokratii v Rossii Seredine XVIIIv.", *Istoricheskie Zapiski,* Volume 89 (1972), 295-352.

K.N.V., "Provintsial'naia Kantseliariia i Cherty narodnoi russkoi Zhizni. (1719-1777)", *Istoricheskii Vestnik,* Volume 18 (1884), 191-200.

A.A. Vasil'chikov, "Semeistvo Razumovskikh i Grafy Aleksei i Kirila Grigorevicha", *Osmnadtsatyi Vek,* Volume 2 (Moscow: Bartenev, 1869), 260-502.

I.I. Vasilev. *Dela pskovskoi provintsial'noi Kantseliarii. Materialy dlia Istorii pskovskoi Strany.* Pskov: Gubernskaia Upravleniia, 1884.

A. Veidemeir. *Tsarstvovanie Elisavety Petrovny.* St. Petersburg, 1835.

V.I. Veretenikov. *Iz Istorii Tainoi Kantseliarii. 1731-1762gg. Ocherk.* Kharkov, 1911.

-----. *Ocherki Istorii General'prokuratury v Rossii Do-ekaterininskago Vremeni.* Kharkov: Adolf Darre, 1915.

F. Veselago. *Kratkaia Istoriia russkago Flota.* Vypusk I. St. Petersburg, 1893.

V.N. Vitevskii. *I.I. Nepliuev i orensburgskii Krai v preshem ego Sostave do 1758g., Istoricheskaia Monografiia.* Kazan: Kliuchnikov, 1897.

M.A. Volkov, "Tamozhennaia Reforma 1753-1757gg.", *Istoricheskie Zapiski,* Volume 71 (1962), 138-172.

S.I. Volkov, "Iz Istorii Upravleniia dvortsovymi Krest'ianami", *K.B. Grekovu ...*, 266-272.

Dimitri S. Von-Mohrenschildt. *Russia in the Intellectual Life of Eighteenth-Century France*. New York: Octagon Books, 1972. Reprint of the 1936 edition.

A.A. Vostokov (Editor). *Proekty ugolovnago Ulozheniia 1754-1766 Godov. Novoulozhennoi Knigi Chast' vtroaia: o pozysknykh Delakh i kakiia za raznyiia Zlodeistva i Prestupleniia Kazni, Nakazaniia i Shtrafy polozheny*. St. Petersburg: Stasiulevich, 1882.

Vnutrenniaia Politika Tsarizma. (Seredina XVI-Nachalo XXv.). Leningrad: "Nauka", 1967.

Voprosy voennoi Istorii Rossii. XVIII i pervaia Polovina XIX Vekov. Moscow: "Nauka", 1969.

G.N. Vul'son, "Poniatie 'Rasnochintsev' v XVIII-pervoi Polovine XIXv", *Ocherki Istoriia Narodov Povolzh'ia i Priural'ia,* Volume 1 (Kazan, 1967), 107-124.

Alexander Vucinich. *Science in Russian Culture. A History to 1860*. Stanford: Stanford University Press, 1963.

Kazimierz Waliszewski. *La dernière des Romanov, Elizabeth 1-ère, 1741-1762*. Paris, 1902. A Russian edition appeared in 1912.

Christian-Freiderich Weber. *Das Veränderte Russland. Dritter Theil. Die Regierung der Kaiserin Catharine [I] und des Kaisers Petri Secundi: und sonst Alle vorgefollens Merkwürdigkeiten in sich Haltend.* Hanover, 1740.

-----. *The Present State of Russia*. London: Taylor, 1723.

George L. Yaney. *The Systematization of the Russian Government. Social Evolution in the Domestic Administration of Imperial Russia.* *1711-1905.* Urbana: University of Illinois Press, 1973.

E.I. Zaozerskaia. *Rabochaia Sila i klassovaia Borba na tekstil'nykh Manufakturakh Rossii v 20-60gg XVIII v.* Moscow: Akademiia Nauk, 1960.

-----. "Sposoby Obespecheniia Rabochei Siloi chastnykh Manufaktur vo vtroi Chertverti XVIIIv.", *Akademiku B.D. Grekovu ...,* 284-293.

V.V. Zvarich. *Numizmaticheskii Slovar'.* Lvov: "Vyscha Shkola", 1957.

937   **DATE DUE**   P. 196-197, 13
11

The Library Store   #47-0103